G000089128

Scandinavian
phrase book

Berlitz Publishing
New York Munich Singapore

Danish

Some basic expressions *Anvendelige udtryk*

Yes/No.	**Ja/Nej.**	ya/nigh
Please.	**Vær så venlig.**	vær $\overline{saw}$ **vehn**leé
Thank you.	**Tak.**	tak
I beg your pardon.	**Undskyld.**	**oon**skewl

Introductions *Præsentationer*

Good morning.	**God morgen.**	goadh**mo͞a**ern
Good afternoon.	**God dag.**	goadh**dai**
Good evening.	**God aften.**	goadh**af**dern
Good night.	**God nat.**	goadh**nat**
Good-bye.	**Farvel.**	far**vehl**
My name is...	**Jeg hedder...**	yigh **hehd**herr
Pleased to meet you!	**Det glæder mig at træffe Dem!**	dɛ **glædh**err migh ah **træf**er dehm
What's your name?	**Hvad hedder De/du?**	vadh **hehd**herr dee/doo
How are you?	**Hvordan har du det?**	vor**dan** har doo dɛ
Fine, thanks. And you?	**Tak, godt. Og hvordan har du det?**	tak god. oa vor**dan** har doo dɛ
Where do you come from?	**Hvor kommer du fra?**	vo͞ar **kom**er doo fra
I'm from...	**Jeg er fra...**	yigh ehr fra
Australia	**Australien**	ow**stral**ee͞ern
Canada	**Canada**	**ka**nada
Great Britain	**Storbritannien**	**stoar**britanyern
United States	**USA**	oo ehs ah
I'm with my...	**Jeg er her sammen med...**	yigh ehr hehr **so͞m**ern mehdh
wife	**min kone**	meen **koa**ner
husband	**min mand**	meen man
family	**min familie**	meen fa**mil**yer
children	**mine børn**	**meen**er børn
parents	**mine forældre**	**meen**er for**æld**rer
boyfriend/girlfriend	**min kæreste**	meen **kærs**der
I'm here on holiday (vacation).	**Jeg er her på ferie.**	yigh ehr hehr paw **fehr**yer

GUIDE TO PRONUNCIATION/EMERGENCIES, see page 30

Questions *Spørgsmål*

When?	**Hvornår?**	vor**nawr**
How?	**Hvordan?**	vor**dan**
What?	**Hvad?**	vadh
Why?	**Hvorfor?**	vor**for**
Who?	**Hvem?**	vehm
Which?	**Hvilken?**	**vil**kern
Where is/are...?	**Hvor er...?**	v$\overline{oo}$ar ehr
Where can I find/ get...?	**Hvor kan jeg finde/ få...?**	v$\overline{oo}$ar kan yigh **fin**ner/faw
How far?	**Hvor langt?**	v$\overline{oo}$ar langt
How long?	**Hvor længe?**	v$\overline{oo}$ar **læng**er
How much/How many?	**Hvor meget/Hvor mange?**	v$\overline{oo}$ar **migh**ert/v$\overline{oo}$ar **mang**er
Can I have...?	**Kan jeg få...?**	kan yigh faw
Can you help me?	**Kan De hjælpe mig?**	kan dee **yehl**per migh
Is there/Are there...?	**Er der...?**	ehr dehr
There isn't/aren't...	**Der er ikke...**	dehr ehr **igg**er
There isn't/aren't any.	**Der er ikke nogen.**	dehr ehr **igg**er n$\overline{oo}$**ā**ern

Do you speak...? *Kan De tale...?*

What does this/that mean?	**Hvad betyder det her/det der?**	vadh ber**tewdh**err dE hehr/dE dehr
Can you translate this for me?	**Kan De oversætte det her for mig?**	kan dee o°°**err**sehder dE hehr for migh
Do you speak English?	**Kan De tale engelsk?**	kan dee **tōl**er **ehng**erlsk
I don't speak (much) Danish.	**Jeg kan ikke tale det (ret meget) dansk.**	yigh kan **igg**er **tōl**er dE (reht **migh**ert) dansk
Could you speak more slowly?	**Kan De tale lidt langsommere?**	kan dee **tōl**er leet **lang**somerrer
Could you repeat that?	**Kan De gentage det?**	kan dee **gehn**tōer dE
Could you write it down, please?	**Kan De være rar og skrive det ned?**	kan dee **væē**rer rar oa **skrēē**ver dE nehdh
I understand.	**Jeg forstår det.**	yigh for**stawr** dE
I don't understand.	**Jeg forstår det ikke.**	yigh for**stawr** dE **igg**er

It's... *Det er...*

better/worse	**bedre/værre**	behdhrer/vehrer
big/small	**stort/lille**	stoart/leeler
cheap/expensive	**billigt/dyrt**	beeleet/dēwrt
early/late	**tidligt/sent**	teedhleet/sɛnt
good/bad	**godt/dårligt**	god/dawleet
hot/cold	**varmt/koldt**	varmt/kolt
old/new	**gammelt/nyt**	gamerlt/newt
right/wrong	**rigtigt/forkert**	rigteet/forkehrt
vacant/occupied	**ledigt/optaget**	lehdheet/optōerdh

Prepositions *Præpositioner*

above	**ovenpå**	o°°ernpaw
after	**efter**	ehfder
at	**ved**	vehdh
before (time)	**før**	før
below	**nedenunder**	nehdhernoonerr
between	**mellem**	mehlerm
down/downstairs	**ned/nedenunder**	nehdh/**nehdh**ernoonerr
from	**fra**	fra
in/inside	**i/indenfor**	ee/**i**nernfor
near	**nær**	nær
on	**på**	paw
outside	**udenfor**	ōōdhernfor
through	**gennem**	gehnerm
to	**til**	til
under	**under**	oonerr
until	**indtil**	intil
up/upstairs	**op/ovenpå**	op/o°°ernpaw
with	**med**	mehdh
without	**uden**	oôdhern

A few more useful words *Nogle flere nyttige ord*

and	**og**	oa
but	**men**	mehn
never	**aldrig**	aldree
not	**ikke**	igger
nothing	**ikke noget**	igger nōaert
now	**nu**	noo
only	**kun**	koon
or	**eller**	ehler
perhaps	**måske**	mosgɛ
soon	**snart**	snart
too (also)	**også**	osser
very	**meget**	mighert

Hotel—Accommodation *Hotel*

I have a reservation.	**Jeg har bestilt værelse.**	yigh har ber**stilt** v**ǣ**rerlser
We've reserved 2 rooms/an apartment.	**Vi har bestilt 2 værelser/en lej-lighed.**	vee har ber**stilt** to v**ǣ**rerlserr/ehn **ligh**leehehdh
Do you have any vacancies?	**Har De nogle ledige værelser?**	har dee **nōā**ler l**e**d**eēē**r v**ǣ**rerlserr
I'd like a...	**Jeg vil gerne have et...**	yigh veel **gehr**ner ha eht
single room	**enkeltværelse**	**ehn**kerldv**ǣ**rerlser
double room	**dobbeltværelse**	**dob**erldv**ǣ**rerlser
with twin beds	**med to senge**	mehdh toa **seh**nger
with a double bed	**med dobbeltseng**	mehdh **dob**erldsehng
with a bath	**med bad**	mehdh badh
with a shower	**med brusebad**	med **brōō**serbadh
Is there...?	**Er der...?**	ehr dehr
air conditioning	**klimaanlæg**	**klēē**ma **an**læg
a laundry service	**tøjvask**	**toi**vask
a private toilet	**toilet på værelset**	to**a**let paw v**ǣ**rerlserdh
a radio/television in the room	**radio/fjernsyn på værelset**	radio/**fyehrn**sewn paw v**ǣ**rerlserdh
room service	**service på værelset**	"service" paw v**ǣ**rerlserdh
a swimming pool	**svømmebasin**	**svøm**merbassæng
washing machine	**en vaskemaskine**	ehn **vas**germaskeener
What's the price...?	**Hvad koster det...?**	vadh **kos**derr dE
Is there a camp site near here?	**Er der en camping-plads i nærheden?**	ehr dehr ehn **kam**pingplas ee n**ǣ**rh**ē**dhern
We'll be staying...	**Vi bliver her...**	vee **blēē**err hehr
overnight only	**en enkel nat**	ehn **ehn**kerlt nat
a few days	**et par dage**	eht par **daer**
a week (at least)	**i (mindst) en uge**	ee (meenst) ehn **ōē**r

Decision *Beslutning*

May I see the room?	**Kan jeg se værel-set?**	kan yigh SE v**ǣ**rerlserdh
That's fine. I'll take it.	**Det er godt. Jeg tager det.**	dE ehr god. yigh tar dE
No. I don't like it.	**Jeg kan ikke lide det.**	yigh kan **igg**er li dE
It's too...	**Det er for...**	dE ehr for...
dark/small	**mørkt/lyst**	mørkt/lewst
noisy	**støjende**	**stoi**erner

NUMBERS, see page 28

Do you have anything...?	**Har De noget...?**	har dee no͞aert
better	**bedre**	behdhrer
cheaper	**billigere**	beele͞e͞eerrer
quieter	**roligere**	roale͞e͞eerrer

Navn/Fornavn	Name/First name
Adresse (by, gade, nummer)	Home town/Street/Number
Nationalitet/Stilling	Nationality/Occupation
Fødselsdato/Fødested	Date/Place of birth
Kommer fra.../Skal videre til...	Coming from.../Going to...
Pasnummer	Passport number
Sted/Dato	Place/Date
Underskrift	Signature

General requirements *Almindelige forespørgsler*

The key to room..., please.	**Nøglen til værelse..., tak.**	noilern til væ͞ærerlser... tak
Could you wake me at... please?	**Kan De vække mig klokken...?**	kan dee vægger migh kloggern
Where's the...?	**Hvor er...?**	vo͞ar ehr
bathroom	**badeværelset**	bo͞dhervæ͞ærerlserdh
dining-room	**spisesalen**	spe͞esersölern
emergency exit	**nødudgangen**	nødhoodhgangern
lift (elevator)	**elevatoren**	ehlehvatoarern
Where are the toilets?	**Hvor er toilettet?**	vo͞ar ehr toalehderdh
Where can I park my car?	**Hvor kan jeg parkere min bil?**	vo͞ar kan yigh parkerer meen beel

Checking out *Afrejse*

May I have my bill, please?	**Må jeg bede om regningen?**	maw yigh be om righningern
Can you get us a taxi?	**Kan De skaffe os en taxa?**	kan dee skaffer os ehn taksa
Could you have our luggage brought down?	**Kunne vi få bagagen ned?**	kooner vee faw bago͞shern nehdh
It's been a very enjoyable stay.	**Vi har nydt opholdet meget.**	vee har newt opholerdh mighert

Eating out *Restauranter*

English	Danish	Pronunciation
Can you recommend a good restaurant?	**Kan De anbefale en god restaurant?**	kan dee anberfoler en goadh rehstoarang
I'd like to reserve a table for 4.	**Jeg vil gerne bestille et bord til 4.**	yigh veel **gehr**ner ber**stil**er eht boar til **feer**er
We'll come at 8.	**Vi kommer klokken 8.**	vee komerr **klogg**ern **oa**der
I'd like..., please.	**Jeg vil gerne have...**	yigh veel **gehr**ner ha
breakfast	**morgenmad**	**moa**ernmadh
lunch	**frokost**	**fro**akost
dinner	**middag**	mid**dai**
What do you recommend?	**Hvad kan De anbefale?**	vadh kan dee **an**berfoler
Do you have a set menu/local dishes?	**Er der en dagens ret/nogle lokale retter?**	ehr dehr ehn **da**erns reht/**loa**kaler **reh**derr
Do you have any vegetarian dishes?	**Er der nogle vegetariske retter?**	ehr dehr **noa**ler vehgeh**ta**risger **reh**derr

Hvad ønsker De?	What would you like?
Jeg kan anbefale det her.	I recommend this.
Hvad ønsker De at drikke?	What would you like to drink?
Vi har ikke...	We don't have...
Ønsker De...?	Would you like...?

English	Danish	Pronunciation
Could we have a/an..., please?	**Kan vi få....**	kan vee faw
ashtray	**et askebæger**	eht **as**gerbæer
cup	**en kop**	ehn kop
fork	**en gaffel**	ehn **gaf**erl
glass	**et glas**	eht glas
knife	**en kniv**	ehn kneev
napkin (serviette)	**en serviet**	ehn sehr**veee**eht
plate	**en tallerken**	ehn ta**lehr**kern
spoon	**en ske**	ehn skE

TELLING THE TIME, see page 27

May I have some...?	**Må jeg bede om...**	maw yigh bɛ om
bread	**noget brød**	nōāert brødh
butter	**noget smør**	nōāert smør
lemon	**noget citron**	nōāert seetroan
oil	**noget spiseolie**	nōāert spēēseroalyer
pepper	**noget peber**	nōāert peh°°er
salt	**noget salt**	nōāert salt
seasoning	**nogle krydderier**	nōāler krewdherrēēerr
sugar	**noget sukker**	nōāert sooggerr
vinegar	**noget eddike**	nōāert ehdhigger

Reading the menu *Læsning af spisekortet*

Børnemenu	Children's menu
Dagens måltid	Meal of the day
Dagens ret/suppe/grønsager	Dish/soup/vegetables of the day
Husets specialiteter	Specialities of the house
Køkkenchefen anbefaler...	The chef recommends...
Serveres med...	Served with...
Vegetar	Vegetarian
Vælg mellem...	Choice of...

desserter	dehs**sehr**derr	desserts
drikkevarer	**drigg**ervarerr	beverages
fisk	fisk	fish
fjerkræ	**fyehr**kræ	poultry
forretter	**for**rehderr	appetizers
frugt	froogt	fruit
grønsager	**grøn**saer	vegetables
is	ēēs	ice cream
koldt bord	kol bordh	smörgåsbord
kylling	**kewl**ling	chicken
ost	oast	cheese
pasta	pasta	pasta
salater	sa**la**derr	salads
skaldyr	**skal**dewr	seafood
småretter	**smaw**rehderr	snacks
smørrebrød	**smør**erbrødh	open sandwich
supper	**soob**berr	soups
vildt	veelt	game
vin	vēēn	wine
ægretter	**æg**rehderr	egg dishes
øl	øl	beer

Breakfast *Morgenmad*

I'll have a/an/ some...	**Jeg vil gerne have...**	yigh veel **gehr**ner ha
bacon and eggs	**bacon og æg**	"bacon" oa æg
bread	**brød**	brødh
butter	**smør**	smør
cereal	**cornflakes**	"cornflakes"
eggs	**æg**	æg
boiled egg	**kogt æg**	kogt æg
fried eggs	**spejlæg**	spighlæg
scrambled eggs	**røræg**	røræg
poached eggs	**pocheret æg**	poshĒrerdh æg
jam	**syltetøj/marmelade**	sewldertoi/marmerlōdher
rolls	**rundstykker**	roonstewgger
toast	**ristet brød**	reesterdh brødh

Starters (Appetizers) *Forretter*

blandet hors d'oeuvre	**blan**erdh "hors d'oeuvre"	assorted appetizers
fyldte tomater	**few**lder toa**mad**err	stuffed tomatoes
omelet	oamer**leht**	omelet
sildesalat	**seel**ersalat	herring salad

kyllingesalat (**kew**leengersahlōt)	chicken meat, macaroni, tomato slices, green peppers, olives, lettuce and mushrooms
smørrebrød (**smør**erbrødh)	large, buttered open-faced sandwich covered with one of a variety of delicacies and gar- nished with various accessories

Soups and stews *Suppe- og labskovsretter*

I'd like some soup.	**Jeg vil gerne have en suppe.**	yigh veel **gehr**ner ha en **soob**ber
aspargessuppe	ah**spars**soobber	asparagus soup
champignonsuppe	sham**pin**yongsoobber	mushroom soup
gule ærter	**gōo**ler ærderr	split-pea soup with salt pork
hummersuppe	**hoom**ersoobber	lobster chowder
hønsekødsuppe	**høns**erkødhsoobber	chicken vegetable soup
æblesuppe	**æbl**ersoobber	apple soup

labskoves (**lab**sko°°s)	beef, diced potatoes, slices of carrots and onions, served with rye bread
frugtsuppe (**froogt**soobber)	"fruit soup", composed of a variety of dried fruits, served chilled or hot.

Fish and seafood *Fisk og skaldyr*

cod	**torsk**	torsk
perch	**aborre**	ahborer
pike	**gedde**	gehdher
smoked herring	**røget sild**	roierdh seel
sole	**søtunge**	søtoonger
trout	**forel**	foarehl

sild i karry
(seel ee **kō**ree)

herring with curry sauce, served with rice, leeks and dark bread

ålesuppe
(**awl**ersoobber)

sweet-and-sour eel soup, with apples and prunes, served with dark rye bread

boiled	**kogt**	kogt
fried	**stegt**	stehgt
grilled	**grillet**	greelerdh
roast	**ovnstegt**	o°°nstehgt
stewed	**stuvet**	stōōerdh
underdone (rare)	**letstegt**	lehtstehgt
medium	**medium**	mehdeeoom
well-done	**gennemstegt**	gehnermstehgt

Meat *Kød*

I'd like some...	**Jeg vil gerne have noget.../nogle...**	yigh veel **gehr**ner ha **nōā**ert.../**nōā**ler
bacon	**bacon**	"bacon"
beef	**oksekød**	okserkødh
chicken	**kylling**	kewling
duck	**and**	an
ham	**skinke**	skeenger
lamb	**lammekød**	lamerkødh
pork	**svinekød**	svēēnerkødh
veal	**kalvekød**	kalverkødh

engelsk bøf
(**ehng**erlsk bøf)

fillet of beef with onions and boiled potatoes

forloren skildpadde
(for**loa**rern **skeel**padher)

"mock turtle": a very traditional Danish dish consisting of meat from a calf's head with meat balls and fish balls

kalkunragout
(kal**koon** ragoo)

jugged turkey in a sweet-and-sour gravy, served with mashed potatoes or chestnuts

æbleflæsk
(**æb**lerflæsk)

smoked bacon with onions and sautéed apple rings

Vegetables *Grøntsager*

beans	**bønner**	bønerr
cabbage	**kål**	kawl
carrots	**gulerødder**	gōolerrødherr
lettuce	**salat**	salat
mushrooms	**champignoner**	shampinyong
onions	**løg**	loi
peas	**ærter**	ærderr
potatoes	**kartofler**	kartoflerr
tomatoes	**tomater**	toamaderr

Cheese *Ost*

danbo	a mild, firm cheese with holes, sometimes
(danbo)	flavoured with caraway seeds
esrom	a mild, slightly aromatic cheese of spongy
(ehsrom)	texture
samsø	a mild, firm cheese with a sweet, nutty flavour
(samsø)	

Fruit and nuts *Frugt og nødder*

apple	**et æble**	eht æbler
cherries	**kirsebær**	keerserbær
lemon	**citron**	seetroan
orange	**en appelsin**	aberlseen
pear	**pære**	pǣrer
plums	**blommer**	blomerr
pumpkin	**græskar**	græskar
raspberries	**hindbær**	heenbær
strawberries	**jordbær**	yoarbær

Desserts–Pastries *Desserter–Bagværk*

eis	ēes	ice-cream
chokoladeis	shoakoaladherēes	chocolate ice-cream
kage	kōer	cake
flødekage	flødherkōer	layer cream cake
Napoleonskage	napoalEonskōer	custard slice with jam
Wienerbrød	vēenerbrødh	Danish pastry

brune kager	spicy, thin crisp brown cake with almond
(brooner kōer)	decoration; a Christmas favourite
bondepige med slør	"veiled country maid": a mixture of rye-bread
(boanerpēēr mehdh slør)	crumbs, apple sauce, cream and sugar

Drinks *Drikkevarer*

beer	**øl**	øl
light/dark beer	**lyst/mørkt øl**	lewst/mørkt øl
brandy	**en brandy**	ehn "brandy"
(hot) chocolate	**(varm) chokolade**	(varm) shoakoa**ladh**er
coffee	**kaffe**	**kaf**er
black/with cream	**sort/med fløde**	soart/mehdh **flødh**er
fruit juice	**frugtsaft**	**froogt**saft
lemonade	**limonade**	leemoan**ōdh**er
milk	**mælk**	mælk
mineral water	**mineralvand**	meenehr**al**van
tea	**te**	tɛ
with milk/lemon	**med mælk/citron**	mehdh mælk/see**troan**
wine	**vin**	vēēn
red/white	**rød/hvid**	rødh/veedh

aquavit
(ahkva**veet**)

traditional Scandinavian drink; colourless grain spirit, usually flavoured with carraway, drunk neat and ice-cold

Complaints–Paying *Klager–Regningen*

The meat is ...	**Kødet er ...**	**kødh**erdh ehr
overdone	**stegt for meget**	stehgt for **migh**ert
underdone	**stegt for lidt**	stehgt for leet
This is too...	**Det her er for ...**	dɛ hehr ehr for
bitter/salty/sweet	**bittert/salt/sødt**	**bi**derdh/salt/søt
That's not what I ordered.	**Det har jeg ikke bestilt.**	dɛ har yigh **igg**er ber**stilt**
The food is cold.	**Maden er kold.**	**madh**ern ehr kol
What's taking you so long?	**Hvorfor tager det så lang tid?**	**vor**for tar dɛ saw lang teedh

The bill (check) *Regningen*

I'd like to pay.	**Jeg vil gerne betale.**	yigh veel **gehr**ner ber**tōl**er
What's this amount for?	**Hvad dækker dette beløb?**	vadh **dægg**err **dehd**er be**lōb**
I think there's a mistake in this bill.	**Der er vist en fejl i denne regning.**	deh ehr vist ehn fighl ee **dehn**er **righ**ning
Can I pay with this credit card?	**Kan jeg betale med dette kreditkort?**	kan yigh ber**tōl**er mehdh **dehd**er kreh**dit**kort
We enjoyed it, thank you.	**Vi har nydt det.**	vee har newt dɛ

NUMBERS, see page 28

Travelling around *Rejse omkring*

Plane *Ifly*

Is there a flight to Rønne?	**Er der et fly til Rønne?**	ehr dehr eht flew til **rø**ner
What time should I check in?	**Hvad tid må jeg checke ind?**	vadh teed maw yigh "check"er in
I'd like to ... my reservation.	**Jeg vil gerne ... min bestilling.**	yigh veel **gehr**ner ... meen beh**stil**ing
cancel	**annullere**	annool**ē**rer
change	**ændre på**	**æn**drer paw
confirm	**bekræfte**	ber**kræf**der

Train *Tog*

Where's the railway station?	**Hvor ligger jern-banestationen?**	vōar **lee**gerr **jehrn**bōnerstashonern

INDGANG	ENTRANCE
UDGANG	EXIT
INFORMATION	INFORMATION

Where is/are ...?	**Hvor er ...?**	vōar ehr
booking office	**pladsreserveringen**	**plas**rehsehrvēringern
left-luggage office (baggage check)	**bagageopbevar-ingen**	ba**gō**sheropbervōringern
lost property (lost and found) office	**hittegodskontoret**	**heed**ergoskontōārerdh
luggage lockers	**bagageboksene**	ba**gō**sherbokserner
platform 7	**perron 7**	peh**rong** sewv
ticket office	**billetlugen**	beelehd**loo**gern
waiting room	**venteværelset**	**vehn**derværerlserdh
Where are the toilets?	**Hvor er toilettet?**	vōar ehr toa**leh**derdh

Inquiries *Forespørgsler*

I'd like a ticket to Copenhagen.	**Jeg vil gerne have en billet til Køben-havn.**	yigh veel **gehr**ner ha ehn bee**lehd** til købern**hown**
single (one-way)	**enkelt**	**ehn**kerlt
return (round trip)	**retur**	reh**tōor**
first/second class	**første/anden klasse**	**førs**der/**an**ern **kla**ser
How long does the journey (trip) take?	**Hvor længe tager turen?**	vōar **læn**ger tar **tōo**rern

TELLING THE TIME, see page 27/NUMBERS, see page 28

When is the... train to Århus?	**Hvornår kører det... tog til Århus?**	vornawr **kö**rerr deht... toa til awrhōōs
first/last/next	**første/sidste/ næste**	**för**sder/**sees**der/**næs**ter
What time does the train to Randers leave?	**Hvad tid afgår toget til Randers?**	vadh teed **ow**gawr to°°erdh til **ran**ers
Is this the right train to Aarhus?	**Kører det her tog til Århus?**	**kö**rerr dɛ hehr toa til awhōōs

Underground (subway) *S-tog*

Where's the nearest underground station?	**Hvor er den nærmeste S-togstation?**	vōār ehr dehn **nær**merster ehs toa sta**shon**
Which line should I take to...?	**Hvilket tog skal jeg tage til...?**	**vil**kert toa skal yigh ta til
Where do I change for...?	**Hvor skal jeg skifte til...?**	vōār skal yigh **skeef**der til

Bus *Bus*

Which bus goes to the town centre?	**Hvilken bus kører til centrum?**	**vil**kern boos **kö**rerr til **sent**room
How much is the fare to...?	**Hvor meget koster det til...?**	vōār **mig**hert **kos**derr dɛ til
Will you tell me when to get off?	**Vil De sige til, hvornår jeg skal af?**	veel dee **sēē**er til vor**nawr** yigh skal ah

Boat service *Bådfart*

When does the next boat for... leave?	**Hvornår går den næste båd til...?**	vor**nawr** gaw dehn **næs**der **bāw**dh til
How long does the crossing take?	**Hvor længe varer overfarten?**	vōār **læng**er **vō**rerr o°°erfardern
I'd like to take a canal tour/ tour of the harbour.	**Jeg vil gerne tage på en kanaltur/en havnerundfart.**	yigh veel **gehr**ner ta paw ehn kan**ōl**tōōr/ehn **how**nerroondfart

Taxi *Taxa*

Where can I get a taxi?	**Hvor kan jeg få en taxa?**	vōār kan yigh faw ehn **tak**sa
What's the fare to...?	**Hvad koster det til...?**	vadh **kos**derr dɛ til
Take me to this address.	**Kør mig til denne adresse.**	kör migh til **deh**ner ah**dreh**ser
Please stop here.	**Stands her.**	stans hehr

Car hire (rental) *Biludlejning*

I'd like to hire (rent) a car.	**Jeg vil gerne leje en bil.**	yigh veel **gehr**ner **ligh**er ehn beel
I'd like it for a day/a week.	**Jeg vil gerne have den en enkel dag/en uge.**	yigh veel **gehr**ner ha dehn ehn **ehnk**erl dai/ehn $\overline{oo}$er
What's the charge per day/week?	**Hvad koster det pr. dag/uge?**	vadh **kos**derr dɛ pehr dai/$\overline{oo}$er
Is mileage included?	**Er det med kilometerpenge?**	ehr dɛ mehdh keeloam**ē**derpehnger

---

Road signs *Vejskilte*

DATOPARKERING	Parking according to date
ENSRETTET	One-way street
JERNBANEOVERSKØRING	Railway level crossing
OMKØRSEL	Diversion, detour
OPHØR AF...	End of restriction
OVERHALING FORBUDT	No overtaking
PAS PÅ	General warning notice
UDKØRSEL	Exit
UJØVN VEJ	Bad road
VEJARBEJDE	Road works

Where's the nearest filling station?	**Hvor er den nærmeste benzinstation?**	v$\overline{oo}$ar ehr dehn **nær**merster behn**seen**stashon
Fill it up, please.	**Fuld tank**	f$\overline{oo}$l tank
Give me... litres of petrol (gasoline).	**... liter benzin.**	... **leed**err ben**seen**
super (premium)/ regular/unleaded/ diesel	**super/normal/ blyfri/diesel**	super/nor**mal**/**blew**free/ diesel
How can I find this place?	**Hvordan kan jeg finde frem til dette sted?**	vor**dan** kan yigh **finn**er frehm til **dehd**er stehdh
How far is it to... from here?	**Hvor langt er der til... herfra?**	v$\overline{oo}$ar langt ehr dehr til... hehr**fra**
I've had a breakdown at...	**Jeg har fået motorstop ved...**	yigh har f$\overline{aw}$erdh **moa**torstop vehdh
Can you send a mechanic?	**Kan De sende en mekaniker?**	kan dee **sehn**ner ehn mehka**nee**kerr

| Can you mend this puncture (fix this flat)? | **Kan De reparere denne punktering?** | kan dee rehpar**ē**rer **deh**ner **poonk**tehring |

You're on the wrong road.	**De har kørt forkert.**
Go straight ahead.	**Kør ligeud.**
It's down there on the left/right.	**Det ligger der til venstre/højre.**
opposite/behind...	**overfor/bagved...**
next to/after...	**ved siden af/efter...**
north/south/east/west	**nord/syd/øst/vest**

Sightseeing *Seværdigheder*

Where's the tourist office?	**Hvor er turistbureauet?**	v**ōā**r ehr too**reest**bewroaert
Is there an English-speaking guide?	**Findes der en engelsktalende guide?**	**fin**ners dehr ehn **ehng**erlskt**ō**lernder "guide"
Where is/are the...?	**Hvor er...?**	v**ōā**r ehr
art gallery	**kunstgalleriet**	**koonst**galer**ēē**ert
botanical gardens	**den botaniske have**	dehn bot**a**neesger h**ō**ver
castle	**borgen**	**bōā**rgern
city centre	**byens centrum**	**bew**erns **sen**troom
church	**kirken**	**keē**rgern
concert hall	**koncertsalen**	kon**sehrt**s**ō**lern
harbour	**havnen**	**how**nern
market	**torvet**	**tōā**rverdh
museum	**museum**	**moosse**oom
palace	**slottet**	**slo**derdh
shopping area	**indkøbscentret**	**in**k**ø**bssentrerdh
square	**pladsen/torvet**	**pla**sern/**torv**erdh
tower	**tårnet**	**tawr**nerdh
town hall	**rådhuset**	**rawdh**h**ōō**serdh
What are the opening hours?	**Hvornår er der åbent?**	vor**nawr** ehr dehr **āw**bern
When does it close?	**Hvornår lukkes der?**	vor**nawr** **loog**gers dehr
How much is the entrance fee?	**Hvor meget koster det i entré?**	v**ōā**r **mig**hert kosderr d**ɛ** ee ang**tr**ē

NUMBERS, see page 28

Landmarks *Landemærker*

bridge	**en bro**	ehn bro
forest/wood	**en skov**	ehn sko°°
garden	**en have**	ehn hōver
hill	**en bakke**	ehn bagger
island	**en ø**	ehn ø
lake	**en sø**	ehn sø
mountain	**et bjerg**	eht byehr
path	**en sti**	ehn stee
river	**en flod**	ehn floadh
sea	**et hav**	eht how
valley	**en dal**	ehn dal
village	**en landsby**	ehn lansbew
waterfall	**et vandfald**	eht vanfal

Relaxing *Forlystelser*

What's playing at the... Theatre?	**Hvad spiller man på ...Teateret?**	vadh **speel**err man paw... tɛatrerdh
Are there any seats for tonight?	**Er der flere pladser tilbage til i aften?**	ehr dehr flɛrer plasserr tilbōer til ee afdern
How much are the seats?	**Hvor meget koster billetterne?**	vōar **mighert kos**derr beelehderner
I'd like to reserve 2 seats for the show on Friday evening.	**Jeg vil gerne bestille 2 billetter til forestillingen fredag aften.**	yigh veel **gehr**ner ber**stil**er to beelehderr til foresteelingern frɛdai afdern
Would you like to go out with me tonight?	**Har du lyst til at gå ud med mig i aften?**	har doo lewst til ah gaw ood mehdh migh ee **af**dern
Thank you, but I'm busy.	**Tak, men jeg er desværre optaget.**	tak mehn yigh ehr dehsværrer optaerdh
Is there a disco-theque in town?	**Findes der et dis-kotek i byen?**	finners dehr eht diskoatēk ee bewern
Would you like to dance?	**Skal vi danse?**	skal vee **dan**ser
Thank you, it's been a wonderful evening.	**Tak, det har været en virkelig hyggelig aften.**	tak dɛ har vāārerdh ehn **veer**kerlee **hewg**gerlee afdern

DAYS OF THE WEEK, see page 27

Sports *Sport*

Is there a football (soccer) match anywhere this Saturday?	**Er der en fodbold- kamp et eller andet sted nu på lørdag?**	ehr dehr ehn fodhboldkamp eht ehllerr annerdh stehdh noo paw lørdai
Can you get me a ticket?	**Kan De skaffe mig en billet?**	kan dee sköfer migh ehn beelehd
Where's the nearest golf course?	**Hvor ligger den nærmeste golf- bane?**	vōar leegerr dehn nærmerster golfbōner
Where are the tennis courts?	**Hvor ligger tennis- banerne?**	vōar leegerr "tennis" bōnerner
What's the charge per...?	**Hvad koster det pr....?**	vadh kosderr de pehr
day/round/hour	**dag/runde/time**	dai/roonder/teemer

cycling	**cykling**	sewgling
football (soccer)	**fodbold**	foadbold
horse racing	**hestevæddeløb**	hehsdervædherløb
horse riding	**ridning**	reedhning
swimming	**svømning**	svømning
tennis	**tennis**	"tennis"

Can one swim in the lake/river?	**Kan man gå i van- det i søen/floden?**	kan man gaw ee vanerdh ee søern/floadhern
Is there a swimming pool here?	**Findes der et svømmebasin her?**	finners dehr eht svömerbassehng hehr
Is there a skating rink near here?	**Findes der en skøj- tebane her i nærhe- den?**	finners dehr ehn skoiderbōner hehr ee nærhēdhern
I'd like to ski.	**Jeg vil gerne stå på ski.**	yigh veel gehrner staw paw ski
downhill/cross- country skiing	**styrtløb/langrend**	stewrtløb/langrehn
I want to hire...	**Jeg vil gerne leje...**	yigh veel gehrner ligher
skates	**et par skøjter**	eht par skoiderr
skiing equipment	**noget skiudstyr**	nōāert skioodhstewr
skis	**et par ski**	eht par ski
I'd like to hire a... bicycle.	**Jeg vil gerne leje en...**	yigh veel gehrner ligher ehn
5-gear	**cykel med gear**	sewgel mehdh geer
mountain	**bjergcykel**	byergsewgel

Shops and services *Butikker og servicevirksomheder*

Where's the nearest...?	**Hvor er den/det nærmeste...**	v$\overline{oo}$r ehr dehn/deht nærmerster
bakery	**bager**	b$\overline{oo}$er
bookshop	**boghandel**	boahanerl
butcher's	**slagter**	slagderr
chemist's/drugstore	**apotek**	apotehk
dentist	**tandlæge**	tanlæer
department store	**stormagasin**	stoarmagaseen
grocery	**købmand**	køman
hairdresser's (ladies/men)	**frisør (dame-/herre-)**	freesør (damer-/hehrrer-)
newsagent's	**bladhandler**	bladhhanlerr
post office	**posthus**	posthoos
souvenir shop	**souvenirbutik**	soovern$\overline{ee}$rbootik
supermarket	**supermarked**	s$\overline{oo}$bermarkerdh

General expressions *Almindelige udtryk*

Where's the main shopping area?	**Hvor er forretningskvarteret**	v$\overline{oo}$r er forrehtningskvartehrerdh

Can I help you?	**Kan jeg hjælpe med noget?**
What would you like?	**Hvad skulle det være?**
What... would you like?	**Hvilken... ønsker De?**
colour/shape/quality	**farve/form/kvalitet**
I'm sorry, we don't have any.	**Jeg beklager, det har vi ikke.**
We're out of stock.	**Der er udsolgt.**
Shall we order it for you?	**Skal vi bestille det til Dem?**
Anything else?	**Skulle der være andet?**
That's... kroner, please.	**Det bliver... kroner.**
The cash desk is over there.	**Kassen er derovre.**

I'd like a... one.	**Jeg vil gerne have en...**	yigh veel **gehr**ner ha ehn
big	**stor**	stoar
cheap	**billig**	beelee
dark	**mørk**	mørk
good	**god**	goadh

heavy	tung	toong
large	stor	stoar
light (weight)	let	leht
light (colour)	lys	lews
oval	oval	oavōl
rectangular	rektangulær	rehktangoolær
round	rund	roon
small	lille	leeler
square	firkantet	fēērkanderdh
sturdy	solid	soleedh

Do you have any...?	Har De nogen...?	har dee nōāern
Don't you have anything...?	Har De ikke noget...?	har dee igger nōāert
cheaper/better	billigere/bedre	beeleēērrer/behdhrer
larger/smaller	større/mindre	størrer/mindrer
Can I try it on?	Kan jeg prøve den?	kan yigh prōver dehn
How much is this?	Hvad koster det?	vadh kosder dE
Please write it down.	Vær rar og skriv det ned.	vær rar oa skreev dE nedh
I don't want to spend more than... kroner.	Jeg vil ikke bruge mere end... kroner.	yigh veel igger brōōer mēhrer ehn... krōānerr
No, I don't like it.	Det bryder jeg mig ikke om.	dE brewdherr yigh migh igger om
I'll take it.	Jeg tager det.	yigh tar dE
Do you accept credit cards?	Tager De kreditkort?	tar dee krehditkort
Can you order it for me?	Kan De bestille det til mig?	kan dee berstiler dE til migh

black	sort	soart
blue	blå	blaw
brown	brun	broon
green	grøn	grøn
grey	grå	graw
orange	orange	oarangsher
red	rød	rødh
white	hvid	veedh
yellow	gul	gool
light...	lyse-	lewser-
dark...	mørke-	mørker-

NUMBERS, see page 28

Chemist's (drugstore) *Apotek*

aspirin	**en æske aspirin**	ehn **æsger** "aspirin"
condoms	**nogle kondomer**	nōāler kon**dom**err
deodorant	**en deodorant**	ehn dEodo**rant**
insect spray (killer)	**en insekt-spray**	ehn in**sehkt**"spray"
moisturizing cream	**fugtighedscreme**	foogteehehdhskrehm
razor blades	**nogle barberblade**	nōāler barbehrblōdher
shampoo	**en shampoo**	ehn "shampoo"
soap	**et stykke sæbe**	eht **stewgger sǣber**
sun-tan cream	**noget solcreme**	nōāert **soal**krehm
tampons	**nogle tamponer**	nōāler tam**pong**er
toothpaste	**en tandpasta**	ehn **tan**pasta

Clothing *Klæder*

blouse	**en bluse**	ehn **blōōser**
bra	**en bh**	ehn be haw
boots	**et par støvler**	eht par stø°°lerr
dress	**en kjole**	ehn kyoaler
gloves	**et par handsker**	eht par hansgerr
jersey	**en ulden trøje**	ehn oolern **troi**er
scarf	**et tørklæde**	eht **tørklædher**
shirt	**en skjorte**	ehn **skyoarder**
skirt	**en nederdel**	ehn **nehdh**erdehl
shoes	**et par sko**	eht par skoa
socks	**et par sokker**	eht par **sogg**err
swimming trunks	**et par badebukser**	eht par **bōdh**erboogserr
swimsuit	**en badedragt**	ehn **bōdh**erdragt
T-shirt	**en T-shirt**	ehn "T-shirt"
tights	**et par strømpe-bukser**	eht par **strømp**erboogserr
trousers	**et par bukser**	eht par **boogs**err
underpants	**et par underbukser**	eht par **oon**erboogserr
What's it made of?	**Hvad er det lavet af?**	vadh ehr dE **laverdh** ah

cotton	**bomuld**	bomool
denim	**denim**	"denim"
lace	**knipling**	**knipling**
leather	**læder**	**lædh**err
linen	**lærred**	**lærerdh**
silk	**silke**	**seel**ker
suede	**ruskind**	**roo**skin
velvet	**fløjl**	floil
wool	**uld**	ool

Grocer's *Madvarer*

I'd like some bread, please.	**Jeg vil gerne have noget brød.**	yigh veel **gehr**ner ha n<u>oa</u>ert brødh
What sort of cheese do you have?	**Hvad slags ost har De?**	vadh slags ost har dee
half a kilo of tomatoes	**et halvt kilo tomater**	eht halt **kee**lo to**mad**err
a litre of milk	**en liter mælk**	ehn **lee**derr mælk
4 slices of ham	**4 skiver skinke**	feerer **skee**verr **skeeng**er
a tin (can) of peaches	**en dåse ferskner**	ehn **daw**ser **fersg**nerr

Miscellaneous *Forskelligt*

I want to buy a/an/ some...	**Jeg vil gerne have...**	yigh veel **gehr**ner ha
bottle opener	**oplukker**	**op**loogger
newspaper	**en avis**	ehn a**vees**
American/English	**amerikansk/ engelsk**	amehree**kansk**/**ehng**erlsk
postcard	**et postkort**	eht **post**kort
torch	**en lommelygte**	ehn **lom**erlewgder
towel	**et håndklæde**	eht **hawn**klædher
I'd like a film for this camera.	**Jeg vil gerne have en film til dette kamera.**	yigh vil **gehr**ner ha ehn film til **dehd**er **ka**merra
black and white	**sort/hvid**	soart/veedh
colour	**farve-**	**far**ver-
Can you repair this camera?	**Kan De reparere dette kamera?**	kan dee rehpar**Ēr**er **dehd**er **ka**merra

Souvenirs *Souvenirer*

ceramics	**keramik**	kehra**mēēk**
costumed doll	**en dukke i folke- dragt**	ehn **doog**ger ee **foal**kerdragt
embroidery	**broderi**	broader**ree**
glassware	**en glasting**	ehn **glas**teeng
hand-painted	**håndmalet**	**hawn**m<u>o</u>lert
modern	**moderne**	moad**Ēr**nert
knitware	**strikvarer**	**streek**v<u>o</u>rerr
shag-rug	**et rya-tæppe**	eht **rēwo**taiber
textiles	**tekstilvarer**	t**ɛk**steelv<u>o</u>rerr
hand-printed	**stortryk**	**stoaf**trewg

DANISH

At the bank *I banken*

Where's the nearest currency exchange office/bank?	**Hvor er det nærmeste vekselkontor/bank?**	võar ehr dɛ **nærmerster vehks**erlkontõar /bank
I want to change some dollars/pounds.	**Jeg ønsker at veksle nogle dollars/pund.**	yigh **ønsgerr at vehks**ler nõaler "dollars"/poon
What's the exchange rate?	**Hvad er vekselkursen?**	vadh ehr **vehks**erlkoorsern
I want to cash a traveller's cheque.	**Jeg ønsker at indløse en rejsecheck.**	yigh **ønsgerr at inløs**er ehn **righ**ser"cheque"

At the post office *Posthus*

I'd like to send this (by)...	**Jeg vil gerne sende det her...**	yigh veel **gehr**ner **seh**ner dɛ hehr
airmail	**(med) luftpost**	(mehdh) **looft**post
express	**expres**	**ehks**prehs
A...-øre stamp, please.	**Et...-øres frimærke.**	eht... **ø**rers **free**mærker
What's the postage for a postcard/letter to Los Angeles?	**Hvad er portoen for et postkort/brev til Los Angeles?**	vadh ehr **porto**ærn for eht **post**kort/breh°° til "Los Angeles"
Is there any post (mail) for me?	**Er der noget post til mig?**	ehr dehr **nõa**ert post til migh

Telephoning *Telefonering*

Where's the nearest telephone booth?	**Hvor er den nærmeste telefonboks?**	võar ehr dehn **nær**merster teh**ler**foanboks
I'd like a telephone card.	**Jeg vil gerne have et telet.**	yigh veel **gehr**ner ha eht **teh**let
May I use your phone?	**Må jeg låne Deres telefon?**	maw yigh **law**ner **dehr**ers teh**ler**foan
Hello. This is...	**Hallo. Det er...**	halloa dɛ ehr
I'd like to speak to...	**Jeg vil gerne tale med...**	yigh veel **gehr**ner **tõl**er mehdh
When will he/she be back?	**Hvornår kommer han/hun tilbage?**	vornawr **koam**err han/hoon til**bõer**
Will you tell him/her I called? My name is...	**Vil De sige til ham/hende, at jeg ringede? Mit navn er...**	veel dee **sõõ**er til ham/**heh**ner at yigh **ring**erdher. meet nown ehr

NUMBERS, see page 28

Dansk

Doctor *Læge*

Where can I find a doctor who speaks English?	**Hvor kan jeg finde en læge, der taler engelsk?**	vōar kan yigh **finner** ehn **læer** dehr **tōlerr ehng**erlsk
Where's the surgery (doctor's office)?	**Hvor har lægen konsultation?**	vōar har **læer**n konsooltas**hon**
Can I have an appointment...?	**Kan jeg komme...?**	kan yigh **komer**
tomorrow	**i morgen**	ee **mōäer**n
as soon as possible	**så snart som muligt**	saw snart som **mool**eet

Parts of the body *Legemsdele*

arm	**armen**	**arm**ern
back	**ryggen**	**rewg**gern
bone	**knoglen**	**knoal**ern
ear	**øret**	**ører**dh
eye(s)	**øjet**	**oier**dh
face	**ansigtet**	**anseeg**derdh
finger	**fingeren**	**feeng**gerern
foot	**foden**	**foad**hern
hand	**hånden**	**hawn**ern
head	**hovedet**	ho°°erdh
heart	**hjertet**	**yehr**derdh
knee	**knæet**	**knäæ**erdh
leg	**benet**	**behn**erdh
lung	**lungen**	**loong**ern
mouth	**munden**	**moon**ern
muscle	**muskelen**	**moosg**lern
neck	**halsen/nakken**	**hals**ern/**nagg**ern
nose	**næsen**	**näæs**ern
shoulder	**skulderen**	**skool**errern
skin	**huden**	**hoodh**ern
stomach	**maven**	**mōv**ern
throat	**halsen**	**hals**ern
tongue	**tungen**	**toong**ern
I've got a/an...	**Jeg har fået...**	yigh har **fāw**erdh
bruise	**et blåt mærke**	eht blawt **mær**ker
burn	**et brandsår**	eht **brans**āwr
cut	**et snitsår**	eht **sneets**āwr
insect bite	**et insektbid**	eht **insehkt**beedh
rash	**udslæt**	**oodhs**læt
sting	**et stik**	eht **steek**
swelling	**en hævelse**	ehn **hæv**erlser
wound	**et sår**	eht **sāwr**

EMERGENCIES, see page 30

Could you have a look at it?	Kan De se på det?	kan dee SE paw dE
It hurts.	Det gør ondt.	dE gør oant
I feel dizzy.	Jeg er svimmel.	yigh err sveemerl
I feel...	Jeg har...	yigh har
nauseous	kvalme	kvalmer
shivery	kuldegysninger	koolergewsningerr
I have a temperature (fever).	Jeg har feber.	yigh har fehberr
I'm diabetic.	Jeg har sukker-syge.	yigh har sooggersewer
Can you give me a prescription for this?	Kan jeg få en recept på det?	kan yigh faw ehn rehsehpt paw dE
May I have a receipt for my health insurance?	Må jeg få en kvit-tering til min syge-forsikring?	maw yigh faw ehn kveettehring til meen sewerforsikring

---

Hvor længe har De følt Dem sådan?	How long have you been feeling like this?
Hvor gør det ondt?	Where does it hurt?
Jeg tager temperaturen/måler blodtrykket.	I'll take your temperature/blood pressure.
Jeg vil give Dem en indsprøjtning.	I'll give you an injection.
Jeg vil have en blodprøve/afføringsprøve/urinprøve.	I want a specimen of your blood/stools/urine.
De skal holde sengen i... dage.	You must stay in bed for... days.
De bør undersøges af en speciallæge.	I want you to see a specialist.

Can you recommend a good dentist?	Kan De anbefale en god tandlæge?	kan dee anberfoler ehn goadh tanlææer
I have toothache.	Jeg har tandpine.	yigh har tanpeener
I've lost a filling.	Jeg har tabt en plombe.	yigh har tabt ehn ploamber

Time and date *Klokken og dato*

It's...	Den er...	dehn ehr
five past one	**fem minutter over et**	fehm mi**noo**derr o°°er eht
ten past two	**ti minutter over to**	tee mi**noo**derr o°°er toa
a quarter past three	**kvart over tre**	kvart o°°er treh
twenty past four	**tyve minutter over fire**	t̄ew̄ver mi**noo**derr o°°er **feer**er
twenty-five past five	**fem minutter i halvseks**	fehm mi**noo**derr ee **hal**sehks
half past six	**halvsyv**	**hal**sewv
twenty-five to seven	**fem minutter over halvsyv**	fehm mi**noo**derr o°°er **hal**sewv
twenty to eight	**tyve minutter i otte**	t̄ew̄ver mi**noo**derr ee **oa**der
a quarter to nine	**kvart i ni**	kvart ee nee
ten to ten	**ti minutter i ti**	tee mi**noo**derr ee tee
five to eleven	**fem minutter i elleve**	fehm mi**noo**derr ee **ehl**ver
twelve o'clock	**tolv/fireogtyve**	toal/**feer**er oa t̄ew̄ver
in the morning	**om morgenen**	om **moa**ernern
in the afternoon	**om eftermiddagen**	om **ehf**dermiddaern
in the evening	**om aftenen**	om **af**dernern
at night	**om natten**	om **nad**dern

Sunday	**søndag**	**søn**dai
Monday	**mandag**	**man**dai
Tuesday	**tirsdag**	**t̄eers**dai
Wednesday	**onsdag**	**oans**dai
Thursday	**torsdag**	**toars**dai
Friday	**fredag**	**freh**dai
Saturday	**lørdag**	**lør**dai
January	**januar**	**yan**ooar
February	**februar**	**fehb**rooar
March	**marts**	marts
April	**april**	a**preel**
May	**maj**	migh
June	**juni**	**ȳoo**nee
July	**juli**	**ȳoo**lee
August	**august**	ow**goost**
September	**september**	sehp**tehm**berr
October	**oktober**	ok**toa**berr
November	**november**	noa**vehm**berr
December	**december**	deh**sehm**berr

NUMBERS, see page 28

yesterday/today	**i går/i dag**	ee gawr/ee dai
tomorrow	**i morgen**	ee mōāern
spring/summer	**forår/sommer**	forawr/somerr
autumn/winter	**efterår/vinter**	ehfderawr/vinderr

Numbers *Tal*

0	**nul**	nool
1	**en**	ehn
2	**to**	toa
3	**tre**	treh
4	**fire**	fēērer
5	**fem**	fehm
6	**seks**	sehks
7	**syv**	sewv
8	**otte**	oader
9	**ni**	nee
10	**ti**	tee
11	**elleve**	ehlver
12	**tolv**	toal
13	**tretten**	trehdern
14	**fjorten**	fyoardern
15	**femten**	fehmdern
16	**seksten**	sighsdern
17	**sytten**	sewdern
18	**atten**	addern
19	**nitten**	needdern
20	**tyve**	tēwver
21	**enogtyve**	ehnotēwver
30	**tredive**	trehdhver
40	**fyrre**	førrer
50	**halvtreds**	haltrehs
60	**tres**	trehs
70	**halvfjerds**	halfyehrs
80	**firs**	fēers
90	**halvfems**	halfehms
100	**hundrede**	hoonrerdher
1000	**tusind**	tōōsin
100,000	**hundrede tusind**	hoonrerdher tōōsin
1,000,000	**en million**	ehn meelyoan
first	**første**	førsder
second	**anden/andet**	anern/anerdh
third	**tredje**	trehdhyer
once/twice	**en gang/to gange**	ehn gang/toa ganger
a half	**en halv/et halvt**	ehn hal/eht halt

Where do you come from? *Hvor kommer De fra?*

Canada	**Canada**	kanada
England	**England**	ehnglan
Finland	**Finland**	finlan
Great Britain	**Storbritannien**	stoarbritanyern
Ireland	**Irland**	irlan
New Zealand	**New Zealand**	"new zealand"
Norway	**Norge**	nōārer
Scotland	**Skotland**	skotlan
South Africa	**Sydafrika**	sewdhafrika
Sweden	**Sverige**	svehrēēer
United States	**USA**	oo ehs ah

Signs and notices *Skilte og opslag*

Åben	Open
Alt optaget	No vacancies
Damer	Ladies
Fare (Livsfare)	Danger (of death)
... forbudt	... forbidden
Forsigtig	Caution
Gratis adgang	Free admittance
Herrer	Gentlemen
Indgangen	Entrance
Information	Information
Ingen adgang/Adgang forbudt	No admittance
I uorden	Out of order
Kasse	Cash desk
Koldt	Cold
Ledig	Vacant
Må ikke berøres	Do not touch
Nødudgang	Emergency exit
Optaget	Occupied
Privat vej	Private road
Reserveret	Reserved
Rygning forbudt	No smoking
Skub	Push
Til leje	To let/for hire
Til salg	For sale
Træk	Pull
Udgang	Exit
Udsalg	Sale
Udsolgt	Sold out
Varmt	Hot
Vent	Please wait
Vil ikke forstyrres	Do not disturb

Emergency *Nødstilfælde*

Call the police	**Tilkald politiet**	tilkal politierdh
Get a doctor	**Tilkald læge**	tilkal lǣer
Go away	**Gå væk**	gaw vehk
HELP	**HJÆLP**	yehlp
I'm ill	**Jeg er syg**	yigh ehr sew
I'm lost	**Jeg er faret vild**	yigh ehr fōōrerdh veel
Leave me alone	**Lad mig være i fred**	ladh migh vǣrer ee frehdh
LOOK OUT	**GIV AGT**	giv agt
STOP THIEF	**STOP TYVEN**	stop tewvern
My ... has been stolen.	**Min/Mit ... er blevet stjålet.**	meen/meet ... ehr blehᵒᵒerdh styawlerdh
I've lost my ...	**Jeg har tabt ...**	yigh har tabt
handbag	**min håndtaske**	meen hāwntasger
passport	**mit pas**	meet pas
wallet	**min tegnebog**	meen tighnerboa
Where can I find a doctor who speaks English?	**Hvor kan jeg finde en læge, der taler engelsk?**	vōar kan yigh finner ehn lǣer dehr tōlerr ehngerlsk

Guide to Danish pronunciation *Udtale*

Consonants

Letter	Approximate pronounciation	Symbol	Example	
b, f, l, m, n, v as in English				
c	1) before **e, i, y, œ** and **ø**, like **s** in **sit**	c	**citron**	seetrōān
	2) before **a, o, u** and a consonant, like **k** in **kite**	k	**café**	kafē
d	1) when at the end of the word after a vowel, or between a vowel and unstressed **e** or **i**, like **th** in **this**	dh	**med**	mɛdh
	2) as in English	d	**dale**	dōler
g	1) at the beginning of a word or syllable, like **g** in **go**	g	**glas**	gals
	2) at the end of a word, usually like **y** in **yet**; sometimes mute after **a, e, o**	y	**sige**	sēēyer

TELEPHONING, see page 24/DOCTOR, see page 25

hv	like **v** in **v**iew	v	**hvot**	v‾oͣr
j, hj	like **y** in **y**et	y	**ja**	y‾æ
k	1) between vowels, generally like **g** in **g**o	g	**ikke**	i**gg**er
	2) otherwise like **k** in **k**ite	k	**kaffe**	**k**ah**f**er
l	always as in **l**eaf, never as in be**ll**	l	**vel**	ve**hl**
ng	as in si**ng**, never as in fi**ng**er, unless **n** and **g** are in separate syllables	ng	**ingen**	**ing**ern
		ngg	**ingre-diens**	**ing**gray-dee**ehnss**
p	1) between vowels, generally like **b** in **b**it	b	**stoppe**	sto**bb**er
	2) otherwise like **p** in **p**ill	p	**pude**	**p**oo**dh**er
r	pronounced in the back of the throat, as in French at the beginnings of words, but otherwise often omitted	r	**rose**	r‾oͣsser
s	always as in **s**ee (never as in ri**s**e)	s	**skål**	**s**kawl
sj	usually like **sh** in **sh**eet (but may also be pronounced like the **ss y** in pa**ss y**ou)	sh	**sjælden**	**sh**ehlern
t	1) between vowels, generally like **d** in **d**o	d	**lytte**	lew**d**er
	2) otherwise like **t** in **t**o (at the end of a word often mute)	t	**torsk**	**t**oarsk

Vowels

a	1) long, like **a** in car	‾o	**klare**	k**l‾o**rer
	2) short, more like **a** in cart	a	**hat**	h**a**t
e	1) when long, as **e** in the French "les" but longer	Ē	**flere**	fl**ē**rer
	2) short, like **i** in hit	ɛ	**fedt**	f**ɛ**t
	3) short, also like **e** in met	eh	**let**	l**eh**t
	4) when unstressed, like **a** in above	er	**hjælpe**	y**e**hlp**er**

i	1) long, like **ee** in b**ee**	e͞e	**ile**	**e͞e**ler
	2) short, between **a** in plate and **i** in p**i**n	i	**drikke**	**dri**gger
o	1) when long, like the **oa** sound in b**oa**t, before you bring your lips together to finish the word	o͞a	**pol**	p**o͞a**l
	2) when short, more or less the same sound	oa	**bonde**	**boa**ner
	3) when short, also like **o** in l**o**t	o	**godt**	god
u	1) when long, like **oo** in p**oo**l	o͞o	**frue**	fr**o͞o**er
	2) when short, like **oo** in l**oo**t	oo	**nu**	noo
y	put your tongue in the position for the **ee** of b**ee**, but round your lips as for the **oo** of p**oo**l	e͞w ew	**nyde** **lytte**	n**e͞w**dher l**ew**der
æ	1) when long, like **ai** in **ai**r	ǣ	**sæbe**	s**ǣ**ber
	2) when short, like **e** in g**e**t	eh	**ægte**	**eh**gter
ø	put your lips together to whistle but make a noise with your voice instead; can be long or short	ø̄ ø	**frøken** **øl**	**frø̄**gern øl
å	1) when long, like **aw** in s**aw**	a͞w	**åben**	**a͞w**bern
	2) when short, like **o** in **o**n	aw	**på**	paw

Diphthongs

av, af	like **ow** in n**ow**	ow	**hav**	how
ef, ej, ij, eg	like **igh** in s**igh**	igh	**nej**	nigh
ev	like **e** in g**e**t followed by a short **oo** sound	eh°°	**levned**	**leh**°°erdh
ou, ov	like **o** in g**o**t followed by a short **oo** sound	o°°	**sjov**	sho°°
øi, øj	like **oi** in **oi**l	oi	**øje**	oier
øv	like **ur** in h**ur**t followed by a short **oo** sound	ø	**søvnig**	sø°°nee

FINNISH

Finnish

Basic expressions *Perusilmaisut*

Yes/No.	**Kyllä/Ei.**	kewllæ/ay¹
Please.	**Olkaa hyvä.**	oalkaa hewvæ
Thank you.	**Kiitos.**	keetoass
I beg your pardon?	**Anteeksi?**	ahntāyksi

Introductions *Esittely*

Good morning.	**(Hyvää) huomenta.**	(hewvāē) h°°oamayntah
Good afternoon.	**(Hyvää) päivää.**	(hewvāē) pæ¹vāē
Good night.	**Hyvää yötä.**	hewvāē ᵉʷurtæ
Good-bye.	**Näkemiin.**	nækaymeen
Hello/Hi!	**Hei/Terve!**	hay¹/tayrvay
My name is...	**Nimeni on...**	nimmayni oan
What's your name?	**Mikä teidän nimenne on?**	mikkæ tay¹dæn nimmaynnay oan
Pleased to meet you.	**Hauska tutustua.**	hah°°skah tootoostooah
How are you?	**Mitä kuuluu?**	mittæ koȯoȯo
Very well, thanks. And you?	**Kiitos, hyvää. Entä sinulle?**	keetoass hewvāē. ayntæ sinnoollay
Where do you come from?	**Mistä päin tulette?**	mistæ pæ¹n toolayttay
I'm from...	**Olen...-sta/...-lta**	oalayn...-stah/...-ltah
Australia	**Australia**	ah°°straaliah
Canada	**Kanada**	kahnahdah
Great Britain	**Iso-Britannia**	isoa-britahnniah
United States	**USA (Yhdysvallat)**	ōōæssaa (ewhdewsvahllaht)
I'm with my...	**Minulla on mukana...**	minnoollah oan mookahnah
wife	**vaimo**	vah¹moa
husband	**aviomies**	ahvioam¹ays
family	**perhe**	payrhay
boyfriend	**poikaystävä**	poa¹kahewstævæ
girlfriend	**tyttöystävä**	tewtturewstævæ
I'm here on business/ vacation.	**Olen täällä liike-matkalla/lomalla.**	oalayn tāēllæ leekaymahtkahllah/ loamahllah

PRONUNCIATION, see page 63/EMERGENCIES, see page 62

Suomi

Questions *Kysymyksiä*

When?/How?	**Milloin?/Kuinka?**	milloa'n/koo'nkah
What?/Why?	**Mitä?/Miksi?**	mittæ/miksi
Who?	**Kuka?**	kookah
Which?	**Mikä?/Kumpi?**	mikkæ/koompi
Where is/are...?	**Missä on/ovat...?**	missæ oan/oavaht
Where can I find/get...?	**Mistä löydän...?**	mistæ lur^{ew}dæn
How far?	**Kuinka kaukana?**	koo'nkah kah^{oo}kanah
How long (time)?	**Kuinka kauan?**	koo'nkah kah^{oo}ahn
How much/many?	**Kuinka paljon/monta?**	koo'nkah pahlyoan/moantah
Can I have...?	**Saanko...?**	saahnkoa
Can you help me?	**Voitteko auttaa minua?**	voa'ttaykoa ah^{oo}ttaa minnooah
Is there/Are there...?	**Onko...?**	oankoa
There isn't/aren't...	**Ei ole...**	ay' oalay
There isn't/aren't any.	**Ei ole yhtään.**	ay' oalay ewhtæn

Do you speak...? *Puhutteko...?*

What does this/that mean?	**Mitä tämä/tuo tarkoittaa?**	mittæ tæmæ/t^{oo}oa tahrkoa'ttaa
Can you translate this for us?	**Voitteko kääntää tämän meille?**	voa'ttaykoa kæntæ tæmæn may'llay
Do you speak English?	**Puhutteko englantia?**	poohoottaykoa aynglahntiah
I don't speak (much) Finnish.	**En puhu (paljon) suomea.**	ayn poohoo (pahlyoan) s^{oo}oamayah
Could you speak more slowly?	**Voisitteko puhua hitaammin?**	voa'sittaykoa poohooah hittaammin
Could you repeat that?	**Voisitteko toistaa sen.**	voa'sittaykoa toa'staa sayn
Could you write it down, please?	**Voisitteko kirjoittaa sen.**	voa'sittaykoa keeryoa'ttaa sayn
I understand.	**Ymmärrän.**	ewmmærræn
I don't understand.	**En ymmärrä.**	ayn ewmmærræ

It's... *Se on...*

better/worse	**parempi/huonompi**	**pah**raympi/**h°°oa**noampi
big/small	**suuri/pieni**	**soo**ri/p'ayni
cheap/expensive	**halpa/kallis**	**hahl**pah/**kahl**liss
early/late	**aikainen/myöhäi-nen**	ah'ka'nayn/**m**ᵉʷurhæ'nayn
good/bad	**hyvä/huono**	**hew**væ/**h°°oa**ŋoa
hot/cold	**kuuma/kylmä**	**kōō**mah/**kewl**mæ
near/far	**lähellä/kaukana**	**læ**hayllæ/**kah°°**kahnah
right/wrong	**oikea/väärä**	**oa**'kaya/**vǣ**ræ
vacant/occupied	**vapaa/varattu**	**vah**paa/**vah**rahttoo

A few more useful words *Muutama hyödyllinen sana lisää*

a little/a lot	**vähän/paljon**	**væ**hæn/**pahl**yoan
and	**ja**	yah
behind	**-n takana/taakse**	-n **tah**kahnah/**taak**say
below	**-n alla/alle**	-n **ahl**lah/**ahl**lay
between	**-n välissä/välillä**	-n **væ**lissæ/**væ**lillæ
but	**mutta**	**moot**tah
down	**alas/alhaalla**	**ahl**lahs/**ahl**haallah
downstairs	**alakerrassa**	**ahl**lahkayrrassah
from	**-n suunnasta**	-n **soon**nahstah
in	**-n sisässä/-llä**	-n **sis**æssæ/-llæ
inside	**sisään/sisälle**	**sis**ǣn/**sis**sællay
near	**lähellä/lähelle**	**læ**hayllæ/**læ**hayllay
never	**ei koskaan**	ay' **koas**kaan
not	**ei**	ay'
nothing	**ei mitään**	ay' **mit**tǣn
now	**nyt**	newt
only	**vain**	**vah**'n
or	**tai**	**tah**'
outside	**ulkona/ulos**	**ool**koanah/**oo**loas
perhaps	**ehkä**	**ayh**kæ
since	**alkaen**	**ahl**kahayn
soon	**pian**	p'ahn
then	**sitten**	**sit**tayn
through	**läpi**	**læ**pi
too (also)	**myös**	mᵉʷurss
towards	**-a kohti**	-a **koah**ti
under	**alla/alle**	**ahl**lah/**ahl**lay
up	**ylös/ylhäällä**	**ewl**urss/**ewlh**ǣllæ
upstairs	**yläkerrassa**	**ewl**ækayrrahssah
very	**tosi**	**toa**si
with	**-n kanssa**	-n **kahns**sah
without	**ilman**	**il**mahn

Hotel—Accommodation *Hotelli*

I have a reservation.	**Minulla on varaus.**	minnoollah oan vahra°°s
We've reserved 2 rooms.	**Olemme varanneet kaksi huonetta.**	oalaymmay vahrahnnayt kahksi h°°oanayttah
Do you have any vacancies?	**Onko teillä vapaita huoneita?**	oankoa tay'llæ vahpah'tah h°°oanay'tah
I'd like a...	**Haluaisin...**	hahlooah'sin
single room	**yhden hengen huoneen**	ewhdayn hayngayn h°°oanāyn
double room	**kahden hengen huoneen**	kahhdayn hayngayn h°°oanāyn
with twin beds	**jossa on kaksi vuodetta**	yaossah oan kahksi v°°oadayttah
with a double bed	**jossa on kaksoisvuode**	yaossah oan kahksoa'sv°°oaday
with a bath	**jossa on kylpyhuone**	yaossah oan kewlpewh°°oanay
with a shower	**jossa on suihku**	yaossah oan soo'hkoo
Is there...?	**Onko...**	oankoa
air conditioning	**ilmastointia**	ilmahstoa'ntiah
a private toilet	**oma wc**	oamah vāysāy
a radio/television in the room	**huoneessa radio/televisio**	h°°oanayssah rahdioa/ taylayvissioa
a sauna	**saunaa**	sah°°naa
What's the price...?	**Mitä hinta on...?**	mittæ hintah oan
Is there a camp site near here?	**Onko lähellä leirin-täaluetta?**	oankoa læhayllæ lay'rintæahlooayttah
Can we camp here?	**Voimmeko leiriytyä tässä?**	voa'mmaykoa lay'riewtewæ tæssæ
We'll be staying...	**Viivymme...**	veevewmmay
overnight only	**vain yhden yön**	vah'n ewhdayn ᵉʷurn
a few days	**muutamia päiviä**	mōōtahmiah pæ'viæ
a week	**viikkon**	veekoan

Decision *Päätös*

May I see the room?	**Saanko nähdä huoneen?**	saankoa næhdæ h°°oanāyn
That's fine. I'll take it.	**Tämä on hyvä. Otan sen.**	tæmæ oan hewvæ. oatahn sayn
No. I don't like it.	**Ei. En pidä siitä.**	ay'. ayn pidæ seettæ
It's too...	**Se on liian...**	say oan leeahn
dark/small	**pimeä/pieni**	pimmᵉʸæ/p'ayni
noisy	**meluisa**	mayloo'sah

NUMBERS, see page 60

Do you have anything...?	Onko teillä mitään...?	oankoa tay'llæ mittæn
better/bigger	parempaa/suurempaa	pahraympaa/sōōraympaa
cheaper	halvempaa	hahlvaympaa
quieter	rauhallisempaa	rah°°hahllissaympaa

Sukunimi/Etunimi	Name/First name
Kotikaupunki/Katu/Numero	Home town/Street/Number
Kansallisuus/Ammatti	Nationality/Occupation
Syntymäaika/-paikka	Date/Place of birth
Tulossa/Menossa	Coming from.../Going to...
Passin numero	Passport number
Paikka/Päivä	Place/Date
Allekirjoitus	Signature

General requirements *Yleisiä tarpeita*

The key to room..., please.	Avain huoneeseen numero..., kiitos.	ahvah'n h°°oanäyssäyn noomayroa... keetoass
Where's the...?	Missä on...?	missæ oan
bathroom	kylpyhuone	kewlpewh°°oanay
dining-room	ruokasali	r°°oakahsahli
emergency exit	hätäuloskäynti	hætæooloaskæ⁰ʷnti
lift (elevator)	hissi	hissi
Where are the toilets?	Missä ovat WC:t?	missæ oavaht väysäyt
Where can I park my car?	Minne voin pysäköidä autoni?	minnay voa'n pewsækur'dæ ah°°toani

Checking out *Lähtö*

May I have my bill, please?	Saisinko laskuni.	sah'sinkoa lahskooni
Can you get us a taxi?	Voitteko hankkia meille taksin?	voa'ttaykoa hahnkkiah may'llay tahksin
It's been a very enjoyable stay.	Olen viihtynyt erinomaisesti.	oalayn veehtewnewt ayrinoamah'saysti

Eating out *Ravintolat*

Can you recommend a good restaurant?	**Voitteko suositella hyvää ravintolaa?**	voa'sittaykoa s°°sittayllah hewvǣ rahvintoalaa
I'd like to reserve a table for 4.	**Varaisin pöydän neljälle.**	vahrahisin p⁗ewdæn nayljællay
We'll come at 8.	**Tulemme kello 8.**	toolaymmay kaylloa kahhdayksahn
I'd like breakfast/ lunch/dinner.	**Saisinko aamiaisen/lounas/päivällinen.**	sah'sinkoa aamiah'ssayn/ loa°°nahss/pǣ'vællinnayn
What do you recommend?	**Mitä suosittelisitte?**	mittæ s°°oasittaylissittay
Do you have a set menu/local dishes?	**Onko teillä vakiolistaa/paikallisia erikoisuuksia?**	oankoa tay'llæ vahkioalistaa/ pah'kahllissiah ayrikoa'sōōksiah
Do you have any vegetarian dishes?	**Onko teillä kasvissyöjän annoksia?**	oankoa tay'llæ kahsvissew⁗yæn ahnnoaksiah

---

Mitä saisi olla?	What would you like?
Suosittelen tätä.	I recommend this.
Mitä haluaisitte juoda?	What would you like to drink?
Meillä ei ole ...	We don't have ...
Ottaisitteko ...?	Would you like ...?

Could we have a/an..., please?	**Voisimmeko saada ...**	voa'simmaykoa saadah
ashtray	**tuhkakupin**	toohhkahkoopin
cup	**kupin**	koopin
fork	**haarukan**	haarookahn
glass	**lasin**	lahsin
knife	**veitsen**	vay'tsayn
napkin (serviette)	**lautasliinan**	lah°°tahsleenahn
plate	**lautasen**	lah°°tahsayn
spoon	**lusikan**	loossikkahn

TELLING THE TIME, see page 59

May I have some ...?	**Voisinko saada...?**	voa'sinkoa saadah
bread	**leipää**	lay'pæ
butter	**voita**	voa'tah
lemon	**sitruunaa**	sitrōōnaa
oil	**öljyä**	urlyewæ
pepper	**pippuria**	pippooriah
salt	**suolaa**	s°°oalaa
seasoning	**mausteita**	mah°°stay'tah
sugar	**sokeria**	soakayriah
vinegar	**viinietikkaa**	veeniayttikkaa

Reading the menu *Ruokalistan luku*

alkupaloja	ahlkoopahloayah	appetizers
äyriäisiä	æ°ʷriæissiæ	seafood
hampurilaisia	hahmpoorillah'sia	burgers
hedelmiä	haydaylmiæ	fruit
jäätelöä	yǣtayl'ᵘʳæ	ice cream
jälkiruokia	yælkirr°°oakiah	desserts
juomat	y°°amaht	beverages
kalaa	kahlaa	fish
kanaa	kahnaa	chicken
keittoja	kay'ttoayah	soups
lintua	lint°°ah	poultry
munaruokia	moonahr°°oakiah	egg dishes
olut	oaloot	beer
pasta	pahstah	pasta
riistaa	reestaa	game
salaatteja	sahlaattayyah	salads
seisova pöytä	say'soavahpur°ʷtæ	smörgåsbord
välipalaa	vælipahlaa	snacks
väliruokia	vælirr°°oakiah	entrees
vihanneksia	vihahnnayksiah	vegetables
viinit	veenit	wine

Breakfast *Aamiainen*

I'd like...	**Saisinko...**	sah'sinkoa
bread/butter	**leipää/voita**	lay'pæ/voa'tah
cheese	**juustoa**	y°°stoaah
eggs	**munia**	mooniah
ham and eggs	**kinkkua ja munia**	kinkkooah yah mooniah
jam/rolls	**hilloa/sämpylöitä**	hilloah/sæampewlur'tæ

Starters (Appetizers) *Alkuruokia*

kaviaaria	kahv^jaariah	caviar
lohta	loahtah	salmon
leikkeleitä	lay^jkkaylaytæ	cold meats
mätiä	mætiæ	roe
parsaa	pahrsaa	asparagus
poronkieltä	poaroank^jaylitæ	reindeer tongue
silakoita	sillahkoa^jtah	Baltic herring

Soups *Keittoja*

I'd like some soup	**Haluaisin jotain keittoa.**	hahlooah^jsin yoatah^jn kay^jttoah
häränhäntäliemi	hæranhæntæl^jaymi	oxtail soup
hernekeitto	hayrnaykay^jttoa	pea soup
kalakeitto	kahlahkay^jttoa	fish soup
kanakeitto	kahnahkay^jttoa	chicken soup
lihamuhennos	lihhahmoohaynnoas	meat stew
pinaattikeitto	pinnaattikay^jttoa	spinach soup

kesäkeitto (kayssaekay^jttoa) — summer soup; a Finnish speciality of vegetables, particularly cauliflower, stewed in milk

Fish and seafood *Kalaa ja äyriäisiä*

ankerias	ahnkayriahss	eel
hummeri	hoommayri	lobster
kaviaari	kahviaari	caviar
kuha	koohah	pike perch
lohi	loahi	salmon
kirjolohi	kiryoaloahi	rainbow trout
meriantura	mayriahntoorah	sole
punakampela	poonahkahmpaylah	plaice
rapu	rahpoo	crayfish/crawfish
sardiinit	sahrdeenit	sardines
silakka	sillahkkah	Baltic herring
silli	silli	herring
taimen	tah^jmayn	trout
tonnikala	toannikahlah	tuna
turska	toorskah	cod

kalakukko (kahlahkookkoa) — 'fish loaf'; sort of loaf of dark bread with *muikku* (sometimes perch) and pork inside and baked in the oven

silaakalaatikko (sillahkkahlaatikkoa) — casserole made of alternating layers of potato slices, onion and Baltic herring, with an egg and milk sauce, baked in the oven

baked	**uunissa paistettu**	ōōnissah **pah'**stayttoo
boiled	**keitetty**	**kay'**tayttew
fried/grilled	**paistettu/grillattu**	**pah'**stayttoo/**grill**ahttoo
roast	**paahdettu**	**paah**dayttoo
underdone (rare)	**puolikypsä**	p°°oalikewpsæ
medium	**keski-kypsä**	**kay**ski-**kewp**sæ
well-done	**hyvin/kypsäksi paistettu**	**hew**vin/**kewp**sæksi **pah'**stayttoo

Meat *Liharuokia*

beef	**naudanlihaa**	nah°°dahnlihaa
chicken	**kana**	**kah**na
duck	**ankka**	**ahnk**kah
lamb	**lammasta**	**lahm**mahstah
pork	**porsaanlihaa**	**poar**saanlihaa
veal	**vasikanlihaa**	**vah**sikkahnlihaa
hanhi	**hahn**hi	goose
hirvenliha	**hir**vaynlihah	elk
kaalikääryleet	(kaalikæærewlāyt)	cabbage leaves stuffed with minced meat and rice
kalkkuna	**kahlk**koonah	turkey
karhunpaisti	**kahr**hoonpah'sti	bear steak
(savustettu) kinkku	(**sah**voostayttoo) **kink**koo	(smoked) ham
makkara	**mahk**kahrah	sausage
palapaisti	**pah**lah**pah'**sti	beef ragout
pekonia	**pay**koaniah	bacon
pihvi	**pih**vi	steak
piparjuuriliha	**pip**pahyōōrilihah	boiled beef with horseradish sauce
poronkäristys	**poa**ronkæristewss	sautéed reindeer stew
poronliha	**poa**roanlihah	reindeer meat

Vegetables and salads *Vihanneksia ja salaatteja*

beans	**pavut**	**pah**voot
beetroot	**punajuuri**	**poo**nahyōōri
broccoli	**parsakaali**	**pahr**sakaali
cabbage	**kaali**	**kaa**li
carrots	**porkkanat**	**poark**kahnaht
cauliflower	**kukkakaali**	**kook**kahkaali
cucumber	**kurkku**	**koork**koo
leeks	**purjo(sipuli)**	**poor**yoa(**sip**pooli)

lettuce	**lehtisalaatti**	**layht**isah**laatti**
mushrooms	**sieni**	s'**ayni**
onions	**sipulit**	**sip**poolit
peas	**herneit**	**hayr**nāÿt
potatoes	**perunat**	**pay**roonaht
swede (rutabaga)	**lanttu**	**lahnt**too
tomatoes	**tomaattit**	**toa**maattit
turnips	**nauriit**	nah°°reet

hapankaalisalaatti	**hahpahnkaalisahlaatti**	sauerkraut salad
lanttulaatikko	**lahnt**too**laatikkoa**	mashed swede casserole
perunalaatikko	**pay**roonah**laatikkoa**	potato bake
pinaattiohukaiset	**pi**nnaatti**oa**hookah'sayt	spinach pancakes
porkkanaohukaiset	**poark**kahnah**oa** hookah'sayt	carrot pancakes
rosolli	**roa**soalli	beetroot salad with salt herring

Fruit *Hedelmiä*

apple	**omena**	**oa**maynah
banana	**banaani**	**bah**naani
blackcurrants	**musta viinimarjat**	**moos**tah **vee**nimahr**yahit**
cherries	**kirsikat**	**keer**sikkaht
grapes	**viinirypäleet**	**vee**nirew**pæli**āÿt
grapefruit	**greippi**	**gay'**ppi
lemon	**sitruuna**	**sit**rōōnah
melon	**meloni**	**may**loani
orange	**appelsiini**	**ahp**paylseeni
peach	**persikka**	**payr**sikkah
pear	**päärynä**	**pæ**rewnæ
plums	**luumut**	**lōō**moot
raspberries	**vadelmat**	**vah**daylmaht
strawberries	**mansikat**	**mahn**sikkaht

karpalo (**kahr**pahloa)	cranberry; also used for making *Polar* liqueur
lakka (**lahk**kah)	Arctic cloudberry; yellow berry growing on the marshes in northern Finland, regarded as the 'queen of berries' in Finland, used in desserts and for making *Lakka* liqueur
mesimarja (**may**ssimahr**yah**)	Arctic bramble; *Mesimarja* liqueur is well known throughout Finland
mustikka (**moos**tikkah)	bilberry, or whortleberry; one of the commonest berries in Finland, used for a variety of desserts and pastries

Desserts—Pastries *Jälkiruokia—Leivonnaisia*

jäätelö	**y**ætaylur	ice-cream
marengit	**mah**rayngit	meringues
mustikkapiirakka	**moos**tikkah**peer**ahkkah	bilberry pie
omenapiirakka	**oa**maynah**peer**ahkah	apple pie
ohukaiset	**oa**hookah'sayt	small pancakes
suklaakakku	**sook**laakah**kkoo**	chocolate cake
vohvelit	**voah**vaylit	waffles
kiisseli (**kees**sayli)	dish made of any fruit or berries and their juice, thickened with potato flour, usually served cold, often with sugar and/or cream and milk
köyhät ritarit (kur^{ew}hæt **ritt**ahrit)	'poor knights'; bread soaked in milk and then fried, served with jam, berries and whipped cream
puolukkapuuro (p^{oo}oalookkah**poo**roa)	porridge made with semolina and lingonberries, served cold with milk

Drinks *Juomia*

beer	**olut**	**oa**loot
(hot) chocolate	**kaakao**	**kaah**kahoa
coffee	**kahvi**	**kahh**vi
black	**mustana**	**moos**tahnah
with milk	**maidon kanssa**	mah'doan **kahns**sah
fruit juice	**hedelmämehu**	haydaylmæmayhoo
lemonade	**limonaatia**	limmoanaatiah
milk	**maito**	mah'to
mineral water	**mineraalivesi**	minnayraali**vay**si
fizzy (carbonated)	**hiilihapollista**	heelihahpoallistah
still	**ilman hiilihappoa**	ilmahn heelihahppoah
sugar	**sokeria**	**soa**kayriah
tea	**tee**	tāy
cup of tea	**kuppi teetä**	**koo**ppi tāytæ
with milk/lemon	**maidon/sitruu-** **nan kanssa**	mah'doan/sitr**oo**nahn **kahns**sah
wine	**viini**	**vee**ni
red/white	**puna/valko**	poonah/vahlkoa
akvaviitti (**ahk**vahveetti)	aquavit, flavoured with caraway seed; originally Danish, now also made in Finland
Pöytäviina (pur^{ew}tæ**vee**nah)	perhaps the most popular of the cheaper varieties of schnapps; distilled from grain
vodka (**voad**kah)	competing with Russian and Polish vodka, the Finns make *Dry Vodka* and, in a special bottle, *Finlandia Vodka*

Complaints *Valituksia*

The meat is ...	Liha on...	lihah oan
overdone	ylikypsää	ewlikewpsǣ
underdone	puolikypsää	p°°oalikewpsǣ
This is too ...	Tämä on liian...	tæmæ oan leeahn
bitter/salty/sweet	kitkerää/suolaista/ makeaa	kitkayrǣ/s°°alah'stah/ mahkayaa
That's not what I ordered.	Tämä ei ole sitä, mitä tilasin.	tæmæ ay' oalay sittæ mittæ tillahsin
The food is cold.	Ruoka on kylmää.	r°°oakah oan kewlmǣ

The bill (check) *Lasku*

I'd like to pay.	Haluaisin maksaa.	hahlooah'sin mahksaa
What's this amount for?	Mihin tämä summa liittyy?	mihin tæmæ soommah leettēw
I think there's a mistake in this bill.	Tässä laskussa taitaa olla virhe.	tæssæ lahskoossah tah'taa oallah veerhay
Is everything included?	Sisältyykö siihen kaikki?	sissæltēwkur seehayn kah'kki
Can I pay with this credit card?	Voinko maksaa tällä luottokortilla?	voa'nkoa mahksaa tællæ l°°attoakoartilla
We enjoyed it, thank you.	Kiitos, pidimme siitä kovasti.	keetoass piddimmay seetæ koavahsti

Snacks—Picnic *Välipalat—Piknik*

Give me two of these and one of those.	Saisinko kaksi täl- laista ja yhden tuollaisen.	sah'sinkoa kahksi tællah'stah yah ewhdayn t°°oallah'sayn
to the left/right	vasemmalle/ oikealle	vahsaymmahllay/ oakayahllay
chips (french fries)	ranskalaisia (peru- noita)	rahnskahlah'siah (payroonoa'tah)
omelet	munakkaan	mooonahkkaan
open sandwich	voileivän	voa'lay'væn
with ham	kinkku	kinkkoo
with cheese	juustovoileivän	yōōstoavoa'lay'væn
piece of cake	palan kakkua	pahlahn kahkkooah
soft drink (soda)	(alkoholittomia) juomia	(ahlkoahoalittoamiah) y°°oamiah

NUMBERS, see page 60

Travelling around *Kulkuneuvot*

Plane *Lento*

Is there a flight to Ivalo?	**Onko lentoa Iva-loon?**	**oan**koa **layn**toah ivvahlōän
What time should I check in?	**Mihin aikaan minun on ilmoit-tauduttava?**	mihin ahⁱkaahn minoon oan **ilm**oaⁱttah°°**doot**tahvah
I'd like to... my reservation.	**Haluaisin... varaukseni.**	hahlooaⁱsiin... vahrahooksayn
cancel	**peruuttaa**	payrō̄ottaa
change	**muuttaa**	mō̄ottaa
confirm	**vahvistaa**	vahhvistaa

Train *Juna*

Where's the railway station?	**Missä on rauta-tieasema?**	missæ oan rah°°tahtiayahsaymah

SISÄÄN	ENTRANCE
ULOS	EXIT
LAITUREILLE	TO THE PLATFORMS
NEUVONTA	INFORMATION

Where is/are (the) ...?	**Missä on/ovat ...?**	missæ oan/oavaht
booking office	**lipunmyynti**	lippoonmēwnti
left-luggage office (baggage check)	**matkatavarasäily-tys**	mahtkahtahvahrahsæi-lewtewss
lost property (lost and found) office	**löytötavaratoi-misto**	lur°ᵂturtahvahrahtoaⁱ-mistoa
luggage lockers	**säilytyslokerot**	sæⁱlewtewsloakayroat
platform 7	**laituri 7**	lahⁱtoori sayⁱtsaymæn
reservations office	**paikanvaraus**	pahⁱkahnvahrah°°s
ticket office	**lipputoimisto**	lippootoaⁱmistoa
waiting room	**odotushuone**	oadoatoosh°°oanay
I'd like a ticket to Pori.	**Saisinko lipun Poriin.**	sahⁱsinkoa lippoon poareen
single (one-way)	**menolippu**	maynoalippoon
return (round trip)	**menopaluu**	maynoapahlō̄o
first/second class	**ensimmäinen/toinen luokka**	aynsimmæⁱnayn/**toa**nayn l°°oakkah

TELLING THE TIME, see page 59

Inquiries *Tiedusteluja*

How long does the journey (trip) take?	**Kuinka kauan matka kestää?**	kooⁱnkah kah°°ahn mahtkah kaystǣ
When is the... train to Tampere?	**Milloin Tampereelle lähtee... juna?**	milloaⁱn tampayrāȳllay lǣhtāȳ... yoonah
first	**ensimmäinen**	aynsimmæⁱnayn
last	**viimeinen**	veemayⁱnayn
next	**seuraava**	say°°raavah
What time does the train to Turku leave?	**Mihin aikaan Turkuun lähtee juna?**	mihin ahⁱkaan toorkōōn lǣhtāȳ yoonah
What time does the train arrive in Mikkeli?	**Mihin aikaan juna saapuu Mikkeliin?**	mihin ahⁱkaan yoonah saapōō mikkayleen
Is there a dining car/ sleeping car on the train?	**Onko junassa ravintolavaunu/ makuuvaunua?**	oankoa yoonassah rahvintoalahvah°°nooah/ mahkōōvah°°nooah
Is this the right train to Tampere?	**Onko tämä Tampereen juna?**	oankoa tæmæ tahmpayrāȳn yoonah
Porter!	**Kantaja!**	kahntahyah
Can you help me with my luggage?	**Voitteko auttaa kantamisessa?**	voaⁱttaykoa ah°°ttaa kahntahmisayssah

Underground (subway) *Metro*

Where's the nearest underground station?	**Missä on lähin metroasema?**	missæ oan lǣhin maytroaahsaymah

Bus—Tram (streetcar) *Bussi—Raitiovaunu*

Which tram (streetcar) goes to the town centre?	**Mikä raitiovaunu menee kaupungin keskustaan?**	mikkæ rahⁱtioavah°°noo maynāȳ kah°°poongin kayskoostaan
How much is the fare to...?	**Mitä on maksu... -n/...-lle?**	mittæ oan mahksoo...-n/ ...-llay
Will you tell me when to get off?	**Sanoisitteko, kun minun täytyy nousta pois?**	sahnoaⁱsittaykoa koon minnoon tæ^{ew}tēw noa°°stah poais
When's the next coach (long-distance bus) to...?	**Milloin lähtee seuraava bussi...-n/ ...-lle?**	milloaⁱn lǣh-tāȳ say°°raavah boossi...-n/ ...-llay

TELLING THE TIME, see page 59

Boat service *Vesiliikenne*

When does the next boat for ... leave?	Milloin lähtee seuraava lautta ...-n/ ...-lle?	milloa'n læhtæȳ say°°raavah lah°°ttah ...-n/ ...-llay
How long does the crossing take?	Kauanko ylitys kestää?	kah°°ahnkoa ewlittews kaystǣ
I'd like to take a cruise/tour of the harbour.	Haluaisin risteilylle/satamaristeilylle.	hahlooah'sin ristay'lewllay/ sahtahmahristay'lewllay

Taxi *Taksi*

Where can I get a taxi?	Mistä voin saada taksin?	mistæ voa'n saadah tahksin
What's the fare to ...?	... – Mitä maksaa ajaa sinne?	mittæ mahksaa ahyaa sinnay
Take me to this address.	Viekää minut tähän osoitteeseen.	v'aykǣ minnoot tæhæn oasoa'ttāyssāyn
Please stop here.	Pysähtykää tässä.	pewssæhtewkǣ tæssæ
Could you wait for me?	Voitteko odottaa?	voa'ttaykoa oadoattaa
I'll be back in 10 minutes.	Tulen takaisin kymmenessä minuutissa.	toolayn tahkah'sin kewmmaynayssæ minnoottissah

Car hire (rental) *Auton vuokraus*

I'd like to hire (rent) a car.	Haluaisin vuokrata auton.	hahlooah'sin v°°oakrahtah ah°°toan
I'd like it for a day/a week.	Haluaisin sen päiväksi/viikoksi.	hahl'°°ah'sin sayn pæ'væksi/ veekoaksi
What's the charge per day/week?	Mikä on päivämaksu/viikkomaksu?	mikkæ oan pæ'væmahksoo/ veekkoamahksoo
Is mileage included?	Kuinka suuri kilometrimäärä sisältyy hintaan?	koo'nkah soori killoamaytrimǣræ sissæltew hintaan
I'd like full insurance.	Haluaisin täysvakuutuksen.	hahlooah'sin tæ°ʷsvahkootooksayn

Where's the nearest filling station?	Missä on lähin bensiiniasema?	missæ oan læhin baynseeniahsaymah
Fill it up, please.	Tankki täyteen, kiitos.	tahnkki tæᵉʷtäyn keetoass
Give me... litres of petrol (gasoline).	Saanko... litraa bensiiniä.	saankoa... litraa baynseeniæ
super (premium)	korkeaoktaanista	koarkayahoaktaahnistah
regular	matalaoktaanista	mahtahlahoaktaahnistah
unleaded	lyijytöntä	lewⁱyewturntæ
diesel	dieselöljyä	dⁱaysaylurlyewæ
How do I get to...?	Miten pääsen...-n/ ...-lle?	mitayn pääsayn...-n/ ...- llay
How far is it to... from here?	Kuinka kaukana täältä on...?	kooⁱnkah kahᵒᵒkahnah tæltæ oan
I've had a break-down at...	Autoni meni epä-kuntoon...-n koh-dalla.	aᵒᵒtoani mayni aypækoontōan...-n koahdahllah
Can you send a mechanic?	Voitteko lähettää korjaajan?	voaittaykoa læhayttæ koaryaayahn
Can you mend this puncture (fix this flat)?	Puhjennut rengas. Voitteko korjata tämän ?	poohyaynnoot rayngahs voaⁱttaykoa koaryahtah tæmæn

---

Road signs *Liikennemerkkejä*

AJA HITAASTI	Drive slowly
AJO SALLITTU OMALLA VASTUULLA	Drive at own risk
ALUERAJOITUS	Local speed limit
KAPEA SILTA	Narrow bridge
KELIRIKKO	Frost damage
KOKEILE JARRUJA	Test your brakes
LIUKAS TIE	Slippery road
NOPEUSRAJOITUS	Speed limit... km
PYSÄKÖINTIPAIKKA	Parking
RYHMITYSMERKKI	Get in lane
TIETYÖ	Road works

Olette väärällä tiellä.	You're on the wrong road.
Ajakaa suoraan eteenpäin.	Go straight ahead.
Se on tuolla vasemmalla/oikealla.	It's down there on the left/right.
Vastapäätä (...-a/...-ta/...-tta)	opposite
...-n takana	behind...
...-n vieressä/...-n jälkeen	next to/after...
pohjoisessa/etelässä	north/south
idässä/lännessä	east/west

Sightseeing *Kiertoajelu*

Where's the tourist office?	**Missä on matkaitoimisto?**	missæ oan ... **maht**kah¹-toa¹**mis**toa
Is there an English-speaking guide?	**Onko siellä englantia puhuva opas?**	oankoa s¹ayllæ ayng**lahn**tiah **poo**hoovah **oa**pahss
Where is/are the ...?	**Missä on/ovat ...?**	missæ oan/**oa**vaht
botanical gardens	**kasvitieteellinen puutarha**	**kahs**vit¹ay**tayl**linnayn **poo**tahrhah
castle	**linna**	**lin**nah
cathedral	**tuomiokirkko**	t°°**ami**oa**keerk**koa
city centre/downtown area	**keskusta**	**kays**koostah
exhibition	**näyttely**	næ°ʷ**ttay**lew
harbour	**satama**	**sah**tahmah
market	**(kauppa)tori**	(kah°°ppah)**toa**ri
museum	**museo**	**moo**ssayoa
shopping area	**ostoskeskus**	**oas**toaskays**kooss**
square	**tori**	**toa**ri
tower	**torni**	**toar**ni
zoo	**eläintarha**	**ay**læ¹n**tahr**hah
When does it open/close?	**Milloin se avataan/suljetaan?**	**mil**loa¹n say **ah**vahtaan/**soon**noontah¹sin
How much is the entrance fee?	**Paljonko pääsymaksu on?**	**pahl**yoankoa **pæ̈se**wmahksoo oan

TELLING THE TIME, see page 59/NUMBERS, see page 60

Landmarks *Maamerkkejä*

bridge	**silta**	**sil**tah
forest	**metsä**	**mayt**sæ
fjord	**vuono**	v°°**oa**noa
glacier	**jäätikkö**	**yǣ**tikkur
island	**saari**	**saa**ri
lake	**järvi**	**yær**vi
mountain	**vuori**	v°°**oa**ri
path	**polku**	**poal**koo
river	**joki**	**yoa**ki
sea	**meri**	**may**ri
waterfall	**vesiputous**	**vay**sipootoa°°ss

Relaxing *Yirkistyminen*

What's playing at the... Theatre?	**Mitä... -teatterissa esitetään?**	**mit**tæ... **ta**yahttayrissah **ay**ssittaytǣn
Are there any seats for tonight?	**Onko täksi illaksi paikkoja?**	**oan**koa **tæk**si **il**lahksi pah¹**kko**ayah
What time does it begin?	**Mihin aikaan se alkaa?**	**mi**hin **ah**¹kaan say **ahl**kaa
I'd like to reserve 2 seats for the show on Friday evening.	**Haluaisin varata 2 paikkaa perjantai-illan näytökseen.**	**hah**looah¹sin **vah**rahtah **kahk**si pah¹**kkaa** **payr**yahntai **il**lahn nǣ^(mw)turksāyn
Would you like to go out with me tonight?	**Lähtisit(te)kö kanssani ulos tänä iltana?**	**læh**tissit(tay)kur **kahns**sahni **oo**loass **tæ**næ **il**tahnah
Thank you, but I'm busy.	**Kiitos, mutta minulle ei sovi.**	**kee**toass **moot**tah **min**noollay ay¹ **soa**vi
Is there a discotheque in town?	**Onko tässä kaupungissa diskoa?**	**oan**koa **tæs**sæ kah°°**poon**gissah **dis**koaah
Would you like to dance?	**Haluaisitteko tanssia?**	**hah**looah¹**sit**taykoa **tahn**ssiah
Thank you, it's been a wonderful evening.	**Kiitos, on ollut ihana ilta.**	**kee**toass oan **oal**loot **ih**hahnah **il**tah

Sports *Urheilu*

Is there a football (soccer) match anywhere this Saturday?	Onko jossain jalka-pallo-ottelua tänä lauantaina?	oankoa **yoass**sah'n **yalkahpahll**loa-**oatt**aylooah tænæ **lah°°**ahntah'nah
What's the admission charge?	Mitä on pääsy-maksu?	**mikk**æ oan **pääsewmahks**oo
Where's the nearest golf course?	Missä on lähin golf-rata?	missæ oan læhin **golf-rah**tah
Where are the tennis courts?	Missä on tennis-kenttiä?	missæ oan **taynniskaynt**tiæ

cycle racing	pyöräkilpailut	pew°°'ræ**kilpah**'loot
football (soccer)	jalkapallo	**yahlkahpahll**loa
ice hockey	jäähockey	y**ā**ē**hoakkay**'
(horse-back) riding	ratsastus	**raht**sahstooss
mountaineering	vuoristokiipeily	v°°oaristoa**keepay**'lew
speed skating	pikaluistelu	pikkahloo'stayloo
ski jumping	mäkihyppy	mækihewppew
skiing	hiihto	**heeht**oa
swimming	uinti	oo'nti
tennis	tennis	**taynn**is

Can one swim in the lake/river?	Voiko tuossa jär-vessä/joessa uida?	voa'koa t°°**oass**sah yærvayssæ/yoa**ay**ssah oo'dah
Is there a swimming pool here?	Onko täällä uima-allasta?	oankoa tǣllæ oo'mahahllahstah
Is there a skating rink near here?	Onko täällä lähellä luistinrataa?	oankoa tǣllæ læhayllæ loo'stinrahtaa
I'd like to ski.	Haluaisin hiihtää.	hahlooah'sin heeht**ǣ**
downhill/cross-country skiing	laskettelu/murto-maahiihto	lahskayttayloo/moortoamaaheehtoa
I want to hire...	Olisivatko... vuok-rattavissa?	oalissivahtkoa... v°°oakrahttahvissah
skates	luistimet	loo'stimmayt
skiing equipment	hiihtovarusteet	heehtoavahroostā**y**t
skis	sukset	sooksayt
I'd like to hire a... bicycle.	Haluaisin vuok-rata...-pyörän.	hahlooah'sin v°°oakrahtah...-pew°°'ræn
5-gear	vaihde	va**ñ**hday
mountain	maasto	maastoa

DAYS OF THE WEEK, see page 59

Shops, stores and services *Myymälät, tavaratalot ja palvelut*

Where's the nearest...?	Missä on lähin...?	missæ oan læhin
baker's	leipomo	laypoamoa
bookshop	kirjakauppa	keeryuaka°°uppah
butcher's	lihakauppa	lihahka°°uppah
chemist's/drugstore	apteekki	ahptāykki
dentist	hammaslääkäri	hahmmahslǣkæri
department store	tavaratalo	tahvahrahtaloa
grocer's	sekatavarakauppa	saykahtahvahrahka°°uppah
hairdresser's (ladies/men)	kampaaja/parturi	kahmpaayah/pahrtoori
market	tori	toari
newsstand	lehtikioski	layhtikioaski
post office	posti	poasti
souvenir shop	matkamuistomyymälä	mahtkamoo'stoamēw-mælæ
supermarket	valintamyymälä	vahlintahmēwmælæ

General expressions *Yleisiä ilmauksia*

Where's the main shopping area?	Missä on tärkein ostosalue?	missæ oan tærkay'n oastoasahlooay
Do you have any...?	Onko teillä...-a?	oankoa tay'llæ...-a

☞	🗣
Voinko auttaa?	Can I help you?
Mitä saisi olla?	What would you like?
Mitä... saisi olla?	What... would you like?
väriä/muotoa/laatua	colour/shape/quality
Tällä hetkellä meillä ei ole sitä varastossa.	We're out of stock at the moment.
Tilaammeko teille sellaisen?	Shall we order it for you?
Entä muuta?/Saako olla muuta?	Anything else?
Kassa on tuolla.	The cashier's is over there.

I'd like a... one.	Minulle saisi olla...	minnullay sah'si oallah
big	iso	issoa
cheap	halpa	hahlpah
dark	tumma	toommah
good	hyvä	hewvæ
heavy	painava	pah'nahvah
large	suurta kokoa	soortah koakoah
light (weight)	kevyt	kayvewt
light (colour)	vaalea	vaalayah
rectangular	suorakulmainen	s°°oarahkoolmah'nayn
round	pyöreä	p°™urrayæ
small	pieni	p'ayni
square	neliskulmainen	nayliskoolmah'nayn
sturdy	tanakka	tahnahkkah
Don't you have anything...?	Eikö teillä olisi jotain...?	aykur tay'llæ oalissi yoatah'n
cheaper/better	halvempaa/parempaa	hahlvaympaa/pahraympaa
larger/smaller	suurempaa/pienempää	sōōraympaa/p'aynaympēē
How much is this?	Paljonko tämä maksaa?	pahlyoankoa tæmæ mahksaa
Please write it down.	Voisitteko kirjoittaa.	voa'sittayko keeryoattaa
No, I don't like it.	Ei, en pidä siitä.	ay' ayn piddæ seetæ
I'll take it.	Otan sen.	oatahn sayn
Do you accept credit cards?	Hyväksyttekö luottokortteja?	hewvæksewttaykur l°°oattoakoarttayyah
Can you order it for me?	Voitteko tilata sen minulle?	voa'ttaykoa tillahtah sayn minnoollay

black	mustaa	moostaa
blue	sinistä	sinnistæ
brown	ruskeata	rooskayahtah
green	vihreää	vihrayēē
grey	harmaata	hahrmaahtah
orange	oranssia	oarahnssiah
red	punaista	poonah'stah
white	valkoista	vahlkoa'stah
yellow	keltaista	kaylltah'stah
light...	vaalean...	vaalayahn
dark...	tumman...	toommahn

NUMBERS, see page 60

Chemist's (drugstore) *Apteekki*

aspirin	**aspiriinia**	aahspireeniah
condoms	**kondomeja**	koandoamayyah
deodorant	**deodoranttia**	dayoadoarahnttiah
insect repellent	**hyttysöljyä**	hewttewsurlyewæ
moisturizing cream	**kosteusvoidetta**	koastay°°svoa¡dayttah
razor blades	**partakoneen teriä**	pahrtahkoanayn tayriæ
shampoo	**shampoota**	shahmpoatah
soap	**saippuaa**	sa¡ppooaa
sun-tan cream	**aurinkovoidetta**	ah°°rinkoavoa¡dayttah
tampons	**tampooneja**	tahmpoanayyah
toothpaste	**hammastahnaa**	hahmmahstahhnaa

Clothing *Vaatetus*

blouse	**puseron**	poosayroan
boots	**saappaat**	saappaat
bra	**rintaliivit**	rintahleevit
dress	**leningin**	layningin
gloves	**hansikkaat**	hahnsikkaat
jersey	**villatakin**	villahtahkin
scarf	**huivin**	hoo¡vin
shirt	**paidan**	pah¡dahn
shoes	**kengät**	kayngæt
skirt	**hameen**	hahmāyn
socks	**(nilkka)sukat**	(nilkkah)sookaht
swimming trunks	**uimahousut**	oo¡mahhoa°°soot
swimsuit	**uimapuvun**	oo¡mahpoovoon
T-shirt	**T-paidan**	tāypah¡dahn
tights	**sukkahousut**	sookkahhoa°°soot
trousers	**(pitkät) housut**	(pitkæt) hoa°°soot
Can I try it on?	**Voinko sovittaa sitä?**	voa¡nkoa soavittaa sittæ
What's it made of?	**Mistä se on tehty?**	mistæ say oan tayhtew

cotton	**puuvillaa**	poovillaa
denim	**farkkukangasta**	fahrkkookahngahstah
lace	**pitsiä**	pitsiæ
leather	**nahkaa**	nahhkaa
linen	**pellavaa**	payllahvaa
silk	**silkkiä**	silkkiæ
suede	**mokkaa**	moakkaa
velvet	**samettia**	sahmayttiah
wool	**villaa**	villaa

NUMBERS, see page 60

Grocer's *Elintarvikemyymälä*

What sort of cheese do you have?	**Mitä eri juustolaatuja teillä on?**	mittæ ayri yoostoalaatooya tay'llæ oan
half a kilo of tomatoes	**puoli kiloa tomaatteja**	p°°oali killoah toamaattayyah
a litre of milk	**litran maitoa**	litrahn mah'toah
4 slices of ham	**4 siivua kinkkua**	naylyæ seevooah kinkkooah
a tin (can) of peaches	**tölkin persikoita**	turlkin payrsikoa'tah

Miscellaneous *Sekalaista*

I'd like a/an/some . . .	**Haluaisin . . .-n/-a**	hahlooah'sin . . .-n/-a
battery	**pariston**	pahristoan
bottle opener	**pullonavaaja**	poolloanahvaayah
bread	**leipää**	lay'pææ
newspaper American/English	**sanomalehden amerikkalaisen/ englantilaisen**	sahnoamahlayhdayn ahmayrikkahlah'sayn/ aynglantillah'sen
postcard	**postikortin**	poastikoartin
torch	**taskulampun**	tahskoolahmpoon
I'd like a film for this camera.	**Haluaisin filmin tähän kameraan.**	hahlooah'sin filmin tæhæn kahmayraan
black and white colour	**mustavalkoista värillistä**	moostahvahlkoa'stah værillistæ
Can you repair this camera?	**Voitteko korjata tämän kameran?**	voa'ttaykoa koaryahtah tæmæn kahmayrahn
I'd like a haircut, please.	**Saisinko tukanleikkuun.**	sah'sinkoa tookahnlay'kkōōn

Souvenirs *Muistoesineitä*

candles	**kyntillät**	kewnttilæt
furs	**turkikset**	toorkiksayt
glass	**lasi**	lahsi
handicrafts	**käsityöt**	kæsit^{ew}urt
reindeer hide	**porontalja**	poaroantahlyah
table linen	**pöytä-ja lautasliinat**	pur^{ew}tæ-yah lah°°tahsleenaht

At the bank *Pankissa*

Where's the nearest bank/currency exchange office?	**Missä on lähin pankki/valuutan-vaihtopaikka?**	missæ oan læhin pahnkki/vahlōōtahnvah'htoapaihk-kah
I want to change some dollars/pounds.	**Haluaisin vaihtaa dollareita/puntia.**	hahlooah'sin vah'htaa doallahray'tah/poontiah
I want to cash a traveller's cheque.	**Haluaisin muuttaa matkasekin rahaksi.**	hahlooah'sin mōōttaa mahtkahshaykin rahhaahksi
What's the exchange rate?	**Mikä on vaihto-kurssi?**	mikkæ oan vah'htoakoorssi

At the post office *Posti*

I'd like to send this (by)...	**Lähettäisin tämän...**	læhayttæisin tæmæn
airmail	**lentopostissa**	layntoapoastissah
express	**pikana**	pikkahnah
What's the postage for a postcard to Los Angeles?	**Mitä maksaa posti-kortti Los Angele-siin?**	mittæ mahksaa poastikoartti loas ahngaylaysseen
Is there any post (mail) for me? My name is...	**Onko minulle pos-tia? Nimeni on...**	oankoa minnoollay poastiah. nimmayni oan

Telephoning *Puhelut*

Where's the nearest telephone booth?	**Missä on lähin puhelinkioski?**	missæ oan læhin poohaylink'oaski
May I use your phone?	**Voinko käyttää puhelintanne?**	voa'nnkoa kæ^{ew}ttæ poohaylintahnnay
Hello. This is...	**Hei. Täällä...**	hay' tæællæ
I'd like to speak to...	**Onko... tavatta-vissa?**	oankoa... tahvahttahvissah
When will he/she be back?	**Milloin hän palaa?**	milloa'n hæn pahlaa
Will you tell him/her I called?	**Kertoisitteko hänelle, että soitin?**	kayrtoa'sittaykoa hænayllaay ayttæ soa'tin
Would you ask him/her to call me?	**Pyytäisittekö häntä soittamaan minulle?**	pewtæisittaykur hæntæ soa'ttahmaan minnoollay
Would you take a message, please?	**Voisinko jättää viestin?**	voa'sinkoa yættæ v'aystin

NUMBERS, see page 60

Suomi

FINNISH

Doctor *Lääkäri*

Where can I find a doctor who speaks English?	**Mistä löytyisi lääkäri, joka puhuu englantia?**	mistæ lur^{ew}tew'si lǣkæri yoakah poohōō aynglahntiah
Where's the surgery (doctor's office)?	**Missä on lääkärin vastaanotto?**	missæ oan lǣkærin vahstaanoattoa
Can I have an appointment... ?	**Voinko saada ajan...?**	voa'nkoah saadah ahyahn
tomorrow	**huomenna**	h^{oo}oamaynnah
as soon as possible	**mahdollisimman pian**	mahhdoallissimmahn p'ahn

Parts of the body *Ruumiinosia*

arm	**käsivarsi**	kæsivahrsi
back	**selkä**	saylkæ
bone	**luu**	lōō
ear	**korva**	koarvah
eye(s)	**silmä(t)**	silmæ(t)
face	**kasvot**	kahsvoat
finger	**sormi**	soarmi
foot	**jalka**	yahlkah
hand	**käsi**	kæsi
head	**pää**	pǣ
heart	**sydän**	sewdæn
knee	**polvi**	poalvi
leg	**sääri**	sǣri
mouth	**suu**	sōō
muscle	**lihas**	lihhahss
nose	**nenä**	naynæ
shoulder	**olkapää**	oalkahpǣ
skin	**iho**	ihhoa
stomach (inside/ outside)	**maha/vatsa**	mahhah/vahtsah
throat (inside/ outside)	**kurkku/kaula**	koorkkoo/kah^{oo}lah
tongue	**kieli**	k'ayli
I've got a/an...	**Minulle on tullut...**	minnoollay oan toolloot
bruise	**mustelma**	moostaylmah
burn	**palohaava**	pahloahaavah
cut	**(viilto)haava**	(veeltoa)haavah
insect bite	**hyönteisen purema**	h^{ew}urntaysayn pooraymah
rash	**ihottumaa**	ihhoattoomah
sting	**pistos**	pistoass
swelling	**turvotusta**	toorvoatoostah
wound	**haava**	haavah

DAYS OF THE WEEK, see page 59

Suomi

Could you have a look at it?	Voisitteko katsoa sitä?	voa'sittaykoa **kaht**soah sittæ
It hurts.	Siihen koskee.	**see**hayn koaskāȳ
I feel...	Minulla on...	**min**noollah oan
dizzy	huimausta	hoo'mah°°stah
nauseous	pahoinvointia	pahhoa'nvoa'ntiah
shivery	puistatuksia	poo'stahtooksiah
I'm diabetic.	Minulla on soker-itauti.	**min**noollah oan soakayritah°°ti
Can you give me a prescription for this?	Voitteko antaa minulle reseptin tätä varten?	voa'ttaykoa **ahn**taa minnoollay **ray**sayptin tætæ **vahr**tayn
May I have a receipt for my health insurance?	Voinko saada kuitin sairausvakuu-tustani varten?	voa'nkoa saadah koo'tin sah'rah°°svahkōōtoostahni **vahr**tayn

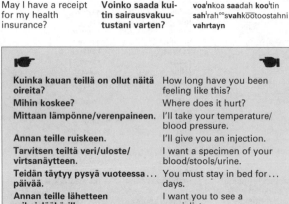

Kuinka kauan teillä on ollut näitä oireita?	How long have you been feeling like this?
Mihin koskee?	Where does it hurt?
Mittaan lämpönne/verenpaineen.	I'll take your temperature/blood pressure.
Annan teille ruiskeen.	I'll give you an injection.
Tarvitsen teiltä veri/uloste/virtsanäytteen.	I want a specimen of your blood/stools/urine.
Teidän täytyy pysyä vuoteessa... päivää.	You must stay in bed for... days.
Annan teille lähetteen erikoislääkärille.	I want you to see a specialist.

Can you recommend a good dentist?	Voitteko suositella hyvää hammaslää-käriä?	voa'sittaykoa s°°asittayllah hewvāē hahmmahslāēkæriæ
I have toothache.	Hammastani sär-kee.	**hahm**mahstahni **sær**kāȳ
I've lost a filling.	Minulta on pudon-nut paikka.	**min**nooltah oan **poo**doannoot pah'kkah

FINNISH

Time and date *Kello ja päivämäärät*

It's...	Se on...	say oan
five past one	viittä yli yksi	veettæ ewli ewksi
ten past two	kymmentä yli kaksi	kewmmayntæ ewli kahksi
a quarter past three	neljännestä/vartin yli kolme	naylyænnaystæ/vahrtin ewli koalmay
twenty past four	kahtakymmentä yli neljä	kahhtahkewmmayntæ ewli naylyæ
twenty-five past five	viittä vaille puoli kuusi	veettæ vahⁱllay p^{oo}oali kōōssi
half past six	puoli seitsemän	p^{oo}oali sayⁱtsaymæn
twenty-five to seven	kahtakymmentävi-ittä vaille seitsemän	kahhtahkewmmayntæ-veettæ vahⁱllay sayⁱtsaymæn
twenty to eight	kahtakymmentä vaille kahdeksan	kahhtahkewmmayntæ vahⁱllay kahhdayksahn
a quarter to nine	viisitoista minuttia vaille yhdeksän	veesitoaⁱstah minoottiah vahⁱllay ewhhdayksæn
ten to ten	kymmentä vaille kymmenen	kewmmayntæ vaⁱllay kewmmaynayn
five to eleven	viittä vaille yksitoista	veettæ vahⁱllay ewksitoaⁱstah
twelve o'clock (noon/ midnight)	kaksitoista (keskipäivällä/ keskiyöllä)	kahksitoaⁱstah (kayskipæⁱvællæ/ kayski^{ew}urllæ)
in the morning	aamulla	aamoollah
afternoon/evening	päivällä/illalla	pæⁱvællæ/illahllah
during the day	päivällä	pæⁱvællæ
at night	yöllä	^{ew}urllæ
yesterday/today	eilen/tänään	ayⁱlayn/yænæn
tomorrow	huomenna	h^{oo}oamaynnah
spring/summer	kevät/kesä	kayvæt/kayssæ
autumn/winter	syksy/talvi	sewksew/tahlvi

Sunday	sunnuntai	soonnoontahⁱ
Monday	maanantai	maanahntahⁱ
Tuesday	tiistai	teestahⁱ
Wednesday	keskiviikko	kayskiveekkoa
Thursday	torstai	toarstahⁱ
Friday	perjantai	payryahntahⁱ
Saturday	lauantai	lah^{oo}ahntahⁱ

NUMBERS, see page 60

Suomi

January	**tammikuu**	tahmmikkōō
February	**helmikuu**	haylmikōō
March	**maaliskuu**	maalisskōō
April	**huhtikuu**	hoohtikkōō
May	**toukokuu**	toaᵒᵒkoakōō
June	**kesäkuu**	kayssækōō
July	**heinäkuu**	hayⁱnækōō
August	**elokuu**	ayloakōō
September	**syyskuu**	sēwskōō
October	**lokakuu**	loakahkōō
November	**marraskuu**	mahrrahskōō
December	**joulukuu**	yoaᵒᵒlookōō

Numbers *Luvut*

0	**nolla**	noallah
1	**yksi**	ewksi
2	**kaksi**	kahksi
3	**kolme**	koalmay
4	**neljä**	naylyæ
5	**viisi**	veessi
6	**kuusi**	kōōssi
7	**seitsemän**	sayⁱtsaymæn
8	**kahdeksan**	kahhdayksahn
9	**yhdeksän**	ewhdayksæn
10	**kymmenen**	kewmmaynayn
11	**yksitoista**	ewksitoaⁱstah
12	**kaksitoista**	kahksitoaⁱstah
13	**kolmetoista**	koalmaytoaⁱstah
14	**neljätoista**	naylyætoaⁱstah
15	**viisitoista**	veessitoaⁱstah
16	**kuusitoista**	kōōssitoaⁱstah
17	**seitsemäntoista**	sayⁱtsaymæntoaⁱstah
18	**kahdeksantoista**	kahhdayksahntoaⁱstah
19	**yhdeksäntoista**	ewhdayksæntoaⁱstah
20	**kaksikymmentä**	kahksikewmmayntæ
21	**kaksikymmentä-yksi**	kahksikewmmayntæewksi
30	**kolmekymmentä**	koalmaykewmmayntæ
40	**neljäkymmentä**	naylyækewmmayntæ
50	**viisikymmentä**	veessikewmmayntæ
60	**kuusikymmentä**	kōōssikewmmayntæ
70	**seitsemänkymmentä**	sayⁱtsaymænkewmmayntæ

| 80 | **kahdeksankym-mentä** | kahdayksahn**kewm**mayntæ |
| 90 | **yhdeksänkymmen-tä** | ewhdayksænkewmmayntæ |

100/1000	**sata/tuhat**	**sah**tah/**too**haht
100,000	**satatuhatta**	**sah**tah**too**hahttah
1,000,000	**miljoona**	mily$\overline{oa}$nah

first	**ensimmäinen**	aynsimmæinayn
second	**toinen**	toa'nayn
third	**kolmas**	koalmahss

| once | **kerran** | kayrrahn |
| twice | **kahdesti** | kahhdaysti |

| a half | **puolikas** | p^{oo}oalikkahs |

Where do you come from? *Mistä tulette?*

Denmark	**Tanska**	tahnskah
England	**Englanti**	aynglahnti
Finland	**Suomi**	s^{oo}oami
Great Britain	**Iso-Britannia**	isoa-britahnniah
Ireland	**Irlanti**	eerlahnti
New Zealand	**Uusi-Seelanti**	$\overline{oo}$si-s$\overline{ay}$lahnti
Norway	**Norja**	noaryah
Scotland	**Skotlanti**	skoatlahnti
South Africa	**Etelä-Afrikka**	eataylæ-ahfrikkah
Sweden	**Ruotsi**	r^{oo}oatsi

Signs and notices *Kylttejä ja varoituksia*

Alennusmyynti/Ale	Sale
Avoinna	Open
Varokaa koiraa	Beware of the dog
Ei saa koskea	Do not touch
Epäkunnossa	Out of order
Hätä/Varauloskäytävä	Emergency exit
(Hengen)vaara	Danger (of death)
Hissi	Lift
Kassa	Cash desk
...kielletty	...forbidden

Kuuma	Hot
Kylmä	Cold
Miehille	Gentlemen
Naisille	Ladies
Neuvonta	Information
Odottakaa	Please wait
Pääsy kielletty	No admittance
Sisään(käynti)	Entrance
Täynnä	No vacancies
Tupakointi kielletty	No smoking
Työnnä	Push
Ulos(käynti)	Exit
Vapaa	Vacant
Vapaa pääsy	Free admittance
Varattu	Occupied
Varattu	Reserved
Varo(kaa)	Caution
Vedä	Pull
Yksityistie	Private road

Emergency *Hätätilanne*

Call the police.	Kutsukaa poliisi.	kootsookaa poaleessi
Get a doctor.	Hakekaa lääkäri.	hahkaykaa lǣkæri
Go away!	Menkää tiehenne!	maynkǣ t'aynaynnay
HELP!	Apua!	ahpooah
I'm ill.	Olen sairas.	oalayn sah'rahs
I'm lost.	Olen eksynyt.	oalayn ayksewnewt
Leave me alone!	Jättäkää minut rauhaan!	yættækǣ minnoot rah°°haan
LOOK OUT!	Varokaa!	vahroakaa
STOP THIEF!	Ottakaa varas kiinni!	oattahkaa vahrahs keenni
My... has been stolen.	...-ni on varastettu	-ni oan vahrahstayttoo
I've lost my...	Olen kadotta-nut...-ni.	oalayn kahdoattahnoot...-ni
handbag/passport	käsilaukku/passi	kæssilah°°kkooni/pahssi
wallet	lompakko	loampahkkoa

TELEPHONING, see page 56

Guide to Finnish pronunciation *Ääntäminen*

Consonants

Letter	Approximate pronunciation	Symbol	Example	
k, m, n, p, t, v as in English				
d	as in rea**d**y, but sometimes very weak	d	**taide**	tah¦day
g	in words of Finnish origin, only found after **n**; **ng** is pronounced as in si**ng**er	ng	**sangen**	sahngayn
h	as in **h**ot, whatever its position in the word	h	**lahti**	lahhti
j	like **y** in **y**ou	y	**ja**	yah
l	as in **l**et	l	**talo**	tahloa
r	always rolled	r	**raha**	rahhah
s	always as in **s**et (never as in pre**s**ent)	s/ss*	**sillä**	sillæ
			kiitos	keetoass

Vowels

a	like **a** in c**a**r; short or long	ah / aa	**matala** / **iltaa**	mahtahlah / iltaa
e	like **a** in l**a**te; but a pure vowel, not a diphthong; short or long	ay / $\overline{ay}$	**kolme** / **teevati**	koalmay / $\overline{tay}$vati
i	like **i** in p**i**n (short) or **ee** in s**ee** (long); **ir** + consonant like **i** in p**i**n (short)	i / ee / eer	**takki** / **siitä** / **kirkko**	tahkki / seetæ / keerkoa
o	a sound between **aw** in l**aw** and **oa** in c**oa**t; short or long	oa / $\overline{oa}$	**olla** / **kookas**	oallah / $\overline{koa}$kahss
u	like **oo** in p**oo**l; short or long	oo / $\overline{oo}$	**hupsu** / **uuni**	hoopsoo / $\overline{oo}$ni
y	like **u** in French s**u**r or **ü** in German **ü**ber; say **ee** as in s**ee**, and round your lips while still trying to pronounce **ee**; it can be short or long	ew / $\overline{ew}$	**yksi** / **syy**	ewksi / s$\overline{ew}$

*To make doubly sure that the Finnish **s** receives its correct pronunciation as **s** in English s**e**t, and not as a z sound in pre**s**ent, we often use **ss** in our phonetic transcriptions. Similarly, we sometimes employ a double consonant after **i** to ensure this is pronounced like **i** in p**i**n, and not like **i** in k**i**te. In these cases you can quickly check with the Finnish spelling whether you should pronounce a single or a double consonant.

ä	like **a** in h**a**t; short or	æ	**äkkiä**	**æ**kkiæ
	long	ǣ	**hyvää**	hewv**ǣ**
ö	like **ur** in f**ur**, but	ur	**tyttö**	tewtt**ur**
	without any **r** sound,	ūr	**likööri**	likk**ūr**ri
	and with the lips			
	rounded; short or long			

N.B. The letters **b, c, f, q, š, sh, w, x, z, ž** and **å** are only found in words from foreign languages, and they are pronounced as in the language of origin.

Diphthongs

In Finnish, diphthongs occur only in the first syllable of a word, except those ending in **-i**, where they can occur anywhere. They should be pronounced as a combination of the two vowel sounds represented by the spelling. The list below shows you how the Finnish diphthongs are written in our imitated pronunciation.

The first vowel is pronounced louder in the following diphthongs:

ai = ah^i	**iu** = i^{oo}	**äi** = æ^i
au = ah^{oo}	**oi** = oa^i	**äy** = æ^{ew}
ei = ay^i	**ou** = oa^{oo}	**öi** = ur^i
eu = ay^{oo}	**ui** = oo^i	**öy** = ur^{ew}
ey = ay^{ew}	**yi** = ew^i	

The second vowel is louder in:

ie = ^{i}ay	**uo** = ^{oo}oa	**yö** = ^{ew}ur

Double letters

Remember that in Finnish *every* letter is pronounced, therefore a letter written double is pronounced long. Thus, the **kk** in ku**kk**a should be pronounced like the two **k** sounds in the words thi**ck c**oat. Similarly the **aa** in k**aa**tua should be pronouced long (like **a** in English c**a**r). These distinctions are important, not least because ku**k**a has a different meaning to ku**kk**a and k**a**tua a different meaning to k**aa**tua.

Icelandic

Basic expressions *Nokkur orð og orðasambönd*

Yes/No.	**Já/Nei.**	yow/nei
Please.	**Afsakið.**	avsakidh
Thank you.	**Takk fyrir.**	takk firir
I beg your pardon?	**Afsakið?/Geturðu endurtekið?**	avsakidh/geduru endurtekidh

Introductions *Kynningur*

Good morning/Good afternoon.	**Góðan dag/Góðan dag.**	goadhan dag/goadhan dag
Good night.	**Góða nótt.**	goadha noat
Hello/Hi.	**Halló/Hæ.**	halloa/huy
Good-bye.	**Bless.**	bless
May I introduce...?	**Má ég kynna...?**	mow yeg kinna
My name is...	**Ég heiti...**	yeg heidi
Pleased to meet you.	**Gaman/Ánægjulegt að sjá þig.**	gaman/ownuyyulekt adh sjow thig
What's your name?	**Hvað heitirðu?**	kvadh heidiru
How are you?	**Hvernig hefurðu það?**	kvernig hefuru thadh
Fine thanks. And you?	**Ég hef það ágætt en þú?**	yeg hef tha owguytt en thoo
Where do you come from?	**Hvaðan ertu?**	kvadhan ertu
I'm from...	**Ég er frá...**	yeg er frow
Australia	**Ástralíu**	owsrtaleeyu
Britain	**Bretlandi**	bretlandi
Canada	**Kanada**	kanada
Ireland	**Írlandi**	eerlandi
USA	**Bandaríkjunum**	bandareekyunum
I'm with my...	**Ég er með...**	yeg er medh
wife	**konunni minni**	konunni minni
husband	**manninum mínum**	manninum meenum
family	**fjölskyldunni**	fyu(r)lskildunni
boyfriend	**vini mínum**	vini meenum
girlfriend	**vinkonu minni**	vinkonu minni
I'm on vacation/on business.	**Ég er á ferðalagi/í viðskiptaerindum.**	yeg er ow ferdhalayi/ee vidhskiftaerindum

GUIDE TO PRONUNCIATION, see page 95/EMERGENCIES, page 94

Questions *Spurnigar*

Where?	**Hvar?**	kvar
How?	**Hvernig?**	**kver**nig
When?	**Hvenær?**	**kve**nuyr
What?	**Hvað?**	kvadh
Why?	**Hvers vegna?**	kvers **veg**na
Who?	**Hver?**	kver
Which?	**Hvaða?**	kva**dha**
Where can I get...?	**Hvar fæ ég...?**	kvar fuy yeg
How far?	**Hversu langt?**	**kver**su lowngt
How long?	**Hversu lengi?**	**kver**su **len**gi
How much?	**Hvað mikið?**	kvadh mikidh
May I?	**Má ég?**	mow yeg
Can I have...?	**Get ég fengið...?**	get yeg **fen**gidh
Can you help me?	**Geturðu hjálpað mér?**	**ge**duru **hyowl**padh meer
Is there/Are there...?	**Er/Eru...?**	er/eru
There isn't/aren't...	**Það er ekki/eru ekki...**	thadh er **ech**i/eru **ech**i
There isn't/aren't any.	**Það er enginn/eru enginn.**	thadh er **ein**ginn/eru **ein**ginn

Do you speak...? *Talarðu...?*

Do you speak English?	**Talarðu ensku?**	talaru **en**sku
What does this mean?	**Hvað þýðir þetta?**	kvað **thee**dhir **thet**ta
Can you translate this for me?	**Geturðu þýtt þetta fyrir mig?**	**ge**duru theett **thet**ta firir mig
Could you speak more slowly?	**Gætirðu talað hægar?**	**guy**dirdhu taladh **huy**gar
Could you repeat that?	**Gætirðu endur-tekið?**	**guy**dirdhu **en**durtekidh
Could you write it down, please?	**Gætirðu vinsam-lega skrifað þetta niður?**	**guy**dirdhu **vin**samlega **skri**fadh **thet**ta nidhur
I understand.	**Ég skil.**	yeg skil
I don't understand.	**Ég skil ekki.**	yeg skil **ech**i

It's...	Það er...	thadh er
better/worse	**bedra/verra**	**bedra**/**ve**rra
big/small	**stór/lítill**	stoar/**lee**didl
cheap/expensive	**ódýrt/dýrt**	**oa**deert/deert
early/late	**snemma/seint**	**snem**ma/seint
good/bad	**gott/slæmt**	gott/sluymt
hot/cold	**heitt/kalt**	heitt/kalt
near/far	**nálægt/langt í burtu**	**now**luygt/langt ee **bur**tu
old/young	**gamalt/ungt**	**ga**malt/oongt
right/wrong	**rétt/rangt**	reett/rowngt
vacant/occupied	**laus/upptekin**	löis/**upp**tekin

A few useful words *Nokkur algeng orð*

a little/a lot	**lítið/mikið**	**lee**didh/**mi**kidh
and	**og**	og
behind	**á eftir**	ow **ef**tir
below	**fyrir neðan**	**fi**rir **ne**dhan
between	**á milli**	ow **mid**li
but	**en**	en
down	**niður**	**ni**dhur
downstairs	**niðri**	**nidh**ri
during	**á meðan**	ow **me**dhan
from	**frá**	frow
inside	**inni**	**in**ni
near	**nálægt**	**now**luygt
never	**aldrei**	**al**drei
not	**ekki**	**ech**i
nothing	**ekkert**	**ech**ert
now	**núna**	**noo**na
only	**aðeins**	**adh**eins
or	**eða**	**e**dha
outside	**úti**	**oo**di
perhaps	**ef til vill**	ef til vidl
since	**síðan**	**seed**han
soon	**bráðum**	**browd**hum
then	**þá**	thow
through	**í gegnum**	ee **geg**num
too (also)	**líka**	**lee**ka
towards	**í áttina til**	ee **owt**tina til
under	**undir**	**un**dir
up	**upp**	upp
upstairs	**uppi**	**up**pi
very	**mjög**	myu(r)g
with	**með**	medh
without	**án**	own

Hotel—Accommodation *Hótel og gisting*

My name is...	**Ég heiti**...	yeg **hei**di
I've a reservation.	**Ég á pantað herbergi.**	yeg ow **pan**tadh **her**bergi
We've reserved two rooms.	**Við pöntuðum tvö herbergi.**	vidh **pu(r)n**tudhum tvu(r) **her**bergi
Here's the confirmation.	**Hér er staðfestingin.**	heer er **stadh**festingin
Do you have any vacancies?	**Eru laus herbergi?**	eru **löis her**bergi
I'd like a... room.	**Ég vildi fá**... **herbergi.**	yeg **vil**di fow **her**bergi
single	**einsmanns**	**eins**manns
double	**tveggja manna**	**tveg**gya **man**na
with twin beds	**með tveim rúmum**	medh tveim **room**um
with a double bed	**með hjónarúmi/ tvíbreiðu rúmi**	medh **hyoa**naroomi/ **tvee**breidhu **roo**mi
with a bath	**með baði**	medh **bad**hi
with a shower	**með sturtu**	medh **stur**tu
with a balcony	**með svölum**	medh **svu(r)**lum
with a view	**með útsýni**	medh **ood**seeni
Is there...?	**Er**...?	er
air conditioning	**loftræstikerfi**	**loft**ruystikervi
a private toilet	**einkasnyrting**	**ein**kasnirting
a radio/television in the room	**útvarp/sjónvarp í herberginu**	**ood**varp/**syoan**varp ee **her**berginu
a sauna	**gufubað**	**guv**ubadh
What's the price...?	**Hvað kostar**...?	kvadh **kos**tar
Is there a campsite near here?	**Er tjaldstæði í nágrenninu?**	er **tyald**stuydhi ee **now**grenninu
Can we camp here?	**Megum við tjalda hér?**	**mei**gum vidh **tyal**da hyer
We'll be staying...	**Við verðum**...	vidh **verd**hum
overnight only	**aðeins yfir nóttina**	**adh**eins **i**vir **noat**tina
a few days	**í nokkra daga**	ee **nok**kra **da**ga
a week (at least)	**í viku (að minnsta kosti)**	ee **vi**ku (adh **minn**sta **kos**ti)

Decision *Ákvörðun*

May I see the room?	**Má ég sjá herbergið?**	mow yeg syow **her**bergidh
That's fine. I'll take it.	**Það er ágætt. Ég ætla að taka það.**	thadh er **owg**uytt. yeg **uyt**la adh **ta**ka thadh

NUMBERS, see page 92

No. I don't like it.	**Nei. Mér líkar það ekki.**	nei. myer leekar thadh echi
It's too...	**Það er of...**	thadh er of
cold/hot	**kalt/heitt**	kalt/heitt
dark/small	**dimmt/lítið**	dimmt/leedidh
noisy	**hávaðasamt**	howvadhasamt
Do you have anything...?	**Áttu eitthvað...?**	owttu eittkvadh
better/bigger	**betra/stærra**	bedra/stuyrra
cheaper/quieter	**ódýrara/rólegra**	oadeerara/roalegra

Nafn/Skírnarnafn	Name/First name
Heimabær/Gata/Númer	Home town/Street/Number
Þjóðerni/Starf	Nationality/Occupation
Dagsetning/Fæðingarstaður	Date/Place of birth
Koma frá.../Fara til...	Coming from.../Going to...
Vegabréfsnúmer	Passport number
Staður/Dagsetning	Place/Date
Undirskrift	Signature

General requirements *Almennar kröfur*

The key to room..., please.	**Get ég fengið lykil að herbergi...**	ged yeg fengidh likil adh herbergi
Where's the...?	**Hvar er...?**	kvar er
bathroom	**baðherbergi**	badhherbergi
dining-room	**borðstofa**	bordhstova
emergency exit	**neyðarútgangur**	neidharoodgowngur
lift (elevator)	**lyfta**	lifta
Where are the toilets?	**Hvar er snyrtingin?**	kvar er snirtingin
Where can I park my car?	**Hvar má ég leggja bílnum?**	kvar moa yeg leggya beelnum

Checking out *Að skrá sig út*

May I have my bill, please?	**Get ég fengið reikninginn?**	get yeg fengidh reikninginn
Can you get us a taxi?	**Geturðu ná í leigu-bíl fyrir okkur?**	gedurdhu nowdh ee leigubeel firir ochur
It's been a very enjoyable stay.	**Dvölin hefur verið ánægjuleg.**	dvu(r)lin hefur veridh ownuyyuleg

Eating out *Borðað úti*

Can you recommend a good restaurant?	**Geturðu mælt með góðum veitingastað?**	gedurdhu muylt medh goadhum veitingastadh
I'd like to reserve a table for 4.	**Ég ætla að panta borð fyrir fjóra.**	yeg uytla adh panta bordh firir fyoara
We'll come at 8.	**Við komum klukkan átta.**	vidh komum klukkan owtta
What do you recommend?	**Með hverju mælirðu?**	medh kveryu muylirdhu
Do you have a set menu/local dishes?	**Eruð þið með fastan matseðil/ þjóðarrétti?**	erudh thidh medh fastan matsedhil/thyoadharryetti
Do you have vegetarian dishes?	**Eruð þið með grænmetisrétti?**	erudh thidh medh gruynmetisreetti

Hvað má bjóða þér?	What would you like?
Ég mæli með þessu.	I recommend this.
Hvað viltu fá að drekka?	What would you like to drink?
... er ekki til.	We don't have...
Viltu/Má bjóða þér...?	Would you like...?

Could we have a/an..., please?	**Gætum við fengið...?**	guydun vidh fengidh
ashtray	**öskubakki**	u(r)skubachi
cup	**bolli**	bodli
fork	**gaffall**	gaffadl
glass	**glas**	glas
knife	**hnífur**	hneevur
napkin (serviette)	**servétta**	servyetta
plate	**diskur**	diskur
spoon	**skeið**	skeidh

TELLING THE TIME, see page 91/NUMBERS, page 92

May I have some...?	Get ég fengið...?	ged yeg fengidh
bread	brauð	bröidh
butter	smjör	smyu(r)
lemon	sítróna	seedroana
oil	olía	oleea
pepper	pipar	pibar
salt	salt	salt
seasoning	krydd	kridd
sugar	sykur	sigur
vinegar	edik	edig

Reading the menu *Að lesa matseðilinn*

ábætisréttir	owbuytisreettir	desserts
ávextir	owvekstir	fruit
bjór	bjoar	beer
borðvín	bordhveen	wine
borgarar	borgarar	burgers
drykkir	drikkir	drinks
eggjaréttir	eggyareettir	egg dishes
fiskréttir	fiskreettir	seafood
fiskur	fiskur	fish
forréttir	forreettir	hors-d'œuvre
fuglakjöt	fuglakyu(r)d	poultry
grænmeti	gruynmedi	vegetables
hrísgrjón	hreesgryoan	rice
ís	ees	ice cream
kjöt	kyu(r)d	meat
kjúklingur	kyooklingur	chicken
milliréttir	midliryettir	entrées
ostar	osdar	cheese
pastaréttir	pastareettir	pasta
sætabrauð	suytabröidh	pastries
salöd	salu(r)d	salads
smáréttir	smowryettir	snacks
súpur	soobur	soups
villibráð	vidlibrowdh	game
vín	veen	wine

Starters *Forréttir*

blönduð sjávarréttarsúpa	blu(r)ndudh **syow**-vareetasooba	mixed seafood soup
djúpsteiktar rækjur	**dyoop**steiktar **ruyk**yur	deep-fried prawns
graflax	**grav**laks	marinated salmon
humar súpa	**humar** sooba	lobster soup
rækju súpa	**ruyk**yusooba	prawn soup
reyktur lax	**reik**tur laks	smoked salmon
villigæsapate	**vid**liguysapade	wild goose paté
blandaðir sjávarréttir (**bland**adhir **syow**vareettir)	mixed seafood plate of prawn, lobster and scallop	

Soups *Súpur*

I'd like some soup	**Ég ætla að fá súpu.**	yeg **uyt**la adh fow **soo**bu
humar súpa	**humar soo**ba	lobster soup
kjötsúpa	**kyu(r)t**sooba	soup with meat and vegetables
rækju súpa	**ruyk**yu **soo**ba	shrimp soup
sjávarréttasúpa	**syow**varreettarree-tarsooba	mixed seafood soup
tómatsúpa	**toa**madsooba	tomato soup
uxahalasúpa	**uk**sahalasooba	oxtail soup

baked	**bakað**	**ba**kadh
boiled	**soðið**	**so**dhidh
fried	**steikt**	steikt
grilled	**glóðað**	**gloa**dhadh
roast	**steikja**	**steik**ya
stewed	**soðið í langan tíma**	**so**dhidh ee **lan**gan **tee**ma
underdone (rare)	**lítið steikt**	**lee**didh steikt
medium	**miðlungs steikt**	**mi**dhlungs steikt
well-done	**vel steikt**	vel steikt

ICELANDIC

Fish and seafood *Fiskur og fiskréttir*

cod	**þorskur**	thoskur
crayfish/crawfish	**krabbadýr**	krabbadeer
haddock	**ýsa**	eesa
halibut	**lúða**	loodha
lobster	**humar**	humar
mussel	**kræklingur**	kruyklingur
plaice	**rauðspretta**	röidhspretta
prawn	**rækja**	ruykya
scallop	**hörpuskelfiskur**	hu(r)rpuskelfiskur
sole	**sólflúru**	soalflooru
trout	**silung**	silung

skata
(**ska**da)

skate; mostly eaten in December, particularly the day before Christmas Eve.

Meat *Kjöt*

I'd like some...	**Ég ætla að fá...**	yeg **uyt**la adh fow
bacon	**beikon**	beikon
beef	**nautakjöt**	nöitakyu(r)d
chicken	**kjúklingur**	kyooklingur
duck	**önd**	u(r)nd
goose	**gæs**	guys
(smoked) ham	**(reykt) svínakjöt**	reikt sveenakyu(r)d
lamb	**lambakjöt**	lambakyu(r)d
pork	**svínakjöt**	sveenakyu(r)d
sausage	**bjúgu**	byooyu
steak	**steik**	steik
turkey	**kalkún**	kalkoon
veal	**kálfakjöt**	kowlvakyu(r)d

lambakóteluttur	lambakoadelettur	lamb chop
nautalundir	nöitalundir	fillet of beef
nautasteik	nöitasteik	beef steak

hangikjöt
(**han**gikyu(r)d)

typical Icelandic dish of smoked lamb; the traditional Christmas dish.

rjúpa
(**ryoo**ba)

ptarmigan; game bird usually only eaten at Christmas time.

íslensk

Vegetables *Grænmeti*

beans	baunir	böinir
beetroot	rauðrófa	röidhroava
broccoli	spergilkál	spergilkowl
cabbage	kál	kowl
carrots	gulrætur	gulruytar
cucumber	agúrka	agoorga
gherkin	gúrka	goorga
leek	blaðlaukur	bladhlöikur
lentils	linsubaunir	linsuböinir
mushroom	sveppur	sveppur
onion	laukur	löigur
peas	baunir	böinir
potatoes	kartöflur	kartu(r)blur
rice	hrísgrjón	hreesgryoan
swede (rutabaga)	rófa	roava
tomato	tómatur	toamadur
turnips	næpa	nuyba

ávaxtasalad	owvakstasalad	fruit salad
eggjakaka	eggyakaka	omelette
grænt salad	gruyn salad	green salad
gulrótarsalad	gulroadarsalad	carrot salad

grænmetisbaka	vegetable pie; served warm, made from a
(gruynmetisbaka)	selection of seasonal vegetables.

Fruit *Ávextir*

apple	epli	epli
banana	banani	banani
blackcurrants	sólber	soalber
grapes	vínber	veenber
grapefruit	greipávöxtur	greibowvu(r)kstur
lemon	sítróna	seetroana
melon	melóna	meloana
orange	appelsína	appelseena
plum	plóma	ploama
raspberries	hindber	hindber
strawberries	jarðaber	yardhaber

bláber	blowber	blueberries
kræ" kiber	kruygiber	crowberries
rifsber	rivsber	redcurrants

Desserts–Pastries *Eftirréttir–Kökur*

ávaxtakaka	owvakstakaka	gateau
ís	ees	ice-cream
jarðarber með rjóma	yardhaber medh ryoama	strawberries and whipped cream
ostakaka	osdakaka	cheese cake
ostar	osdar	mixed cheese plate
súkkulaði kaka	sookuladhi kaka	chocolate cake

Drinks *Drykkir*

(hot) chocolate	**(heitt) súkkulaði**	(heitt) sookuladhi
coffee	**kaffi**	kaffi
black	**svart**	svart
with milk	**með mjólk**	medh myoalk
fruit juice	**ávaxtadjús**	owvakstadyoos
orange	**appelsínudjús**	appelseenudyoos
apple	**epladjús**	epladyoos
lemonade	**sítrónudrykkur**	seetroanudrichur
mineral water	**sódavatn**	soadavatn
fizzy (sparkling)	**með gosi**	medh gosi
still	**án goss**	own gosi
tea	**te**	te
cup of tea	**tebolli**	tebodli
with milk	**með mjólk**	medh myoalk
iced tea	**íste**	eeste
beer	**bjór**	byoar
gin and tonic	**gin og tónik**	gin og toanik
liqueur	**líkjör**	leekyu(r)r
port	**púrtvín**	poortveen
rum	**romm**	romm
sherry	**sherrí**	syerree
wine	**vín**	veen
red/white	**rauðvín/hvítvín**	röidhveen/kveetveen
vodka	**vodka**	vodka
brennivín (brenniveen)		Icelandic schnapps (sometimes called 'Black Death')
neat (straight)	**óblandað**	oablandadh
on the rocks	**á ís**	ow ees
with a little water	**með smávegis af vatni**	medh smowvegis av vatni
Cheers!/To your health!	**Skál!**	skowl

Complaints and paying *Kvartanir og greiðsla*

The meat is...	**Kjötið er...**	kyu(r)tidh er
overdone	**of steikt**	ov steikt
underdone	**of lítið steikt**	ov leedidh steikt
This is too...	**Þetta er of...**	thetta er of
bitter/salty/sweet	**beiskur/saltur/ sætur**	beiskur/saltur/suydur
That's not what I ordered.	**Ég pantaði ekki þetta.**	yeg pantadhi ekki thetta
The food is cold.	**Maturinn er kaldur.**	madurinn er kaldur

The bill (check) *Reikninginn*

I'd like to pay.	**Ég ætla að borga.**	yeg uytla adh borga
What's this amount for?	**Fyrir hvað er þessi upphæð?**	firir hvadh er thessi upphuydh
I think you made a mistake in the bill.	**Ég held að reik- ningurinn sé ekki réttur.**	yeg held adh reiknin- gurinn see ekki reetur
Can I pay with this credit card?	**Get ég borgað með þessu greiðslu- korti?**	get yeg borgadh medh thessu greidhslukorti
Is service included?	**Er þjónustugjald innifalið?**	er thyoanustugyald innifalidh
We enjoyed it, thank you.	**Þetta var góð máltíð.**	thetta var goadh mowlteedh

Snacks—Picnic *Smáréttir—Lautarferð*

Give me two of these and one of those.	**Ég ætla að fá tvo af þessum og einn af þessu.**	yeg uytla adh fow tvo av thessum og eidn av thessu
to the left/right	**til vinstri/hægri**	til vinstri/huygri
above	**fyrir ofan**	firir ovan
below	**fyrir neðan**	firir nedhan
chips (french fries)	**franskar kartöflur**	franskar kartu(r)blur
soft drink (soda)	**gosdrykkir**	gosdrikkir
omelette	**eggjakaka**	eggyakaka
open sandwich	**brauðsneið**	bröidhsneidh
with ham	**með skinku**	medh skinku
with cheese	**með osti**	medh osdi
piece of cake	**kökusneið**	ku(r)kusneidh

NUMBERS, see page 92

Travelling around *Ferðast*

Plane *Flugvél*

Is there a flight to Reykjavík?	**Er flogið til Reykjavíkur?**	er flogidh til **reik**yaveekur
What time do I check in?	**Klukkan hvað á ég að skrá mig inn?**	**kluk**kna kvað ow yeg adh skrow mig inn
I'd like to... my reservation on flight no. ...	**Ég vil gjarnan... pöntun mín í flug númer...**	yeg vil **gyar**na... **pu(r)**ntun meen ee flug **noo**mer
cancel	**aflýsa**	av**lee**sa
change	**breyta**	**brei**ta
confirm	**staðfesta**	**stadh**festa

Coach (long-distance bus) *Rúta (Lanferðabíll)*

Where's the coach station?	**Hvar er brautastöðin?**	kvar er **brö**idarstu(r)dhin

INNGANGUR	ENTRANCE
ÚTGANGUR	EXIT
TIL BRAUTARPALLA	TO THE COACH BAYS
UPPLÝSINGAR	INFORMATION

Where is/are (the)...?	**Hvar er/eru...?**	kvar er/eru
left-luggage office (baggage check)	**farangursgeymsla (farangurssko-ðun)**	**far**owngursgeimsla (**far**owngursskodhun)
lost property (lost and found) office	**tapað fundið**	tapadh **fun**didh
luggage lockers	**farangursskápar**	**far**owngursskowbar
reservations office	**pantanir**	**pan**tanir
ticket office	**miðasala**	**midh**asala
waiting room	**biðstofa**	**bidh**stova
I want a ticket to Akureyri.	**Ég ætla að fá miða til Akureyrar.**	yeg **uyt**la adh fow **midh**a til akureirar
single (one-way)	**aðra leiðina**	**adh**ra **leidh**ina
return (roundtrip)	**báðar leiðir/fram og til baka**	**boadh**ar leidhir/fram og til baka
first/second class	**fyrsta/annað farrými**	**fir**ta/**an**nadh **far**reemi

TELLING THE TIME, see page 91

ICELANDIC

Inquiries *Fyrirspurnir*

How long does the journey (trip) take?	Hvað tekur ferðin langan tíma?	kvadh tekur ferdhin langan teema
When is the... coach to Húsavik?	Hvenær fer... rútan til Húsavíkur?	kvenuyr fer... roodan til hoosaveekur
first/next	fyrst/næst	first/nuyst
last	síðast	seedhast
What time does the coach to Akranes leave?	Hvenær fer rútan til Akraness?	kvenuyr fer roodan til akraness
What time does the coach arrive in Keflavík?	Hvenær kemur rútan til Keflavíkur?	kvenuyr kemur roodan til keblaveekur
Is this the right coach for Isafjöður?	Er þetta rútan til Ísafjarðar?	er thetta roodan til eesafyardhar
Porter!	Burðarmaður!	burdharmadhur
Can you help me with my luggage?	Geturðu hjápað mér með farangur- inn?	gedurdhu hyowlpadh möir medh farowngurinn

Bus—Tram (streetcar) *Strætó—Sporvagn*

What bus do I take to the centre?	Hvaða strætó tek ég niður í bæ?	kvadha struydoa tek eeg nidhur ee buy
How much is the fare to...?	Hvað kostar...?	kvadh kostar
Will you tell me when to get off?	Viltu segja mér hvenær ég á að fara út úr strætisvagni- num?	viltu segya meer kvenuyr yeg ow adh fara oot oor struydisvagninum
When's the next coach (long-distance bus) to Geysir?	Hvenær er næsta rúta (langferðabíll) að Geysi?	kvenuyr er nuysda rooda (langferdhabeedl) adh geisi

Boat service *Báta þjónusta*

When does the next boat for... leave?	Hvenær fer næsti bátur til...?	kvenuyr fer nuysdi bowdur til
How long does the crossing take?	Hvað tekur ferðin langan tíma?	kvadh tekur ferdhin lowngan teema
I'd like to take a tour of the harbour.	Ég vildi gjarnan fara í ferð um höf- nina.	yeg vildi gyarnan fara ee ferdh um hu(r)bnina

íslensk

TELLING THE TIME, see page 91/NUMBERS, see page 92

Taxi *Leigubíll*

Where can I get a taxi?	Hvar næ ég í leigu-bíl?	kvar nuy yeg ee leigubeel
How much is it to...	Hvað kostar til...	kvadh kostar til
Take me to this address.	Viltu gjöra svo vel að aka mér á þennan stað.	viltu gyu(r)a svo vel adh aka meer ow thennan stadh
Please stop here.	Viltu gjöra svo vel að stoppa hér.	viltu gyu(r)a svo vel adh stoppa heer
I'll be back in 10 minutes.	Ég kem eftir tíu mínútur.	yeg kem eftir teeyu meenoodur

Car hire *Bíla leiga*

I'd like to hire (rent) a car.	Ég ætla að leigja bíl.	yeg uytla adh leigya beel
I'd like it for a day/week.	Ég vildi hafa hann í einn dag/eina viku.	yeg vildi hafa hann ee einn dag/eina viku
What's the charge per day/week?	Hvað kostar á dag/í viku?	kvað kostar ow dag/ee viku
Is mileage included?	Er kílómetragjald innifalið?	er keeloametragyald innifalidh

Road signs *Vegvísar*

Akið hægt	Drive slowly
Akið á eigin ábyrgð	Drive at own risk
Athugið hemlana	Test your brakes
Bílastæði	Parking
Farið á þessa akrein	Get in lane
Frost skemmdir	Frost damage
Hálir vegir (hálka)	Slippery road
Hámarkshraði... km	Speed limit... km
Kröpp beygja	Road works
Lausamöl	Loose gravel
Malarvegur	Dangerous bend
Þröng brú	Narrow bridge
Tímabundinn hámarkshraði	Local speed limit

| Where's the nearest filling station? | Hvar er næsta ben-sínstöð? | kvar er nuysta benseenstu(r)dh |
| Full tank, please. | Fylla, takk. | fidla, takk |

Give me ... litres of petrol (gasoline).	Ég ætla að fá ... lítra af bensíni.	yeg uytla adh fow... leetra af benseeni
super (premium)/regular/unleaded/diesel	súper/venjulegt/blýlaust/dísel	soober/venyulegt/bleelöist/deesel
Where can I park?	Hvar má ég leggja?	kvar moa yeg leggya
How do I get to ...?	Hvernig kemst ég til ...?	kvernig kemst yeg til
How far is it to ... from here?	Hvað er langt héðan til ...?	kvadh er langt hyedhan til
I've had a breakdown at ...	Bíllinn bilaði við/í ...	beedlinn biladhi vidh/ee
Can you send a mechanic?	Geturðu sent viðgerðarmann?	gerurdhu sent vidhgerdharmann
Can you mend this puncture (fix this flat)?	Geturðu gert við sprungið dekk?	geturdhu gert vidh sprungidh dekk
Please check the ...	Vinsamlega athugið ...	vinsamlega athugidh
anti-freeze	frostlögur	frostlu(r)gur
battery	rafgeymir	ravgeimir
brake fluid	bremsuvökvi	bremsuvu(r)kvi
oil/coolant	olía/kælivökvi	oleea/kuylivu(r)vi
wheel chains	keðjur	kedhyur
windscreen water	gluggaúði	gluggaoodhi
Would you check the tyre pressures?	Viltu mæla loftið í dekkinu?	viltu muyla loftidh ee dechinu

---

You're on the wrong road.	Þú ert ekki á réttum vegi.
Go straight ahead.	Haltu beint áfram.
It's down there on the ...	Það er þarna niður til ...
left/right	vinstri/hægri
next to/after ...	næsta við/ fyrir aftan ...
north/south	norður/suður
east/west	austur/vestur
Turn left at the traffic lights.	Beygðu til vinstri við umferðaljósin.

NUMBERS, see page 92

Sightseeing *Skoðunarferð*

Where's the tourist office?	**Hvar er ferðaskrifstofan?**	kvar er **ferdhaskrifstofan**
What are the main points of interest?	**Hverjir eru athyglisverðustu staðirnir?**	**kver**yir eru **athyglisverdhustu stadhirnir**
Is there an English-speaking guide?	**Er leiðsögumaðurinn enskumælandi?**	er **leidh**su(r)gumadhurinn enskumuylandi
Where is/are the...?	**Hvar er/eru...?**	kvar er/eru
beach	**strönd**	stru(r)nd
botanical gardens	**grasagarðurinn**	**grasa**gardhurinn
cathedral	**dómkirkja**	**doam**kirkya
city centre	**miðbær**	**midh**buyr
exhibition	**sýning**	**see**ning
harbour	**höbn**	hu(r)bn
market	**markaður**	**marka**dhur
museum	**safn**	safn
shops	**verslanir**	**vers**lanir
zoo	**dýragarður**	**deer**agardhur
When does it open?	**Hvenær er opnað?**	**kven**uyr er **opnadh**
When does it close?	**Hvenær er lokað?**	**kven**uyr er **lokadh**
How much is the entrance fee?	**Hvað kostar inn?**	kvað **kostar** inn

Landmarks *Kennileiti*

bridge	**brú**	broo
fjord	**fjörður**	**fyu(r)**dhur
geyser	**goshver**	**gos**kver
glacier	**jökull**	**yu(r)**kudl
island	**eyja**	**ei**ya
lake	**stöðuvatn**	**stu(r)**dhuvadn
mountain	**fjall**	**fyadl**
path	**stígur**	**stee**gur
river	**á**	ow
sea	**sjór**	syoar
waterfall	**foss**	foss
wood	**skógur**	**skoa**gur

TELLING THE TIME, see page 91

Entertainment *Skemmtanir*

What's showing at the cinema tonight?	Hvað er í bíó í kvöld?	kvadh er ee **bee**oa ee kvu(r)ld
What's playing at the theatre?	Hvað er í leikhúsinu í kvöld?	kvadh er ee leik**hoo**sinu ee kvu(r)ld
How much are the seats?	Hvað kostar miðinn?	kvað **kost**ar midhinn
What time does it begin?	Hvenær byrjar það?	**kven**uyr **bir**yar thadh
Are there any seats left for tonight?	Eru einhverjir miðar til í kvöld?	eru **eink**veryir **mid**har til ee kvu(r)ld
I'd like to reserve 2 seats for the show on Friday evening.	Ég ætla að láta taka frá tvo miða á föstudagssýninguna.	yeg **uyt**la adh **low**da taka frow tvo **mid**ha ow fu(r)sdudagsseeninguna
Would you like to go out with me tonight?	Viltu koma út með mér í kvöld?	**vil**tu **ko**ma oot medh myer ee kvu(r)ld
Thank you, but I'm busy.	Takk fyrir en ég er upptekin.	Tach **fir**ir en yeg er **upp**tekin
Is there a discotheque in town?	Er diskótek í bænum?	er **dis**koatek ee **buy**num
Would you like to dance?	Viltu dansa?	**vil**tu **dan**sa
Thank you. It's been a wonderful evening.	Takk fyrir. Þetta var dásamlegt kvöld.	takk **fir**ir. **thet**ta var **dow**samlegt kvu(r)ld

Sports *Íþróttir*

Is there a football (soccer) match anywhere this Saturday?	Er fótboltaleikur einhvers staðar á laugardaginn?	er **foad**boltaleikur **eink**vers stadhar ow **löi**gardaginn
What's the admission charge?	Hvað kostar inn?	kvað **kost**ar inn
Where's the nearest golf course?	Hvar er næsti golfvöllur?	kvar er **nuys**di golf**vu(r)d**lur
Where are the tennis courts?	Hvar eru tennisvellirnir?	kvar eru **ten**nisvedlirnir

cycle racing	hjólreiðakeppni	hjoalreidhakeppni
fishing	veiðar	veidhar
football (soccer)	fótbolti	foadbolti
ice hockey	ís hokkí	ees hochee
(horse-back) riding	útreiðar	oodreidhar
mountaineering	fjallganga	fyadlgownga
speed skating	skautahlaup	sköidahlöip
ski jumping	skíðastökk	skeedhastu(r)ch
skiing	skíðamennska	skeedhamennska
swimming	sund	sund
tennis	tennis	tennis

Can one swim in the lake/river?	Má synda í vatninu/ánni?	mow sinda ee vadninu/ownni
Is there a swimming pool here?	Er sundlaug hér?	er sundlöig hyer
Is there a skating rink near here?	Er skautasvell hér í nágrenninu?	er sköidasvedl hyer ee nágrenninu
I'd like to ski.	Mig langar á skíði.	mig lowngar ow skeedhi
downhill/cross-country skiing	brun/skíðaganga	brun/skeedhagownga
I want to hire . . .	Ég ætlaði að leigja . . .	yeg uytladhi adh leigya
skates	skautar	skaöidar
skiing equipment	skíðaútbúnaður	skeedhaoodboonadhur
skis	skíði	skeedhi
I'd like to hire a . . . bicycle.	Ég vildi leigja . . . hjól.	yeg vildi leigya hjoal
5-gear	fimm-gíra	fimm-geera
mountain	fjalla	fyadla

Shops, stores and services *Verslanir og þjónusta*

Where's the nearest...?	**Hvar er næsta...?**	kvar er nuysta
baker's	**bakarí**	bakaree
bookshop	**bókaverslun**	boakaverslun
butcher's	**kjötbúð**	kyu(r)tboodh
chemist's	**apótek**	aboatek
delicatessen	**verslun með tíl-búna rétti**	verslun medh tilboona reetti
dentist	**tannlæknir**	tannluyknir
department store	**stórmarkaður**	stoarmarkadhur
grocery	**grænmetisverslun**	gruynmetisverslun
hairdresser	**hárgreiðslustofa**	howrgreidhslustofa
liquor store	**vínbúð**	veenboodh
newsagent	**blaðasala**	bladhasala
post office	**pósthús**	poasthoos
souvenir shop	**minjagripaverslun**	minyagripaverslun
supermarket	**stórmarkaður**	stoarmarkadhur

General expressions *Almennar spurningar*

Where's the main shopping area?	**Hvar er aðal verslunarsvæðið?**	kvar er adhal verslunarsvuydhidh
Do you have any...?	**Eru til...?**	eru til

Can I help you?	Get ég aðstoðað þig?
What would you like?	Hvað viltu?
What... would you like?	Hvað... mundirðu vilja?
colour/shape/quality	litur/lögun/gæði
We're out of stock at the moment.	Varan er uppseld í augnablikinu.
Shall we order it for you?	Eigum við að panta þetta fyrir þig?
Anything else?	Er það eitthvað annað?
That's... crowns, please.	Þetta kostar... krónur, takk fyrir.
The cash desk is over there.	Kassinn er þarna.

big	**stór**	stoar
cheap	**ódýr**	oadeer
dark	**dimmur**	dimmur
good	**góður**	goadhur
heavy	**þungur**	thoongur
large	**stór**	stoar
light (weight)	**létt**	leett
light (colour)	**ljós**	lyoas
rectangular	**rétthyrndur**	reetthirndur
round	**kringlóttur**	kringloattur
small	**lítill**	leedidl
square	**ferhyrndur**	ferhirndur

Can you show me this/that?	**Geturðu sýnt mér þetta?**	**ge**turdhu seent myer **thet**ta
Do you have anything...?	**Eru til...?**	**eru** til
cheaper/better	**ódýrara/betra**	oa**dee**rara/**bed**ra
larger/smaller	**stærra/minna**	**stuyr**ra/**min**na
Can I try it on?	**Má ég máta?**	mow yeg **mow**da
Where's the fitting room?	**Hvar er mátunar-klefinn?**	kvar er **mow**dunarklefinn
How long will it take?	**Hvað tekur það langan tíma?**	kvadh **tek**ur thadh **low**gan **tee**ma
How much is this?	**Hvað kostar þetta?**	kvadh **kost**ar **thet**ta
Please write it down.	**Viltu gjöra svo vel að skrifa það niður.**	**vil**tu **gyu**(r)a svo vel adh **skrif**a thadh **nidh**ur
No, I don't like it.	**Nei, mér líkar það ekki.**	nei, myer **lee**kar thadh **ek**ki
I'll take it.	**Ég ætla að fá þetta.**	yeg **uyt**la adh fow **thet**ta
Do you accept credit cards?	**Tekurðu greiðslu-kort?**	**tek**urdhu **greidh**slukort
Can you order it for me?	**Geturðu pantað það fyrir mig?**	**ge**turdhu **pan**tadh thadh **fir**ir mig

black	**svart**	svart
blue	**blátt**	blowtt
brown	**brúnt**	broont
green	**grænt**	gruynt
grey	**grátt**	growtt
orange	**appelsínugult**	**ap**pelseenugult
red	**rautt**	röitt
yellow	**gult**	gult
white	**hvítt**	kveett

NUMBERS, see page 92

Chemist's (drugstore) *Apótek*

aspirin	**aspirín**	**as**pereen
condoms	**smokkar**	**smoc**har
deodorant	**svitakrem**	**svi**dakrem
insect repellent/spray	**skordýra fæla/eitur**	**skor**deera **fuy**la/**ei**dur
moisturizing cream	**rakakrem**	**ra**gakrem
razor blades	**rakvélablöð**	**rag**veelablu(r)dh
shampoo	**sjampó**	**syam**poa
sun-tan cream	**sól krem**	soal krem
soap	**sápa**	**sow**ba
tampons	**tíðatappar**	**teed**hatappar
toothpaste	**tannkrem**	**tann**krem

Clothing *Fatnaður*

blouse	**blússa**	**bloos**sa
boots	**stígvél**	**steeg**vyel
bra	**brjóstahaldari**	**bryoa**stahaldari
coat	**kápa**	**kow**ba
dress	**kjóll**	**kjoadl**
fur hat	**loðhattur**	**lodh**hattur
gloves	**hanskar**	**hans**kar
jersey	**prjónapeysa**	**pryoa**napeisa
scarf	**slæða**	**sluy**dha
shirt	**skyrta**	**skir**da
shoes	**skór**	skoar
skirt	**pils**	pils
socks	**sokkar**	**sok**kar
swimming trunks	**sundskýla**	**sund**skeela
swimsuit	**sundbolur**	**sund**bolur
T-shirt	**stuttermabolur**	**stut**termabolur
tights	**sokkabuxur**	**sok**kabuksur
trousers	**síðbuxur**	**seedh**buksur
underpants	**undirbuxur**	**un**dirbuksur
What's it made of?	**Úr hverju er það?**	oor **kver**yu er thadh

cotton	**bómull**	**boa**mudl
denim	**denímefni**	**de**neemebni
lace	**blúnda**	**bloon**da
leather	**leður**	**led**hur
linen	**lín**	leen
silk	**silki**	**sil**ki
suede	**rúskinn**	**roo**skinn
velvet	**flauel**	**flöi**el
wool	**ull**	udl

Grocer's *Grænmetisverslun*

What sort of cheese do you have?	**Hvaða ostategundir eru til?**	kvadha **os**dategundir eru til
half a kilo of apples	**hálft kíló af epplum**	howlft **keel**oa af **epp**lum
a litre of milk	**einn mjólkurlíter**	einn **myoal**kurleeter
4 slices of ham	**fjórar sneiðar af skinku**	fyoarar sneidhar av skinku
a tin (can) of peaches	**ein dós af ferskjum**	ein doas av ferskyum

Miscellaneous *Almennar*

I want to buy...	**Ég ætla að fá...**	yeg **uyt**la adh fow
batteries	**rafhlöður**	**rafh**lu(r)dhur
film	**filmu**	**fil**mu
newspaper	**dagblað**	**dagt**hladh
English/American	enskt/**bandarískt**	enskt/**bandareest**
torch	**blys**	blis
I'd like... film for this camera.	**Ég ætla að fá... filmu í þessa myndavél.**	yeg **uyt**la adh fow **fil**mu ee **thessa** mindavyel
black and white	**svart hvíta**	svart **kvee**da
colour	**lit**	lit
I'd like a haircut.	**Ég ætla að láta klippa mig.**	yeg **uyt**la adh **low**ta **klipp**a mig

Souvenirs *Minjagripir*

askur
(asgur)
carved wooden dinner bowl that Icelanders traditionally used as plates.

keramik
(keramik)
ceramics; bowls, vases, cups and plates made by Icelandic artists.

lopapeysa
(lobapeisa)
lopi sweater; an ordinary handknitted sweater made of Icelandic wool.

sauðskinnskór
(söidhskinnskoar)
shoes made of sheep skin; small imitations of the kind of shoes traditionally worn in Iceland.

silfurskartgripir
(silvurskartgribir)
silver jewellery; made to old designs by Icelandic silversmiths.

þjóðbúningsdúkka
(thyoadh-booningsdoocha)
national doll; dolls of different sizes dressed in various costumes. The costumes depend on social status and period in history.

Þórshamar
(thoarshamar)
Thorshammer; a small statue of the Nordic God Thor holding his hammer.

At the bank *Í bankanum*

Where's the nearest bank?	Hvar er næsti banki?	kvar er **nuysti bown**ki
I want to change some dollars/pounds into krona.	Ég ætla að skipta nokkrum dollurum/ pundum í krónur.	yeg **uyt**la adh **skip**ta **nokkrum dollurum**/ **pundum** ee **kroa**nur
What's the exchange rate?	Hvað er gengið?	kvadh er **gengið**

At the post office *Á pósthúsinu*

I want to send this by...	Ég ætla að senda þetta með...	yeg **uyt**la adh **senda thetta** medh
airmail	flugpósti	**flug**poasti
express	hraðpósti	**hradh**poasti
registered mail	ábyrgðarpósti	**owbirgdhar**poasti
I want... -krona stamps.	Ég ætla að fá... króna frímerki.	yeg **uyt**la adh fow... **kroa**na **free**merki
What's the postage for a letter/postcard to the United States?	Hvað er póstbur- ðargjald fyrir bréf/ póstkort til Banda- ríkjanna?	kvadh er **poastburdhaegyald** firir breef/**poastkort** til **bandareekyanna**
Is there any mail for me? My name is...	Er einhver póstur til mín? Ég heiti...	er **einkveer poas**tur til meen. yeg **heiti**
Can I send a telegram/fax?	Get ég sent skeyti/ símbréf?	get yeg sent **skeidi**/ **seem**breef

Telephoning *Sími*

Where's the nearest public phone?	Hvar er næsti símaklefi?	kvar er **nuys**di **seem**aklevi
May I use your phone?	Má ég hringja?	mow yeg **hring**ya
Hello. This is... speaking.	Halló. Þetta er... sem talar.	halloa. **thetta** er... sem talar
I want to speak to...	Get ég fengið að tala við...	get yeg **fengidh** adh **tala** vidh
When will he/she be back?	Hvenær kemur hann/hún aftur?	**kvenuyr ke**mur hann/hoon aftur
Will you tell him/her that I called?	Viltu segja honum/ henni að ég hringdi?	**vil**tu **seg**ya **ho**num/henni adh yeg **hreeng**di
Would you take a message, please?	Viltu gjöra svo vel að taka skilaboð?	**vil**tu **gyu**(r)a svo vel adh taka **skilabodh**

NUMBERS, see page 92

Doctor *Læknir*

Where can I find a doctor who speaks English?	**Hvar er ensku-mælandi læknir?**	kvar er **ensku**muylandi **luyk**nir
Where's the surgery (doctor's office)?	**Hvar er lækna-stofan?**	kvar er **luyk**nastovan
Can I have an appointment... ?	**Get ég fengið tíma...?**	get yeg **fen**gidh **tee**ma
tomorrow	**á morgun**	ow **mor**gun
as soon as possible	**eins fljótt og mögulegt er**	eins flyoatt og **mu(r)**gulegt er

Parts of the body *Líkamshlutar*

arm	**handleggur**	**hand**leggur
back	**bak**	bak
bone	**bein**	bein
ear	**eyra**	**eira**
eye	**auga**	**öiga**
face	**andlit**	**andlid**
finger	**fingur**	**fingur**
foot	**fótur**	**foa**dur
hand	**hönd**	hu(r)nd
head	**höfuð**	**hu(r)**vudh
heart	**hjarta**	**hyarta**
knee	**hné**	hnye
leg	**fótleggur**	**foad**leggur
lung	**lunga**	**loon**ga
mouth	**munnur**	**munn**ur
muscle	**vöðvi**	**vu(r)dh**vi
nerve	**taug**	töig
nose	**nef**	nev
shoulder	**öxl**	u(r)ksl
skin	**húð**	hoodh
stomach	**magi**	**mayi**
throat	**háls**	howls
tongue	**tunga**	**toon**ga
I've got a/an...	**Ég er með...**	yeg er medh
bruise	**mar**	mar
burn	**brunasár**	**brina**sowr
cut	**skurð**	skurdh
insect bite	**skordýrabit**	**skor**deerabid
rash	**útbrot**	**ood**brod
sting	**sár eftir stungu**	aowr **evtir stoon**gu
swelling	**bólga**	**boal**ga
wound	**sár**	sowr

Could you have a look at it?	Gætirðu litið á það?	guydirdhu litidh ow thadh
It hurts.	Ég finn til.	yeg finn til
I feel...	Mér líður...	myer leedhur
dizzy	Mig svimar	mig svimar
nauseous	Mér er flögurt	myeer er flu(r)gurt
shivery	Ég er með skjálfta	yeg er medh skyowlfda
I'm diabetic.	Ég er sykursjúkur.	yeg er sigursyoogur
Can you give me a prescription for this?	Get ég fengið lyfseðil fyrir þetta?	ged yeg fengið lifsedhil firir thetta
May I have a receipt for my health insurance?	Get ég fengið kvittun fyrir sjúkratryggingunni?	ged yeg fengidh knittun firir syookratriggingunni

How long have you been feeling like this?	Hvað lengi hefur þér liðið svona?
Where does it hurt?	Hvar finnurðu til?
I'll take your temperature/blood pressure.	Ég ætla að mæla þig/blóðþrýstinginn.
I'll give you an injection.	Ég ætla að sprauta þig.
I want a specimen of your blood/stools/urine.	Ég þarf að fá blóð/hægðar/þvagsýni
You must stay in bed for... days.	Þú verður að vera í rúminu í... daga.
I want you to see a specialist.	Ég vil gjarnan hitta sérfræðing.

Can you recommend a good dentist?	Geturðu mælt með góðum tannlækni?	gedurdhu muylt medh goadhum tannluykni
I have toothache.	Ég er með tannpínu.	yeg er medh tannpeenu
I've lost a filling.	Það hefur dottið fylling úr tönn.	thadh hevur dottidh filling oor tu(r)nn

91

ICELANDIC

Time and date *Klukkan og dagsetning*

It's...	Hún er...	hoon er
five past one	**fimm mínútur yfir eitt**	fimm **mee**noodur ivir eitt
ten past two	**tíu mínútur yfir tvö**	teeyu **mee**noodur ivir tvu(r)
a quarter past three	**korter yfir þrjú**	**kor**ter ivir thryoo
twenty past four	**tuttugu mínútur yfir fjórir**	**tut**tugu **mee**noodur ivir fjórir
twenty-five past five	**tuttugu og fimm mínútur yfir fimm**	**tut**tugu og fimm **mee**noodur ivir fimm
half past seven	**hálf átta**	howlf **owt**ta
twenty to eight	**tuttugu mímútur í átta**	**tut**tugu **mee**noodur ee **owt**ta
twenty-five to nine	**tuttugu og fimm mínútur í níu**	**tut**tugu of fimm **mee**noodur ee neeyu
ten to ten	**tíu mínútur í tíu**	teeyu **mee**noodur ee teeyu
five to eleven	**fimm mínútur í ellefu**	fimm **mee**noodur ee ellevu
noon/midnight	**hádegi/miðnætti**	**how**degi/**midh**nuytti
in the morning	**um morgun**	um **mor**gun
during the day	**um daginn**	um **dag**inn
in the evening	**um kvöldið**	um **kvu(r)l**didh

Sunday	**sunnudagur**	**sunn**udagur
Monday	**mánudagur**	**mown**udagur
Tuesday	**þriðjudagur**	**thridh**yudagur
Wednesday	**miðvikudagur**	**midh**vikudagur
Thursday	**fimmtudagur**	**fimm**tudagur
Friday	**föstudagur**	**fu(r)**studagur
Saturday	**laugardagur**	**löi**gardagur
January	**janúar**	**yan**ooar
February	**febrúar**	**feb**rooar
March	**mars**	mars
April	**apríl**	**apr**eel
May	**maí**	maee
June	**júní**	**yoo**nee
July	**júlí**	**yoo**lee
August	**ágúst**	**owg**oost
September	**september**	**sep**tember
October	**október**	**okt**oaber
November	**nóvember**	**noa**vember
December	**desember**	**des**ember

NUMBERS, see page 92

at night	um nóttina/á nót-tinni	um **noatt**ina/ow **noatt**inni
yesterday	í gær	ee gyuyr
today	í dag	ee dag
tomorrow	á morgun	ow **mor**gun
spring	vor	vor
summer	sumar	**su**mar
autumn (fall)	haust	höist
winter	vetur	**ve**tur

Numbers *Tölur*

0	núll	nooll
1	einn	eidn
2	tveir	tveir
3	þrír	threer
4	fjórir	**fyoa**rir
5	fimm	fimm
6	sex	seks
7	sjö	syu(r)
8	átta	**owt**ta
9	níu	**nee**yu
10	tíu	**tee**yu
11	ellefu	**edle**vu
12	tólf	toalf
13	þrettán	**thrett**town
14	fjórtán	**fyoar**town
15	fimmtán	**fimm**town
16	sextán	**seks**town
17	sautján	**söi**dyown
18	átján	**owd**yown
19	nítján	**need**yown
20	tuttugu	**tuttu**gu
30	þrjátíu	**thryow**teeyu
40	fjörtíu	**fyu**(r)teeyu
50	fimmtíu	**fimm**teeyu
60	sextíu	**seks**teeyu
70	sjötíu	**syu**(r)teeyu
80	áttatíu	**owtta**teeyu
90	níutíu	**nee**teeyu
100	hundrað	**hund**radh
101	hundrað og einn	**hund**radh og eidn
200	tvöhundruð	**tvu**(r)hundrudh
500	fimmhundruð	**fimm**hundrudh
1,000	þúsund	**thoo**sund
100,000	hundrað þúsund	**hund**radh **thoo**sund
1,000,000	milljón	**millyoan**

first	fyrsti	firsti
second	annar	annar
third	þriðji	thridhyi
once	einu sinni	einu sinni
twice	tvisvar	tvisvar
three times	þrisvar	thrisvar
a half	hálfur	howlvur
a quarter	fjórðungur	fyoardhungur
one third	einn þriðji	eidn thri-dhyi

Where do you come from? *Hvaðan kemurðu?*

Australia	Ástralíu	owstraleeyu
Canada	Kanada	kanada
Denmark	Danmörku	danmu(r)rku
England	Englandi	englandi
Finland	Finnlandi	finnlandi
Great Britain	Stóra Bretlandi	stoara bredlandi
Iceland	Íslandi	eeslandi
Ireland	Írlandi	eerlandi
New Zealand	Nyja Sjálandi	neeya syowlandi
Norway	Noregi	noreigi
Scotland	Skotlandi	skodlandi
South Africa	Suður Afríku	sidhur afreeku
Sweden	Svíþjóð	sveethyosdh
USA	Bandaríkjunum	bandareekyunum

Signs and notices *Merki og tilkynningar*

Aðgangur bannaður	No admittance
Aðgangur ókeypis	Free admittance
... bannað	... forbidden
Bilað	Out of order
Draga	Pull
Einkavegur	Private road
Ekkert laust	No vacancies
Frátekið	Reserved
Gjaldkeri	Cash desk
Hætta (lífshætta)	Danger (of death)
Heitt	Hot
Herrasnyrting	Gentlemen (toilets)

Inngangur	Entrance
Kalt	Cold
Kvennasnyrting	Ladies (toilets)
Laust	Vacant
Lifta	Lift
Neyðarútgangur	Emergency exit
Opið	Open
Reykingar bannaðar	No smoking
Snertið ekki	Do not touch
Upplýsingar	Information
Upptekið	Occupied
Útgangur	Exit
Útsala	Sale
Varist hundinn	Beware of the dog
Varúð	Caution
Vinsamlega bíðið	Please wait
Yta	Push

Emergency *Neyðarástand*

Call the police	Hringið í lögregluna	hringidh ee lu(r)gregluna
Get a doctor	Náið í lækni	noaidh ee luykni
Go away	Farið í burtu	faridh ee burtu
HELP	Hjálp	hyowlp
I'm ill	Ég er lasin	yeg er lasin
I'm lost	Ég er villtur (villt)	yeg er viltur (vilt)
Leave me alone	Látið mig í friði	lowdidh mig ee fridhi
LOOK OUT	Varúð	varoodh
STOP THIEF	Stöðvið þjófinn	stu(r)dhvidh thyoavinn
My ... have been stolen.	... minni hefur verið stolið.	minni hefur veridh stolidh
I've lost my ...	Ég hef týnt ... minni.	yeg hef teent ... minni
handbag	töskunni	tu(r)skunni
passport	vegabréfinu	vagabreevinu
luggage	farangrinum	farowngrinum
wallet	veskinu	veskinu

TELEPHONING, see page 88/DOCTOR, see page 89

Guide to Icelandic pronunciation

In Icelandic the first syllable is always stressed. There is hardly any intonation, so there is no difference between the intonation of questions and statements.

Consonants

Letter	Approximate pronunciation	Symbol	Example	
b,d,f, g,h,m, n,p,t,v	as in English			
ð	like **th** in to**geth**er	dh	**með**	medh
h	when preceding **v** then like **k** in **k**eep	k	**hvar**	kvar
j	like **y** in **y**et	y	**já**	yow
k	1) at the beginning of a word like **k** in **k**eep	k	**kápa**	**kow**pa
	2) double **k** in the middle of a word is like **ch** in Scottish lo**ch**	ch	**ekki**	e**chi**
l	1) at the beginning of a word like **l** in **l**eg	l	**lá**	low
	2) double **l** like **dl** of we**dl**ock	dl	**hella**	he**dl**a
ng	as in si**ng** never as in fi**ng**er	ng	**ganga**	**gow**nga
pp	close to **b** in **b**ed with a slight aspiration; not like **pp** in ski**pp**ed	b(h)	**keppa**	ke**bh**a
r	more like the Scottish **r** (hard **r** or rolling **r**) than the English one, it is always pronounced; it is never like **r** in arm	r	**rúm**	room
s	always like **s** in **s**ee (never like **s** in ri**s**e)	s	**skál**	skowl
þ	like **th** in **th**ought	th	**þá**	thow

Vowels

Note that the vowels with accents – **á, é, í, ó, ú, ý** – are pronounced quite differently from those without.

a	always short like **a** in cat	a	**gaf**	gaf
á	like **ow** in n**ow**	ow	**fá**	fow
e	like **e** in g**e**t	e	**ef**	ef
é	like the word **yeah**	ye	**él**	yel
i	like **i** in d**i**d	i	**il**	il
í	like **ee** in s**ee**	ee	**ís**	ees
o	like **o** in g**o**t	o	**oft**	oft
ó	like **oa** in g**oa**t	oa	**hóll**	hoadl
u	like **u** in p**u**t, but with the lips rounded	u	**upp**	uph
ú	like **oo** in p**oo**l	oo	**út**	oot
y	like **i** in d**i**d	i	**frysta**	fristna
ý	like **ee** in s**ee**	ee	**ýsa**	eesa
æ	like **uy** in g**uy**	uy	**særa**	suyra
ö	like **ur** in f**ur**, but with the lips rounded and without the r-sound	u(r)	**öl**	u(r)l

Diphthongs

| au | there is no exact equivalent in English; quite like the **ur** of f**ur**, followed by the **i** of d**i**d | öi | **sundlaug** | **sund**löig |
| ei, ey | like **a** in g**a**me | ei | **heim** | heim |

Norwegian

Basic expressions *Vanlige uttrykk*

Yes/No.	**Ja/Nei.**	yaa/næ
Please.	**Vær (så) snill å.../..., takk.**	vǣr (saw) snil aw/... tahk
Thank you.	**Takk.**	tahk
I beg your pardon?	**Unnskyld?**	**ewn**shewl

Introduction *Presentasjon*

Good morning.	**God morgen.**	goo**maw**r'n
Good afternoon.	**God dag.**	goo**daag**
Good night.	**God natt.**	goo**naht**
Goodbye.	**Adjø.**	ah**dyūr**
Hello/Hi!	**Hallo/Hei!**	hah**loo**/hæi
My name is...	**Mitt navn er...**	mit nahvn ær
What's your name?	**Hva heter du?**	vah **hay**terr dew
Pleased to meet you!	**Hyggelig å treffes!**	**hew**gerli aw **treh**ferss
How are you?	**Hvordan står det til?**	**voo**'dahn stawr deh til
Very well, thanks. And you?	**Bare bra, takk. Og med deg?**	**baa**rer braa tahk. o(g) meh(d) dæi
Where do you come from?	**Hvor kommer du fra?**	voor **kom**mer dew fraa
I'm from...	**Jeg kommer fra...**	yæi **kom**mer fraa
Australia	**Australia**	ou**straa**leeah
Canada	**Kanada**	**kah**nahdah
Great Britain	**Storbritannia**	**stoor**brittahneeah
United States	**USA**	ēw-ehss-**aa**
I'm with my...	**Jeg er her med...**	yæi ær hǣr meh(d)
wife	**min kone**	meen **kōō**ner
husband	**min mann**	meen mahn
family	**min familie**	meen fah**mee**lyer
boyfriend	**min venn**	meen vehn
girlfriend	**min venninne**	meen veh**nin**ner
I'm here on business/vacation.	**Jeg er her i forretninger/på ferie.**	yæi ær hǣr ee forreht**ning**err/paw **fay**ryer

PRONUNCIATION/EMERGENCIES, see page 126

Questions *Spørsmål*

When?	**Når?**	nor
How?	**Hvordan?/Hvor?**	**voo'**dahn/voor
What?/Why?	**Hva?/Hvorfor?**	vaa/**voor**for
Who?/Which?	**Hvem?/Hvilken?**	vehm/**vil**kern
Where is/are...?	**Hvor er...?**	voor ær
Where can I find...?	**Hvor finner jeg...?**	voor **finn**err yæi
How far?	**Hvor langt?**	voor lahngt
How long?	**Hvor lenge?**	voor **leh**nger
How much/many?	**Hvor mye/mange?**	voor **mew**er/**mahn**ger
Can I have...?	**Kan jeg få...?**	kahn yæi faw
Can you help me?	**Kan du hjelpe meg?**	kahn dew **yehl**per mæi
Is there/Are there...?	**Er det...?**	ær deh
There isn't/aren't...	**Det er ikke...**	deh ær **ik**ker

Do you speak...? *Snakker du...?*

What does this/that mean?	**Hva betyr dette/ det?**	vaa ber**tewr** **deh**ter/deh
Can you translate this for us?	**Kan du oversette dette for oss?**	kahn dew **aw**vershehter **deh**ter for oss
Do you speak English?	**Snakker du engelsk?**	**snah**kerr dew **ehn**gerlsk
I don't speak (much) Norwegian.	**Jeg snakker ikke (så bra) norsk.**	yæi **snah**kerr **ik**ker (saw braa) noshk
Could you speak more slowly?	**Kan du snakke litt langsommere?**	kahn dew **snah**ker lit **lahng**sommerrer
Could you repeat that?	**Kan du gjenta det?**	kahn dew **yehn**tah deh
I understand.	**Jeg forstår.**	yæi fo**shtawr**
I don't understand.	**Jeg forstår ikke.**	yæi fo**shtawr** **ik**ker

It's... *Det er...*

better/worse	**bedre/verre**	**bay**drer/**vær**
big/small	**stor/liten**	**stoor**/**lee**tern
cheap/expensive	**billig/dyr**	**bil**li/**dewr**
early/late	**tidlig/sen**	**teel**i/**sayn**
good/bad	**bra/dårlig**	braa/**daw**li
hot/cold	**varm/kald**	vahrm/kahl

near/far	**nær/fjern**	nǣr/fyǣ'n
right/wrong	**riktig/feil**	rikti/fæil
vacant/occupied	**ledig/opptatt**	lāydi/optaht

A few more useful words *Noen flere nyttige ord*

a little/a lot	**lite/mye**	leeter/mēwer
above	**over**	awverr
after	**etter**	ehterr
and	**og**	o(g)
at	**ved**	veh(d)
before	**før**	fūrr
behind	**bak**	baak
below	**under**	ewnerr
between	**mellom**	mehlom
but	**men**	mehn
down	**ned**	nāy(d)
downstairs	**nede**	nāyder
from	**fra**	fraa
in	**i**	ee
inside	**inne**	inner
near	**nær**	nǣr
never	**aldri**	ahldri
next to	**ved siden av**	veh(d) seedern ahv
none	**ingen**	ingern
not	**ikke**	ikker
nothing	**ingenting, ikke noe**	ingernting, ikker nōōer
now	**nå**	naw
on	**på**	paw
only	**bare**	baarer
or	**eller**	ehlerr
outside	**ute**	ewter
perhaps	**kanskje**	kahnsher
since	**siden**	seedern
soon	**snart**	snaa't
then	**da**	dah/daa
through	**gjennom**	yehnom
too	**også**	osso
towards	**mot**	mōōt
under	**under**	ewnerr
until	**til**	til
up	**opp**	op
upstairs	**oppe**	opper
very	**meget**	māygert
with	**med**	meh(d)
without	**uten**	ewtern
yet	**ennå**	ehnaw

Hotel—Other accommodation *Hotell*

I have a reservation.	**Jeg har bestilt rom.**	yæi haar ber**stilt** room
We've reserved 2 rooms.	**Vi har bestilt 2 rom.**	vee haar ber**stilt** 2 room
Do you have any vacancies?	**Har dere noen ledige rom?**	haar **day**rer **noo**ern **lay**deeyer room
I'd like a...	**Jeg vil gjerne ha et...**	yæi vil **yæ'**ner eht
single room	**enkeltrom**	**ehng**kerltroom
double room	**dobbeltrom**	**dobber**ltroom
with twin beds	**med to senger**	meh(d) too **sehng**err
with a double bed	**med dobbeltseng**	meh(d) **dobber**ltsehng
with a bath	**med bad**	meh(d) baad
with a shower	**med dusj**	meh(d) dewsh
Is there...?	**Fins det...?**	finss deh
air conditioning	**air-conditioning**	**ayr**-kondisherning
a private toilet	**toalett på rommet**	tooah**leht** paw **room**mer
a radio/television in the room	**radio/TV på rommet**	**raad**yoo/**tay**veh paw **room**mer
a sauna	**badstue/sauna**	**bah**stew/**sou**nah
How much does it cost...?	**Hvor mye koster det...?**	voor **mew**er **kost**err deh
Is there a camp site near here?	**Er det en camping-plass i nærheten?**	ær deh ehn **kæm**ping-plahss ee **nær**hehtern
Can we camp here?	**Kan vi campe her?**	kahn vee **kæm**per hær
We'll be staying...	**Vi blir...**	vee bleer
overnight only	**bare natten over**	**baa**rer **nah**tern **aw**verr
a few days	**ett par dager**	eht pahr **daa**gerr
a week	**en uke**	ehn **ew**ke

Decision *Beslutning*

May I see the room?	**Kan jeg få se rommet?**	kahn yæi faw say **room**mer
That's fine. I'll take it.	**Det er bra. Jeg tar det.**	deh ær braa. yæi taar deh
No. I don't like it.	**Nei. Jeg liker det ikke.**	næi. yæ **lee**kerr **ik**ker
It's too...	**Det er for...**	deh ær for
dark/small	**mørkt/lite**	**murrk**t/**lee**ter
noisy	**støyende**	**stoy**erner

NUMBERS, see page 124

Do you have anything...?	**Har dere noe...?**	haar **dayr**er **noo**er
better/bigger	**bedre/større**	**bay**drer/**stur**rer
cheaper	**rimeligere**	**ree**merleeyerrer
quieter	**roligere**	**roo**leeyerrer

Etternavn/Fornavn	Name/First name
Hjemsted	Home town
Nasjonalitet/Yrke	Nationality/Occupation
Fødselsdato/Fødested	Date/Place of birth
Passnummer	Passport number
Dato for ankomst til Norge/ Skandinavia	Date of arrival in Norway/ Scandinavia
Hensikt med oppholdet	Reason for visit
Underskrift	Signature

General requirements *Allmenne forespørsler*

The key to room..., please.	**Nøkkelen til rom...,takk.**	**nur**kerlern til room... tahk
Where's the...?	**Hvor er...?**	voor ær
bathroom	**badet**	**baa**der
dining-room	**spisesalen**	**spee**sserssaalern
emergency exit	**nødutgangen**	**nur**dewtgahngern
lift (elevator)	**heisen**	**hæi**ssern
Where are the toilets?	**Hvor er toalettet?**	voor ær tooah**leht**er
Where can I park my car?	**Hvor kan jeg park- ere bilen?**	voor kahn yæi pahr**kay**rer **bee**lern

Checking out *Avreise*

May I have my bill, please?	**Kan jeg få regn- ingen?**	kahn yæi faw **ræi**ningern
Can you get us a taxi?	**Kan du skaffe oss en drosje?**	kahn dew **skah**fer oss ehn **dro**sher
It's been a very enjoyable stay.	**Det har vært ett meget hyggelig opphold.**	deh haar væ't eht **may**gert **hew**gerli **op**hol

Eating out *Mat og drikke*

Can you recommend a good restaurant?	**Kan du anbefale en bra restaurant?**	kahn dew **ahn**berfaaler ehn braa rehstew**rahng**
I'd like to reserve a table for 4.	**Jeg vil gjerne bestille et bord til 4.**	yæi vil y**ææ**'ner ber**still**er eht b**oo**r til 4
We'll come at 8.	**Vi kommer kl. 8.**	vee **komm**err **klok**kern 8
I'd like breakfast/ lunch/dinner.	**Jeg vil gjerne ha frokost/lunsj/ middag.**	yæi vil y**ææ**'ner haa fr**oo**kost/lurnsh/**mid**dah(g)
What do you recommend?	**Hva kan du anbefale?**	vaa kahn dew **ahn**berfaalerr
Do you have a set menu/local speciality?	**Har dere en meny/ lokal spesialitet?**	haar d**ay**rer ehn meh**new**/ look**aal** spehsseeahlit**ay**t
Do you have any vegetarian dishes?	**Har dere noen vegetariske retter?**	haar d**ay**rer n**oo**ern vehger**taa**risker **reh**terr

---

Hva skal det være?	What would you like?
Jeg kan anbefale dette.	I recommend this.
Hva vil du/dere ha å drikke?	What would you like to drink?
Vi har ikke ...	We don't have ...
Vil du ha ...?	Would you like ...?

Could we have a/an ..., please?	**Kan vi få ...?**	kahn vee faw
ashtray	**et askebeger**	eht **ahs**kerb**ay**gerr
cup	**en kopp**	ehn kop
fork	**en gaffel**	ehn **gah**ferl
glass	**et glass**	eht glass
knife	**en kniv**	ehn kneev
napkin (serviette)	**en serviett**	ehn sehrv**yeht**
plate	**en tallerken**	ehn tahl**lær**kern
spoon	**en skje**	ehn sh**ay**

NUMBERS, see page 124

May I have some...?	**Kan jeg få litt...?**	kahn yæi faw lit
bread	**brød**	brūr
butter	**smør**	smurr
oil	**olje**	olyer
pepper	**pepper**	pehperr
salt	**salt**	sahlt
seasoning	**krydder**	krewderr
sugar	**sukker**	sookkerr
vinegar	**eddik**	ehdik

Reading the menu *Å lese spisekartet*

dessert	dehssær	dessert
drikker	drikkerr	drinks
fisk	fisk	fish
forretter	forrehterr	appetizers
frukt	frewkt	fruit
fugl	fēwl	poultry
hovedretter	hōōverdrehterr	main courses (entrées)
is(krem)	ees(krāym)	ice cream
kaker	kaakerr	pastries/cakes
kjøtt	khurt	meat
koldtbord	koltbōōr	smorgasbord
leskedrikk	lehskerdrik	soft drinks
ost	oost	cheese
pastaretter	pahstahrehterr	pasta dishes
risretter	reesrehterr	rice dishes
salatbar	sahlaatbaar	salad bar
smørbrød	smurrbrūr	open sandwiches (smørbrød)
supper	sewperr	soups
varme smørbrød	vahrmer smurrbrūr	sandwiches with hot meat, fish, etc.
varmretter	vahrmrehterr	hot dishes
vilt	vilt	game

Breakfast *Frokost*

I'd like...	**Jeg vil gjerne...**	yæi vil yǣ'ner
bread/butter	**brød/smør**	brūr/smurr
cheese	**ost**	oost
eggs	**egg**	ehg
ham and eggs	**skinke og egg**	shingker o(g) ehg
jam	**syltetøy**	sewltertoy
roll	**et rundstykke**	eht rewnstewker

Norsk

Starters (Appetizers) *Forrett*

blåskjell	blawshehl	mussels
froskelår	froskerlawr	frogs' legs
gåselever	gawsserlehverr	goose liver
snegler	snæilerr	snails
sursild	sewshil	marinated herring
østers	urstersh	oysters
ål i gelé	awl ee shehlay	jellied eel

Soups *Supper*

I'd like some soup.	**Jeg vill gjerne ha en suppe.**	yæi vil yæe'ner haa ehn sewper
betasuppe	baytahsewper	thick meat-and-vegetable soup
fiskesuppe	fiskersewper	fish soup
grønnsaksuppe	grurnsaaksewper	vegetable soup
gul ertesuppe	gewl æ'tersewper	yellow pea soup
hummersuppe	hoommerrsewper	lobster soup
neslesuppe	nehshlersewper	nettle soup
oksehalesuppe	ookserhahlersewper	oxtail soup

Fish and seafood (shellfish) *Fisk og skalldyr*

ansjos	ahngshooss	marinated sprats
blekksprut	blehksprewt	octopus
blåskjell	blawshehl	mussels
brasme	brahsmer	bream
flyndre	flewndrer	flounder
gjedde	yehder	pike
hellefisk	hehlerfisk	halibut
hummer	hoommerr	lobster
hyse	hewsser	haddock
kamskjell	kahmshehl	scallop
karpe	kahrper	carp
kolje	kolyer	haddock
krabbe	krahber	crab
laks	lahkss	salmon
tunfisk	tewnfisk	tuna

gravet laks/gravlaks
(**graa**vert lahkss/
graavlahkss)
salt-and-sugar-cured salmon flavoured with dill; often served with sliced potatoes in a white sauce

seibiff med løk
(**sæ**ibif meh(d) l$\overline{u}$rk)
fried fillets of coalfish (pollack) with onions, served with boiled potatoes and vegetables or salad

spekesild
(**spay**kersil)
salted herring; served with boiled potatoes, onion rings, pickled beetroot, butter and often cabbage or mashed swedes (rutabaga)

baked	**bakte**	bahkt
boiled	**kokt**	kookt
fried	**stekt**	stehkt
grilled	**grillet/grillstekt**	**grill**ert/**gril**stehkt
roast	**ovnsstekt**	**ovns**stehkt
underdone (rare)	**råstekt**	**raw**stehkt
medium	**medium stekt**	**may**diewm stehkt
well-done	**godt stekt**	got stehkt

Meat *Kjøtt*

I'd like some...	**Jeg vil gjerne ha...**	yæi vil y$\overline{æ}$'ner haa
beef	**oksekjøtt**	**ook**serkhurt
chicken/duck	**kylling/and**	**khew**ling/ahn
lamb	**lammekjøtt**	**lah**merkhurt
pork	**svinekjøtt**	**svee**nerkhurt/**kahl**verkhurt
veal	**kalvekjøtt**	

biff	bif	beef steak
gås	gawss	goose
kalkun	kahl**kew**n	turkey
pølse	**purl**ser	sausage
spekeskinke	**spay**kershingker	smoked, cured ham
svineribbe	**svee**nerribber	sparerib
elgstek	**ehlg**st$\overline{ay}$k	roast elk
kjøttpudding	**khurt**pewding	meat loaf
lungemos	**loong**erm$\overline{oo}$s	minced pork lungs and onions
medisterkaker	meh**dis**terrkaakerr	small pork-and-veal hamburgers
medisterpølse	meh**dis**terrpurlser	pork-and-veal sausage
okserulader	**ook**serrewlaaderr	braised beef rolls
reinsdyrmedaljonger	**ræins**d$\overline{ew}$-rmehdahlyongerr	small round fillets of reindeer

Vegetables and salads *Grønnsaker og salater*

beans	bønner	burnerr
beetroot	rødbeter	rūrbehterr
cabbage	kål	kawl
carrots	gulrøtter	gewlrurterr
cauliflower	blomkål	blomkawl
cucumber	agurk	ahgewrk
leeks	purre	pewrer
lettuce	hodesalat	hōōdersahlaat
mushrooms	sopp	sop
onions	løk	lūrk
peas	erter	æ'terr
potatoes	poteter	pootayterr
spinach	spinat	spinnaat
swede (rutabaga)	kålrabi/kålrot	kawlraabi/kawlrōōt
tomatoes	tomater	toomaaterr
turnips	nepe	nāyper

agurksalat
(ah**gewrk**sahlaat)
cucumber salad, usually with a vinegar-sugar dressing

blandet salat
(**blah**nert sah**laat**)
mixed salad (lettuce, tomatoes, cucumber, etc., with oil-and-vinegar dressing); accompanies many main courses

sildeball
(**sill**erbahl)
potato dumplings with a filling of minced salted herring, onion, bacon and flour; served with pickled beetroot

størje-/tunfisksalat
(**sturr**yer-/**tewn**fisk sahlaat)
tuna fish salad – Norwegian version of salad Niçoise

skalldyrsalat
(**skahl**dewrsahlaat)
seafood salad (mostly mussels and prawns, but also lobster or crab)

Fruit *Frukt*

apple	eple	ehpler
arctic cloudberries	multer	mewlterr
banana	banan	bahnaan
blackberries	bjørnebær	byūr'nerbær
cherries	kirsebær	khisherbær
cranberries	tyttebær	tewterbær
gooseberries	stikkelsbær	stikkerlsbær

grapes	**druer**	dre̅werr
black	**blå**	blaw
white	**grønne**	grurner
grapefruit	**grapefrukt**	gra̅ypfrewkt
lemon	**sitron**	sitro̅on
melon	**melon**	mehlo̅on
orange	**appelsin**	ahperlseen
peach	**fersken**	fæshkern
pear	**pære**	pærer
plums	**plommer**	ploommerr
raspberries	**bringebær**	bringerbær
rowanberries	**rognebær**	rongnerbær
strawberries	**jordbær**	yoorbær
wild strawberries	**markjordbær**	mahrkyoorbær

Dessert *Dessert*

(varm) eplekake med krem	(vahrm) **eh**plerkaaker meh(d) kra̅ym	(hot) apple pie with whipped cream
frityrstekt camembert med solbærsyltetøy	frite̅wshtehkt kahmangbær meh(d) so̅olbærsewltertoy	deep-fried camembert with blackcurrant jam
fruktkompott	**frewkt**koompot	stewed fruit
is(krem)	eess(kra̅ym)	ice cream
mandelkake	**mahn**derlkaaker	almond cake
multer med krem	**mewl**terr meh(d) kra̅ym	arctic cloudberries with whipped cream
pannekaker	**pahn**erkaakerr	pancakes
riskrem	**rees**kra̅ym	creamed rice with red berry sauce
rødgrøt	**ru̅r**grurt	fruit pudding with cream
vafler med syltetøy	**vahf**lerr meh(d) **sewl**tertoy	waffles with jam

Hoffdessert (**hof**dehssær)	layers of meringue and whipped cream, topped with chocolate sauce and toasted almonds
pære Belle Helene (**pæ**rer behl hehla̅yn)	poached pears with vanilla ice cream and chocolate
tilslørte bondepiker (**til**shur'ter **boon**nerpeekerr)	layers of stewed apples, biscuit (cookie) crumbs, sugar and whipped cream

Norsk

Drinks *Drikkevarer*

A bottle of mineral (spring) water, please.	**En flaske naturlig mineralvann, takk.**	ehn flahsker nahtew'li minerraalvahn tahk
fizzy (sparkling)	**med kullsyre**	meh(d) kewlsewrer
still (natural)	**uten kullsyre**	ewtern kewlsewrer
apple juice	**eplesaft**	ehplersahft
aquavit	**akevitt**	ahkervit
beer	**øl**	url
(hot) chocolate	**(varm) sjokolade**	(vahrm) shookoolaader
coffee	**kaffe**	kahfer
espresso	**en espresso**	ehn ehsprehssoo
with cream	**med fløte**	meh(d) flurter
grapefruit juice	**grapefruktjuice**	graypfrewktyewss
lemonade	**sitronbrus**	sitroonbrewss
(glass of) milk	**(et glass) melk**	(eht glahss) mehlk
sugar	**sukker**	sookkerr
tea	**te**	tay
a cup of	**en kopp**	ehn kop
with lemon	**med sitron**	meh(d) sitroon
with milk	**med melk**	meh(d) mehlk
vodka	**vodka**	vodkah
whisky	**whisky**	viski
wine	**vin**	veen
red/white wine	**rødvin/hvitvin**	rurveen/veetveen
May I have the wine list, please?	**Kan jeg få se vinkartet?**	kahn yæi faw say veenkah'ter
neat (straight)	**bar**	baar
on the rocks	**med is**	meh(d) eess
with water	**med vann**	meh(d) soodah

Complaints *Klager*

The meat is...	**Kjøttet er...**	khurter ær
overdone	**for mye stekt**	for mewer stehkt
underdone	**for lite stekt**	dor leeter stehkt
This is too...	**Dette er for...**	dehter ær for
bitter/salty/sweet	**beskt/salt/søtt**	behskt/surt/sahlt
That's not what I ordered.	**Dette er ikke det jeg bestilte.**	dehter ær ikker deh yæi berstilter
The food is cold.	**Maten er kald.**	maatern ær kahl

The bill (check) *Regningen*

I'd like to pay.	Jeg vil gjerne betale.	yæi vil yǽ'ner bertaaler
What's this amount for?	Hva står dette beløpet for?	vah stawr dehter berlürper for
I think there's a mistake in this bill.	Jeg tror det er en feil på regningen.	yæi trōōr deh ær ehn fæil paw ræiningern
Is everything included?	Er alt inkludert?	ær ahlt inklewdāy't
Can I pay with this credit card?	Kan jeg betale med dette kredittkortet?	kahn yæi bertaaler meh(d) dehter krehdit-ko'ter
We enjoyed it, thank you.	Det var meget godt.	deh vaar māygert got

Snacks—Picnic *Småretter—Picnic*

I'll have one of those.	Jeg vil gjerne ha en av dem.	yæi vil yǽ'ner haa ehn ahv dehm
to the right/left above/below	til høyre/venstre ovenfor/nedenfor	til hoyrer/vehnstrer awvernfor/nāydernfor
Danish pastry	et wienerbrød	eht veenerrbrür
doughnut	en smultring	ehn smewltring
fish pudding	fiskepudding	fiskerpewding
fried sausage	en grillpølse	ehn grilpurlser
liver sausage	leverpølse	lehverrpurlser
(slice of) pizza	en (skive) pizza	ehn (sheever) pitsah
a potato pancake	lompe	loomper
soft drink	leskedrikk	lehskerdrik
spring (egg) roll	vårrull	vawrrewl

| **fastelavnsbolle** (fahsterlaavnsboller) | lenten bun; bun cut in half, filled with whipped cream and topped with icing (confectioners') sugar |
| **kransekake** (krahnserkaaker) | cone-shaped pile of almond-macaroon rings decorated with icing (frosting), marzipan flowers, etc. |

NUMBERS, see page 124

Norsk

Travelling around *På reise*

Plane *Fly*

Is there a flight to Tromsø?	**Går det et fly til Tromsø?**	gawr deh eht flew til troomsur
What time should I check in?	**Når må jeg sjekke inn?**	nor maw yæi **sheh**ker in
I'd like to... my reservation.	**Jeg vil gjerne... reservasjon.**	yæi vil yæ'ner rehssævahshoonern
cancel	**annullere**	ahnewlayrer
change	**endre**	ehndrer
confirm	**bekrefte**	berkrehfter

Train *Tog*

Where's the railway station?	**Hvor er jernban-estasjonen?**	voor ær yæ'nbaanerstahshoonern
Where is/are (the)...?	**Hvor er...?**	voor ær
booking office	**billettkontoret**	bil**leht**koontoorer
left-luggage office (baggage check)	**bagasjeoppbevar-ingen**	bah**gaas**heropbervaaringern
lost property (lost and found) office	**hittegodskontoret**	**hit**tergoodskoontoorer
luggage (baggage) lockers	**oppbevaringsbok-sene**	opbervaaringsbokserner
platform 2	**perrong 2**	peh**rong** 2
ticket office	**billettluken**	bil**leht**lewkern
waiting room	**venterommet**	**vehn**tersaalern

INNGANG	ENTRANCE
UTGANG	EXIT
INFORMASJON	INFORMATION

I'd like a ticket to...	**Jeg vil gjerne ha en billett til...**	yæi vil yæ'ner ehn bil**leht** til
single (one-way)	**enkeltbillett**	**ehng**kerltbilleht
return (round-trip)	**tur-returbillett**	tewr-reh**tewr**billeht
first/second class	**første/andre/annen klasse**	**fursh**ter/**ahn**drer/**aae**rn klahsser

Inquiries *Forespørsler*

When is the... train to Halden?	**Når går... tog til Halden?**	nor gawr... tawg til **hahl**dern
first/last/next	**første/siste/neste**	**fursh**ter/**nehs**ter/**sis**ter

NUMBERS, see page 124

What time does the train to Oslo leave?	**Når går toget til Oslo?**	nor gawr **taw**ger til **oosh**loo
Is there a dining car/ sleeping car on the train?	**Fins det en spise- vogn/sovevogn på toget?**	finss deh ehn **spee**sservongn/ **saw**vervongn ee **taw**ger
Is this the train to Geilo?	**Er dette toget til Geilo?**	ær **deh**ter **taw**ger til **yæi**loo
I'd like a time-table, please.	**Jeg vil gjerne ha en rutetabell.**	yæi vil **yæ'**ner haa ehn **rēw**tertahbehl

Underground (subway) *T-bane*

| Where's the nearest underground station? | **Hvor er nærmeste T-banestasjon?** | voor ær **nær**mehster **tāy**- baanerstahshoo&n |
| Where do I change for...? | **Hvor må jeg bytte for å komme til...?** | voor maw yæi **bew**ter for aw **kom**mer til |

Bus—Tram (Streetcar) *Buss—Trikk*

Which tram (streetcar) goes to the town centre?	**Hvilken trikk går til sentrum?**	**vil**kern trik gawr til **sehn**trewm
How much is the fare to...?	**Hvor mye koster det til...?**	voor **mēw**er **kos**terr deh til
Will you tell me when to get off?	**Kan du si fra når jeg skal gå av?**	kahn dew see fraa nor yæi skahl gaw ahv

Boat service *Båt*

When does the next boat/ferry for... leave?	**Når går båten/ fergen til...?**	nor gawr **baw**tern/ **fær**ggern til
How long does the crossing take?	**Hvor lang tid tar overfarten?**	voor lahng teed taar **aw**verrfah'rtern
I'd like to take a boat trip.	**Jeg vil gjerne ta en båttur.**	yæi vil **yæ'**ner taa ehn **bawt**tēwr

Taxi *Drosje/Taxi*

Where can I get a taxi?	**Hvor kan jeg få tak i en drosje?**	voor kahn yæi faw taak ee ehn **dro**sher
What's the fare to...?	**Hva koster det til...?**	vaa **kos**terr deh til
Take me to this address.	**Kjør meg til denne adressen?**	khūrr mæi til **deh**ner ah**dreh**ssern
Please stop here.	**Stans her.**	**stahnss** hær

Car hire (rental) *Bilutleie*

I'd like to hire (rent) a car.	**Jeg vil gjerne leie en bil.**	yæi vil y**æ**'ner l**æ**ier ehn beel
I'd like it for a day/a week.	**Jeg vil ha den en dag/en uke.**	yæi vil haa dehn ehn daag/ehn **ew**ker
What's the charge per day/week?	**Hvor mye koster det pr. dag/uke?**	voor m**ew**er **kos**terr deh pær daag/**ew**ker
Is mileage included?	**Er kjørelengden inkludert?**	ær k**hur**rerlehngdern inklew**day**'t
I'd like full insurance.	**Jeg vil ha full for-sikring.**	yæi vil haa fewl fo**shik**ring

---

Road signs *Trafikkskilt*

ALL STANS FORBUDT	No stopping
FERIST	Cattle grid
GRUSVEI	Gravelled road
INNKJØRSEL FORBUDT	No entry
KJØR SAKTE	Drive slowly
MØTEPLASS	Road passing place
FORBIKJØRING FORBUDT	No overtaking (passing)
OMKJØRING	Diversion (Detour)
PARKERING (FORBUDT)	(No) Parking
RASFARE	Falling rocks
SVAKE KANTER	Soft shoulders
TOLL	Customs
UTKJØRSEL	Exit
VEIARBEID/VEGARBEID	Roadworks

Where's the nearest filling station?	**Hvor er nærmeste bensinstasjon?**	voor ær **nær**mehster behn**seen**stahsh**oo**n
Fill it up, please.	**Full tank, takk.**	fewl tahngk tahk
Give me... litres of petrol (gasoline).	**... liter bensin, takk.**	... **lee**terr behn**seen** tahk
super (premium)/ regular/unleaded/ diesel	**super/normal/ blyfri/diesel**	**sew**perr/**noor**maal/ bl**ew**free/**dee**sserl
How do I get to...?	**Hvordan kommer jeg til...?**	**voo**'dahn **kom**merr yæi til
How far is it to... from here?	**Hvor langt er det til... herfra?**	voor lahngt ær deh til... **hær**frah

I've had a break-down at...	**Jeg har fått motor-stopp ved...**	yæi haar fot **mōo**tooshtop veh(d)
Can you send a mechanic?	**Kan du sende en mekaniker?**	kahn dew **seh**nerr ehn meh**kaa**nikkerr
Can you mend this puncture (fix this flat)?	**Kan du reparere denne punkter-ingen?**	kahn dew rehpah**rāy**rer **deh**ner poong**tāy**-ringern

Du har kjørt feil.	You're on the wrong road.
Kjør rett frem.	Go straight ahead.
Det er der borte til høyre / venstre.	It's down there on the right/ left.
midt imot/bak...	opposite/behind...
ved siden av/etter...	next to/after...
nord/sør	north/south
øst/vest	east/west

Sightseeing *Sightseeing*

Where's the tourist office?	**Hvor er turistkon-toret?**	voor ær tew**rist**-koont**ōō**rer
Is there an English-speaking guide?	**Fins det en engelsk-talende guide der?**	finss deh ehn **ehng**erlsk-taalerner "guide" dær
Where is/Where are the...?	**Hvor er...?**	voor ær
botanical gardens	**den botaniske hagen**	dehn boo**taa**nisker **haa**gern
castle	**slottet**	**shlo**tter
cathedral	**domkirken**	**dom**khirkern
city centre	**sentrum**	**sehn**trewm
exhibition	**utstillingen**	**ēwt**stillingern
harbour	**havnen**	**hahv**nern
market	**torghandelen**	**torg**hahnderlern
museum	**museet**	mewss**āy**er
shopping area	**handlestrøket**	**hahn**dlerstrũkerr
square	**plassen/torget**	**plahss**ern/**tor**gger
tower	**tårnet**	**taw**'nerr
zoo	**dyrehagen**	**dēw**rerhaagern
When does it open/ close?	**Når åpner/stenges det?**	nor **awp**nerr/**stehn**gerr deh

TELLING THE TIME, see page 123

Landmarks *Landemerker*

farm	en bondegård	ehn **boon**ergawr
fjord	en fjord	ehn fy$\overline{oo}$r
forest	en skog	ehn sk$\overline{oo}$g
island	en øy	ehn oy
meadow	en eng	ehn ehng
mountain	et fjell	eht fyehl
path	en sti	ehn stee
river	en elv	ehn ehlv
sea	en sjø	ehn sh$\overline{u}$r
valley	en dal	ehn daal
waterfall	en foss	ehn foss

Relaxing *Underholdning*

What's playing at the... Theatre?	Hva spilles på... Theatret?	vah **spill**erss paw... t$\overline{ay}$aatrer
Are there any tickets for tonight?	Fins det fremdeles billetter for i kveld?	finss eh frehmd$\overline{ay}$lerss bill**eh**terr til ee kvehl
What time does it begin/finish?	Når begynner/ slutter det?	nor ber**yew**nerr/**shlew**ter deh
I'd like to reserve 2 tickets for the show on Friday evening.	Jeg vil gjerne bestille 2 billetter til forestillingen på fredag kveld.	yæi vil **yæ'**ner ber**still**er 2 bill**eh**terr til **faw**rerstillingern paw fr$\overline{ay}$dah(g) kvehl
Would you like to go out with me tonight?	Skal vi gå ut i kveld?	skahl vee gaw $\overline{ewt}$ ee kvehl
Thank you, but I'm busy.	Takk, men jeg er dessverre opptatt.	tahk mehn yæi ær dehsv**æ**rer **op**taht
Is there a discotheque in town?	Fins det et diskotek i byen?	finss deh eht diskoot$\overline{ay}$k ee **bew**ern
Would you like to dance?	Skal vi danse?	skahl vee **dahn**ser
Thank you, it's been a wonderful evening.	Takk, det har vært en veldig hyggelig kveld.	tahk deh haar væ't ehn **vehl**di **hew**gerli kvehl

TELLING THE TIME/DAYS OF THE WEEK, see page 123

Sports *Sport*

Is there a football (soccer) match anywhere this Saturday?	**Er det en fotball-kamp noe sted på lørdag?**	ær deh ehn **foot**bahlkahmp nŏŏer stay(d) paw **lūr**'dah (g)
What's the admission charge?	**Hva koster inn-gangsbilletten?**	vah **kost**err **in**gahngsbillehtern
Is there a golf course/ tennis court nearby?	**Fins det en golf-bane/tennisbane i nærheten?**	finss deh ehn **golf**baaner/ **teh**nisbaaner ee **nær**hehtern

bicycling	**sykling**	**sewk**ling
football (soccer)	**fotball**	**foot**bahl
fishing	**fiske**	**fisk**er
ice hockey match	**ishockeykamp**	**ees**hokkikahmp
rowing	**roing**	**rōō**ing
sailing	**seiling**	**sæ**iling
speed skating	**skøyteløp**	**shoy**terlūrp
ski jumping	**skihopping**	**shee**hopping
swimming	**svømming**	**svur**ming

Can one swim in the lake/river?	**Kan man svømme i (inn)sjøen/elven?**	kahn mahn **baa**der ee **(in)**shūrern/**ehl**vern
Is there a swimming pool here?	**Er det et svømme-basseng her?**	ær deh eht **svur**merbahssehng hær
Is there a skating rink near here?	**Fins det en skøyte-bane i nærheten?**	finss seh ehn **shoy**terbaaner ee **nær**hehtern
I'd like to ski.	**Jeg vil gjerne gå på ski.**	yæi vil **yæ**'ner gaw paw shee
downhill/cross-country skiing	**utforkjøring/lan-grenn**	**ewt**forkhūrring/**lahng**rehn
Are there any good ski tracks (trails) nearby?	**Fins det noen gode skiløyper i nærhe-ten?**	finss deh **nōō**ern **gōō**(d)er **shee**loyperr ee **nær**hehtern
I'd like to hire...	**Jeg vil gjerne leie...**	yæi vil **yæ**'ner **læ**ier
skates	**skøyter**	**shoy**terr
ski boots	**skistøvler**	**shee**sturvlerr
skis	**ski**	shee
I'd like to hire (rent) a bicycle.	**Jeg vil gjerne leie en sykkel.**	yæi vil **yæ**'ner **læ**ier ehn **sewk**erl

Shops, stores and services *Butikker og servicenæringer*

Where's the nearest...?	**Hvor er nærmeste...?**	voor ær **nær**mehster
baker's	**et bakeri**	eht baaker**ree**
bookshop	**en bokhandel**	ehn **boo**khahnderl
butcher's	**en slakter**	ehn **shlahk**terr
chemist's/drugstore	**et apotek**	eht ahpoo**tāȳk**
dentist	**en tannlege**	ehn **tahn**lāȳger
department store	**et stormagasin**	eht **stoor**mahgahsseen
grocer's	**en matvarehandel**	ehn **maat**vaarerhahnderl
hairdresser's (ladies/men)	**en frisør (dame-/herre-)**	ehn friss**ūrr** (**daa**mer-/**hær**rer-)
market	**en torghandel**	ehn **torg**hahnderl
newsstand	**en aviskiosk**	ehn ah**vees**khyosk
post office	**et postkontor**	eht **post**koon**toor**
souvenir shop	**en suvenirbutikk**	ehn sewver**neer**bewtik
supermarket	**et supermarked**	eht **sew**perrmahrkerd

General expressions *Vanlige uttrykk*

Where's the (main) shopping area?	**Hvor er (det største) handlestrøket?**	voor ær deh **sturs**hter **hah**ndlerstr**ūr**ker
Do you have any...?	**Har du noen...?**	har dew **noo**ern

Kan jeg hjelpe deg?	Can I help you?
Hva skal det være?	What would you like?
Hvilken... vil du ha?	What... would you like?
farge/form	colour/shape
Det er vi utsolgt for.	We're out of stock.
Skal vi bestille det?	Shall we order it for you?
Skal det være noe annet?	Anything else?
Det blir... kroner, takk.	That comes to... kroner.
Kassen er der borte.	The cash desk is over there.

I'd like a ... one.	**Jeg vil gjerne ha en ...**	yæi vil **yæ'**ner haa ehn
big	**stor**	stoor
cheap	**rimelig**	**ree**merli
dark	**mørk**	murrk
good	**god**	goo(d)
heavy	**tung**	toong
large	**stor**	stoor
light (weight)	**lett**	leht
light (colour)	**lys**	lewss
rectangular	**rektangulær**	rehktahngew**lær**
round	**rund**	rewn
small	**liten**	**lee**tern
square	**firkantet**	**fir**kahntert
sturdy	**robust/solid**	roo**bewst**/soo**leed**
Don't you have anything ...?	**Har du ikke noe ...?**	haar de ikker **noo**er
cheaper/better	**rimeligere/bedre**	reemerleeyerrer/**bayd**rer
larger/smaller	**større/mindre**	**stur**rer/**min**drer
How much is this?	**Hvor mye koster dette?**	voor **mew**er **kos**terr **deh**ter
Please write it down.	**Kan du skrive det?**	kahn dew **skree**ver deh
I don't want to spend more than ... kroner.	**Jeg vil ikke gi mer enn ... kroner.**	yæi vil **ik**ker yee **mayr** ehn ... **kroo**nerr
No, I don't like it.	**Nei, jeg liker det ikke.**	næi yæi **lee**kerr deh **ik**ker
I'll take it.	**Jeg tar det.**	yæi taar deh
Do you accept credit cards?	**Tar dere kreditt-kort?**	taar **day**rer kreh**dit**ko't
Can you order it for me?	**Kan du bestille det til meg?**	kahn dew ber**stil**ler deh til mæi

black	**svart**	svah't
blue	**blå**	blaw
brown	**brun**	brewn
green	**grønn**	grurn
grey	**grå**	graw
orange	**oransje**	oo**rahngsh**
red	**rød**	rur
white	**hvit**	veet
yellow	**gul**	gewl
light ...	**lyse ...**	**lew**sser
dark ...	**mørke ...**	**murr**ker

NUMBERS, see page 124

Chemist's (Drugstore) *Apotek*

aspirin	**aspirin**	ahspir**reen**
condoms	**kondomer**	koon**dōō**merr
deodorant	**en deodorant**	ehn dehoodoo**rahnt**
insect repellent	**et insektmiddel**	eht **in**sehktmidderl
moisturizing cream	**en fuktighetskrem**	ehn **fook**tihehtskrāym
razor blades	**barberblader**	bahr**bāy**rblaaderr
shampoo	**en sjampo**	ehn **shahm**poo
soap	**en såpe**	ehn **saw**per
sun-tan oil	**en sololje**	ehn **sōō**lolyer
tampons	**tamponger**	tahm**pong**err
toothpaste	**en tannpasta**	ehn **tahn**pahstah

Clothing *Klær*

blouse	**en bluse**	ehn **blew**sser
boots	**støvler**	**sturv**lerr
coat	**en frakk/kåpe**	ehn frahk/**kaw**per
dress	**en kjole**	ehn **khōō**ler
pair of gloves	**et par hansker**	eht pahr **hahn**skerr
scarf	**et skjerf**	eht shærf
shirt	**en skjorte**	ehn **shoo'**ter
shoes	**sko**	skōō
skirt	**et skjørt**	eht shur't
socks	**et par sokker**	eht pahr **sokk**err
sweater	**en genser**	ehn **gehn**serr
swimming trunks	**et badebukse**	eht **baa**derbookser
swimsuit	**en badedrakt**	ehn **baa**derdrahkt
T-shirt	**en T-skjorte**	ehn **tāy**-shoo'ter
tights	**en strømpebukse**	ehn **strurm**perbookser
trousers	**et par langbukser**	eht pahr **lahng**bookserr
Can I try it on?	**Kan jeg få prøve den?**	kahn yæi faw **prūr**ver dehn
What's it made of?	**Hva er det laget av?**	vaa ær deh **laa**gert ahv

cotton	**bomull**	**boo**mewl
denim	**denim**	deh**neem**
lace	**knipling**	**knip**ling
leather	**lær**	lǣr
linen	**lin**	leen
silk	**silke**	**sil**ker
suede	**semsket skinn**	**sehm**skert shin
velvet	**fløyel**	**floy**erl
wool	**ull**	ewl

Grocer's *Matvarehandel*

What sort of cheese do you have?	**Hva slags ostesorter har du?**	vaa shlakss **oos**terso'terr haa dew
half a kilo of tomatoes	**1/2 kg tomater**	ehn hahl **kheel**oo toom**aa**terr
a litre of milk	**1 l melk**	ehn **lee**terr mehlk
4 slices of ham	**4 skiver skinke**	**feer**er **sheev**err **shing**ker
some bread	**litt brød**	lit brür
a tin (can) of peaches	**en boks fersken**	ehn bokss **fæsh**kern

Miscellaneous *Forskjellig*

I'd like a/an/some...	**Jeg vil gjerne ha...**	yæi vil **yæ**'ner haa
battery	**et batteri**	eht bahter**ree**
bottle-opener	**en flaskeåpner**	ehn **flah**skerawpnerr
newspaper	**en avis**	ehn ah**veess**
American/English	**amerikansk/ engelsk**	ahm(eh)ri**kaansk**/ **ehng**erlsk
postcard	**et postkort**	eht **post**ko't
torch	**en lommelykt**	ehn **loom**merlewkt
I'd like a film (for this camera).	**Jeg vil gjerne ha en film (til dette apparatet).**	yæi vil **yæ**'ner haa ehn film (til **deh**ter ahpah**raa**ter)
black and white	**svart-hvitt**	**svah't**-vit
colour	**farge**	**fahr**gger
Can you repair this camera?	**Kan du reparere dette apparatet?**	kahn dew rehpah**rāy**rer **deh**ter ahpah**raa**ter
I'd like a haircut, please.	**Klipping, takk.**	**klip**ning tahk

Souvenirs *Suvernirer*

drinking horn	**et drikkehorn**	eht **drikk**erhōō'n
hunting knife	**en jaktkniv**	ehn **yahkt**kneev
reindeer skin	**et reinsdyrskinn**	ehn **ræins**dēwrshin
sealskin slippers	**et par selskinnstøfler**	eht pahr **sāyl**shinsturflerr
troll	**et troll**	eht trol
Viking ship	**et vikingskip**	eht **vee**kingsheep

At the bank *I banken*

Where's the nearest bank/currency exchange office?	**Hvor er nærmeste bank/veksling- skontor?**	voor ær **nær**mehster bahngk/ **vehk**shlingskoontoōr
I'd like to change some dollars/pounds.	**Jeg vil gjerne veksle noen dollar/ pund.**	yæi vil yæˉner **vehk**shler nōōern dollahr/pewn
I'd like to cash a traveller's cheque.	**Jeg vil gjerne løse inn en reisesjekk.**	yæi vil yæˉner **lü**rsser in ehn ræissershehk
What's the exchange rate?	**Hva er veksling- skursen?**	vaa ær **vehk**shlingskewshern

At the post office *Postkontor*

I'd like to send this ...	**Jeg vil gjerne sende dette ...**	yæi vil yæˉner **seh**ner dehter
airmail/express	**med fly/ekspress**	meh(d) flewˉ/ehks**prehss**
A ...-kroner stamp, please.	**Et ...-kroners fri- merke, takk.**	eht ... -krōōnersh **free**mærker tahk
What's the postage for a postcard to the U.S.?	**Hva er portoen for et postkort til USA?**	vah ær poo'tooern for eht **post**koˈt til ēwˉ-ehss-aa
Is there any post (mail) for me? My name is ...	**Har det kommet noe post til meg? Mitt navn er ...**	har deh **kom**mert nōōer post til mæi. mit nahvn ær

Telephoning *Telefon*

Where's the nearest telephone booth?	**Hvor er nærmeste telefonkiosk?**	voor ær **nær**mehster tehler**fōōn**khyosk
May I use your phone?	**Kan jeg få låne telefonen?**	kahn yæi faw **law**ner tehler**fōō**nern
Hello. This is ...	**Hallo. Dette er ...**	hah**lōō**. **deh**ter ær
I'd like to speak to ...	**Kan jeg få snakke med ...?**	kahn yæi faw **snah**ker meh(d)
When will he/she be back?	**Når kommer han/ hun tilbake?**	nor kommer hahn/hewn til**baa**ker
Will you tell him/her I called?	**Kan du si til ham/ henne at jeg ringte?**	kahn dew see til hahm/ **heh**ner aht yæi haar ringt
Would you ask her to phone me?	**Kan du be henne om å ringe meg?**	kahn dew bāy **heh**ner om aw **ring**er mæi
Would you take a message?	**Kan du ta imot en beskjed?**	kahn dew taa ee**mōōt** ehn ber**shāy**

NUMBERS, see page 124

Doctor *Lege*

Where can I find a doctor who speaks English?	Hvor kan jeg få tak i en lege som snakker engelsk?	voor kahn yæi faw taak ee ehn lāÿger som snahkerr ehngerlsk
Where's the surgery (doctor's office)?	Hvor er legekonto-ret?	voor ær lāÿgernkoontoōrer
Can I have an appointment...?	Kan jeg få bestille en time til...?	kahn yæi faw teemer
tomorrow	i morgen	ee mawer'n
as soon as possible	så snart som mulig	saw snaa't som mēwli

Parts of the body *Kroppsdeler*

arm	armen	ahrmern
back	ryggen	rewgern
bone	benet (i kroppen)	bāÿner (ee kroppern)
ear	øret	ūrrer
eye	øye	oyer
face	ansiktet	ahnsikter
finger	fingeren	fingerrern
foot	foten	foōtern
hand	hånden	honern
head	hodet	hoōder
heart	hjertet	yæ'ter
knee	kneet	knāÿer
leg	benet	bāÿner
lung	lungen	loongern
mouth	munnen	mewnern
muscle	muskelen	mewskerlern
neck	nakken	nahkern
nose	nesen	nāÿssern
shoulder	skulderen	skewlderrern
skin	huden	hewdern
stomach	magen	maagern
throat	halsen	hahlsern
tongue	tungen	toongern
I've got a/an...	Jeg har fått...	yæi haar fot
blister	en blemme	ehn blehmer
bruise	et blått merke	eht blot mærker
burn	et brannsår	eht brahnsawr
cut	et kutt	eht kewt
rash	et utslett	eht ēwtshleht
sting	et stikk	eht stik
swelling	en hevelse	ehn hāÿverlser
wound	et sår	eht sawr

Could you have a look at it?	**Kan du undersøke det?**	kahn dew **ewn**ershürker deh
It hurts.	**Det gjør vondt.**	deh yürr voont
I feel...	**Jeg føler meg ...**	yæi **fü**rlerr mæi
dizzy	**svimmel**	**svim**merl
nauseous	**kvalm**	kvahlm
I feel shivery.	**Jeg har kulde-gysninger.**	yæi haar **kewl**erye͞wsningerr
I'm diabetic.	**Jeg er diabetiker.**	yæi ær deeah**bay**tikkerr
Can you give me a prescription for this?	**Kan du gi meg en resept på dette?**	kahn dew yee mæi ehn reh**sehp**t paw **deh**ter
May I have a receipt for my health insurance?	**Kan jeg få en kvittering for sykeforsikringen?**	kahn yæi faw ehn kvit**tay**ring for **se͞w**kerfoshikringern

---

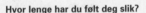

Hvor lenge har du følt deg slik?	How long have you been feeling like this?
Hvor gjør det vondt?	Where does it hurt?
Jeg skal ta temperaturen/måle blodtrykket.	I'll take your temperature/ blood pressure.
Jeg skal gi deg en sprøyte.	I'll give you an injection.
Jeg vil ha en blodprøve/ avføringsprøve/urinprøve.	I want a specimen of your blood/stools/urine.
Du bør holde sengen i ... dager.	You must stay in bed for... days.
Du bør oppsøke en spesialist.	I want you to see a specialist.

Can you recommend a good dentist?	**Kan du anbefale en god tannlege?**	kahn dew **ahn**berfaaler ehn goo(d) **tahn**layger
I have toothache.	**Jeg har tannpine.**	yæi haar **tahn**peener
I've lost a filling.	**Jeg har mistet en plombe.**	yæi haar **mis**tert ehn **ploom**ber

What time is it? *Hvor mange er klokken?*

It's...	Den er...	dehn ær
five past one	**fem over ett**	fehm **aw**verr eht
ten past two	**ti over to**	tee **aw**verr too
a quarter past three	**kvart over tre**	kvah't **aw**verr tray
twenty past four	**tjue over fire/ti på halv fem**	khewer **aw**verr feerer/tee paw hahl fehm
twenty-five past five	**fem på halv seks**	fehm paaw hahl sehkss
half past six	**halv sju**	hahl shew
twenty-five to seven	**fem over halv sju**	fehm **aw**verr hahl shew
twenty to eight	**ti over halv åtte/ tjue på åtte**	tee **aw**verr hahl **ot**ter/ **khew**er paw **ot**ter
a quarter to nine	**kvart på ni**	kvah't paw nee
ten to ten	**ti på ti**	tee paw tee
five to eleven	**fem på elleve**	fehm paw **ehl**ver
twelve o'clock	**klokken tolv**	**klok**kern tol
in the morning	**om morgenen**	om **maw'**nern
in the afternoon	**om ettermiddagen**	om **ehterr**middaagern
in the evening	**om kvelden**	om **kveh**lern
at night	**om natten**	om **nah**tern
yesterday/today	**i går/i dag**	ee gawr/ee daag
tomorrow	**i morgen**	ee **maw**er'n
spring/summer	**vår/sommer**	vawr/**som**merr
autumn/winter	**høs/vinter**	hurst/**vin**terr

Sunday	**søndag**	**surn**dah(g)
Monday	**mandag**	**mahn**dah(g)
Tuesday	**tirsdag**	**teesh**dah(g)
Wednesday	**onsdag**	**oons**dah(g)
Thursday	**torsdag**	**tawsh**dah(g)
Friday	**fredag**	**fray**dah(g)
Saturday	**lørdag**	**lur'**dah(g)
January	**januar**	yahnewa**waar**
February	**februar**	fehbrewa**waar**
March	**mars**	mahsh
April	**april**	ah**preel**
May	**mai**	maay
June	**juni**	**yew**nee
July	**juli**	**yew**lee
August	**august**	ou**gewst**
September	**september**	sehp**tehm**berr
October	**oktober**	ok**taw**berr
November	**november**	noo**vehm**berr
December	**desember**	dehs**sehm**berr

Numbers *Tall*

0	**null**	newl
1	**en**	ayn
2	**to**	too
3	**tre**	tray
4	**fire**	feerer
5	**fem**	fehm
6	**seks**	sehkss
7	**sju**	shew
8	**åtte**	otter
9	**ni**	nee
10	**ti**	tee
11	**elleve**	ehlver
12	**tolv**	tol
13	**tretten**	trehtern
14	**fjorten**	fyoo'tern
15	**femten**	fehmtern
16	**seksten**	sæistern
17	**sytten**	surtern
18	**atten**	ahtern
19	**nitten**	nittern
20	**tjue**	khewer
21	**tjueen**	khewerayn
30	**tretti**	trehti
40	**førti**	fur'ti
50	**femti**	fehmti
60	**seksti**	sehksti
70	**sytti**	surti
80	**åtti**	otti
90	**nitti**	nitti
100	**hundre**	hewndrer
1000	**tusen**	tewssern
100,000	**hundre tusen**	hewndrer tewssern
1,000,000	**en million**	ehn milyoon

first	**første**	furshter
second	**annen/andre**	aaern/ahndrer
third	**tredje**	traydyer
once	**en gang**	ehn gahng
twice	**to ganger**	too gahngerr
a half	**en halv**	ehn hahl
a quarter	**en fjerdedel**	ehn fyærerdayl
a third	**en tredjedel**	ehn traydyerdayl
a pair	**et par**	eht pahr
a dozen	**et dusin**	eht dewsseen

Where do you come from? *Hvor kommer du fra?*

Canada	**Kanada**	**kah**nahdah
Denmark	**Danmark**	**dahn**mahrk
England	**England**	**ehng**lahn
Finland	**Finland**	**fin**lahn
Great Britain	**Storbritannia**	**stoor**brittahneeah
Iceland	**Island**	**ees**lahn
Ireland	**Irland**	**eer**lahn
New Zealand	**Ny-Zealand**	n$\overline{\text{ew}}$-**say**lahn
Norway	**Norge**	**nor**gger
Scotland	**Skottland**	**skot**lahn
South Africa	**Sør-Afrika**	**s$\overline{\text{ur}}$r**aafreekah
Sweden	**Sverige**	**sveer**yer
United States	**USA**	$\overline{\text{ew}}$-ehss-**aa**

Signs and notices *Skilt og oppslag*

Damer	Ladies
Forsiktig	Caution
Forsiktig, trapp	Mind the step
Gratis adgang	Free admittance
Herrer	Gentlemen
Høgspenning	High voltage
I uorden	Out of order
Kaldt	Cold
Kasse	Cash desk (Cashier)
Ledig	Free/Vacant
Livsfare	Danger (of death)
Nymalt	Wet paint
Nødutgang	Emergency exit
Opptatt	Occupied
Privat	Private
Privat vei/veg	Private road
Reservert	Reserved
Røyking forbudt	No smoking
Røyking (ikke) tillatt	(Non)Smoker
Stengt	Closed
Skyv	Push
Trekk	Pull
Utgang	Exit
Varmt	Hot
Vokt deg/Dem for hunden	Beware of the dog
Åpent	Open
Åpningstider	Opening hours

Emergency *Nødsfall*

Call the police	**Ring til politiet**	ring til poolitteeyer
Get a doctor	**Hent en lege**	hehnt ehn lāyger
Go away	**Gå vekk**	gaw vehk
HELP	**HJELP**	yehlp
I'm ill	**Jeg er syk**	yæi ær sēwk
I'm lost	**Jeg har gått meg bort**	yæi haar got mæi boo't
Leave me alone	**La meg være i fred**	lah mæi vǣrer ee frāy(d)
LOOK OUT	**SE OPP**	sāy op
STOP THIEF	**STOPP TYVEN**	stop tēwvern
My... has been stolen.	**... er blitt stjålet.**	... ær blit styawlert
I've lost my...	**Jeg har mistet ...**	yæi haar mistert
handbag	**håndvesken**	honvehskern
passport	**passet**	pahsser
wallet	**lommeboken**	loommerbōōkern

Guide to Norwegian pronunciation *Uttale*

Consonants

Letter	Approximate pronunciation	Symbol	Example	
b,c,d, f,h,l, m,n,p, q,t,v,x	as in English			
g	1) before **ei, i** and **y**, generally like **y** in **y**es	y	**gi**	yee
	2) before **e** and **i** in some words of French origin, like **sh** in **sh**ut	sh	**geni**	sheh**nee**
	3) elsewhere. like **g** in **g**o	g	**gått**	got
gj	like **y** in **y**es	y	**gjest**	yehst
j	like **y** in **y**es	y	**ja**	yaa

TELEPHONING, see page 120

k	1) before **i**, and **y**, generally like **ch** in German i**ch** (quite like **h** in **h**uge, but with the tongue raised a little higher)	kh	**kino**	**kh**eenoo
	2) elsewhere, like **k** in ki**t**	k	**kaffe**	**kah**fer
kj	like **ch** in German i**ch**	kh	**kjøre**	**kh**ūrrer
r	rolled near the front of the mouth	r	**rare**	**r**aarer
rs	like **sh** in **sh**ut	sh	**norsk**	no**sh**k
s	like **s** in **s**it	s/ss	**spise**	**s**peesser
sj	generally like **sh** in **sh**ut	sh	**stasjon**	stah**sh**ōōn
sk	1) before **i**, **y** and **ø**, generally like **sh** in **sh**ut	sh	**ski**	**sh**ee
	2) elsewhere, like **sk** in **sk**ate	sk	**skole**	**sk**ōōler
skj	like **sh** in **sh**ut	sh	**skje**	**sh**āy
w	like **v** in **v**ice	v	**whisky**	**vi**ski
z	like **s** in **s**it	s	**zoom**	**s**ōōm

Vowels

a	1) when long, like **a** in car	aa	**dag**	d**aa**g
	2) when short, between **a** in car and **u** in cut	ah	**takk**	t**ah**k
e	1) when long, like **ay** in say, but a pure vowel, not a diphthong	āy	**sent**	s**āy**nt
	2) when followed by **r**, often like **a** in man (long or short)	ǣ / æ	**her** / **herre**	h**ǣ**r / h**æ**rer
	3) when short, like **e** in get	eh	**penn**	p**eh**n
	4) when unstressed, like **a** in about	er	**betale**	b**er**taaler
i	1) when long, like **ee** in bee	ee	**hit**	h**ee**t
	2) when short, like **i** in sit	i	**sitt**	s**i**t

o	1) when long, often like **oo** in s**oo**n, but with the lips more tightly rounded	o͞o	**ord**	o͞ord
	2) the same sound can be short, like **oo** in f**oo**t	oo	**ost**	oost
	3) when long, sometimes like **aw** in s**aw**	aw	**tog**	tawg
	4) when short, sometimes like **o** in g**o**t (British pronunciation)	o	**stoppe**	stopper
u	1) something like **ew** in f**ew**, or Scottish **oo** in g**oo**d (long or short)	e͞w ew	**mur** **busk**	me͞wr bewsk
	2) occasionally like **oo** in f**oo**t	oo	**nummer**	noommerr
y	very much like the sound described under **u** (1) above (long or short); put your tongue in the position for the **ee** in b**ee**, and then round your lips as for the **oo** in p**oo**l	e͞w ew	**by** **bygge**	be͞w bewger
æ	like **a** in **a**ct (long or short)	a͞e	**lære**	la͞erer
ø	like **ur** in f**ur**, but with the lips rounded (long or short)	u͞r ur	**dør** **sønn**	du͞rr surn
å	1) when long, like **aw** in s**aw**	aw	**såpe**	sawper
	2) when short, like **o** in g**o**t (British pronunciation)	o	**sånn**	son

Diphthongs

au	rather like **ou** in l**ou**d, though the first part is the Norwegian ø-sound	ou	**sau**	sou
ei, eg, egn	like **ai** in w**ai**t, though first part is the Norwegian æ-sound	æi	**geit** **jeg** **tegne**	yæit yæi tæiner

Swedish

Some basic expressions *Användbara uttryck*

Yes/No.	**Ja/Nej.**	yaa/nay
Please.	**Var snäll och .../..., tack.**	vaar snehl ok/tahk
Thank you.	**Tack.**	tahk
I beg your pardon?	**Förlåt?**	fur'lawt

Introductions *Presentation*

Good morning.	**God morgon.**	goo(d) morron
Good afternoon.	**God middag.**	goo(d) middah(g)
Good night.	**God natt.**	goo(d) naht
Good-bye.	**Adjö.**	ahy͞ur
Hello/Hi!	**Hej!**	hay
My name is ...	**Mitt namn är ...**	mit nahmn ǣr
What's your name?	**Vad heter ni/du?**	vaad hāyterr nee/dēw
Pleased to meet you!	**Trevligt att träffas!**	trāyvlli(g)t aht trehfahss
How are you?	**Hur mår ni/du?**	hēwr mawr nee/dēw
Very well, thanks. And you?	**Bara bra, tack. Och ni/du?**	baarah braa tahk. ok nee/dēw
Where do you come from?	**Varifrån kommer du?**	vaarifrawn kommer dēw
I'm from ...	**Jar är från ...**	yaa(g) ǣr frawn
Australia	**Australien**	aaewstraaliern
Canada	**Kanada**	kahnahdah
Great Britain	**Storbritannien**	st͞oorbrittahniern
United States	**USA**	ēwehssaa
I'm with my ...	**Jar är här med ...**	yaa(g) ǣr hǣr māyd
wife	**min fru**	min frēw
husband	**min man**	min mahn
family	**min familj**	min fahmily
boyfriend	**min pojkvän**	min poykvehn
girlfriend	**min flickvän**	min flikvehn
I'm here on business/vacation.	**Jag är här i affärer/på semester.**	yaa(g) ǣr hǣr ee ahfǣrerr/paw sehmehsterr

PRONUNCIATION, see page 158/EMERGENCIES, page 157

Questions *Frågor*

When?/How?	**När?/Hur?**	nǣr/hēwr
What?/Why?	**Vad?/Varför?**	vaad/**vahr**furr
Who?	**Vem?**	vehm
Which?	**Vilken?**	**vil**kern
Where is/are ...?	**Var är/Var finns/ Var ligger ...?**	vaar ǣr/vaar finss/vaar **lig**gerr
Where can I find ...?	**Var hittar jag?**	vaaar **hit**tahr yaa(g)
Where can I get ...?	**Var kan jag få tag på ...?**	vaar kahn yaa(g) faw taag paw
How far?	**Hur långt?**	hēwr longt
How long?	**Hur länge?**	hēwr **lehng**er
How much/many?	**Hur mycket/ många?**	hēwr **mewk**er(t)/**mong**ah
Can I have ...?	**Kan jag få ...?**	kahn yaa(g) faw
Can you help me?	**Kan ni hjälpa mig?**	kahn nee **yehl**pah may
Is there/Are there ...?	**Finns det ...?**	finss dāy(t)
There isn't/aren't ...	**Det finns inte ...**	dāy(t) finss **in**ter
There isn't/aren't any.	**Det finns ingen/ inga.**	dāy(t) finss **ing**ern/**ing**ah

Do you speak ...? *Talar ni ...?*

What does this/that mean?	**Vad betyder det här/det där?**	vaa(d) ber**tew**derr dāy(t) hǣr/dāy(t) dǣr
Can you translate this for us?	**Kan ni översätta det här för oss?**	kahn nee **ūr**ver'sehtah dāy(t) hǣr fūrr oss
Do you speak English?	**Talar ni engelska?**	**taa**lahr nee **ehng**erlskah
I don't speak (much) Swedish.	**Jag talar inte (så bra) svenska.**	yaa(g) **taa**lahr **in**ter (saw braa) **svehn**skah
Could you speak more slowly?	**Kan ni tala lite långsammare?**	kahn nee **taa**lah **li**ter **long**sahmahrer
Could you repeat that?	**Kan ni upprepa det där?**	kahn nee **ewp**rāypah dāy(t) dǣr
Could you write it down, please?	**Skulle ni kunna skriva det?**	**skew**ler nee **kew**nnah **skree**vah dāy(t)
I understand.	**Jag förstår.**	yaa(g) furr'**stawr**
I don't understand.	**Jag förstår inte.**	yaa(g) furr'**stawr in**ter

It's ...	Den är ...	
better/worse	**bättre/sämre**	be**h**trer/**sehm**rer
big/small	**stor/liten**	st**ōō**r/**lee**tern
early/late	**tidig/sen**	**tee**di(g)/s**ay**n
good/bad	**bra/dålig**	braa/**dawl**i(g)
hot/cold	**varm/kall**	vahrm/kahl
near/far	**nära/långt (bort)**	n**ǣ**rah/longt (bo**r**t)
right/wrong	**rätt/fel**	re**h**t/**fayl**
vacant/occupied	**ledig/upptagen**	l**āy**di(g)/**ewp**taagern

A few more useful words *Några fler användbara ord*

a little/a lot	**lite/mycket**	**lee**ter/**mew**ker(t)
above	**ovanför**	**awv**ahnf**ū**rr
after	**efter**	**ehf**terr
and	**och**	ok
behind	**bakom**	**baa**kom
below	**nedanför**	n**āy**dahnf**ū**rr
between	**mellan**	**meh**lahn
but	**men**	mehn
downstairs	**där nere**	d**ǣ**r **nāy**rer
during	**under**	**ewn**derr
for	**för**	f**ū**rr
from	**från**	frawn
inside	**inne**	**inn**er
near	**nära**	**nǣ**rah
never	**aldrig**	**ahl**drig
next to	**bredvid**	br**āy**(d)**veed**
none	**ingen**	**ing**ern
not	**inte**	**int**er
nothing	**ingenting, inget**	**ing**ernting **ing**ert
now	**nu**	n**ew**
on	**på**	paw
only	**bara**	**baa**rah
or	**eller**	**ehl**err
outside	**ute**	**ēw**ter
perhaps	**kanske**	**kahn**sher
soon	**snart**	snaa**r**t
then	**då, sedan**	daw sehn
through	**genom**	**yāy**nom
too	**också**	**ok**so
towards	**mot**	m**ōō**t
under	**under**	**ewn**derr
until	**till**	til
upstairs	**där uppe**	d**ǣ**r **ewp**er
very	**mycket**	**mew**ker(t)
with	**med**	m**āy**d
without	**utan**	**ēw**tahn

Hotel—Other accommodation *Hotell*

I have a reservation.	**Jag har beställt rum.**	yaa(g) haar ber**stehlt** rewm
We've reserved 2 rooms.	**Vi har beställt 2 rum.**	vee haar ber**stehlt** 2 rewm
Do you have any vacancies?	**Har ni några lediga rum?**	har nee **naw**grah **lay**diggah rewm
I'd like a ...	**Jag skulle vilja ha ett ...**	yaa(g) **skew**ler **vil**yah haa eht
single room	**enkelrum**	**ehn**kerlrewm
double room	**dubbelrum**	**dew**berlrewm
with twin beds	**med två sängar**	mayd tvaw **sehng**ahr
with a double bed	**med dubbelsäng**	mayd **dew**berlsehng
with a bath	**med bad**	mayd baad
with a shower	**med dusch**	mayd dewsh
Is there ...?	**Finns det ...?**	finss **day**(t)
air conditioning	**luftkonditionering**	**lewft**kondishonnayring
a private toilet	**toalett på rummet**	tooah**leht** paw **rew**mert
a radio/television in the room	**radio/TV på rummet**	**raay**do/**tay**veh paw **rew**mert
a sauna	**bastu**	**bah**stew
What's the price ...?	**Vad kostar det ...?**	vaad **kos**tahr **day**(t)
Is there a camp site near here?	**Finns det nagon campingplats i närheten?**	finss **day**(t) **naw**gon **kahm**pingplahtss ee **nær**haytern
Can we camp here?	**Kan vi campa här?**	kahn vee **kahm**pah hær
We'll be staying ...	**Vi tänker stanna ...**	vee **tehn**kerr **stah**nah
overnight only	**bara över natten**	**baa**rah **ür**verr **nah**tern
a few days	**några dagar**	**naw**grah **daa**(gah)r
a week	**en vecka**	ehn **veh**kah

Decision *Beslut*

May I see the room?	**Kan jag få se på rummet?**	kahn yaa(g) faw say paw **rew**mert
That's fine. I'll take it.	**Det är bra. Jag tar det.**	**day**(t) ær braa. yaa(g) taar **day**(t)
No. I don't like it.	**Nej. Jag tycker inte om det.**	nay. yaa(g) **tew**kerr **in**ter om **day**(t)
It's too ...	**Det är för ...**	**day**(t) ær fürr
cold	**kallt**	kahlt
dark/small	**mörkt/litet**	**murr**kt/**lee**tert

NUMBERS, see page 156

Do you have anything ...?	**Har ni något ...?**	haar nee **naw**got
better/bigger	**bättre/större**	**beht**rer/**stur**rer
cheaper	**billigare**	**bil**liggahrer
quieter	**tystare**	**tews**tahtrer

Efternamn/Förnamn	Name/First name
Hemort/Gata/Nummer	Home town/Street/Number
Nationalitet/Yrke	Nationality/Occupation
Födelsedatum/Födelseort	Date/Place of birth
Inrest ...	Arrived on ...
Passnummer	Passport number
Ort/Datum	Place/Date
Underskrift	Signature

General requirements *Allmänna förfrågningar*

The key to room ..., please.	**Nyckeln till rum ..., tack.**	**newk**er(l)n til rewm ... tahk
Where's the ...?	**Var är ...?**	vaar ær
bathroom	**badrummet**	**baad**rewmert
dining-room	**matsalen**	**maat**saalern
emergency exit	**nödutgång**	**nūrd**ewtgawngern
lift (elevator)	**hissen**	**his**sern
Where are the toilets?	**Var är toaletten?**	vaar ær tooah**leh**tern
Where can I park my car?	**Var kan jag parkera bilen?**	vaar kahn yaa(g) pahr**kāy**rah **bee**lehn

Checking out *Avresa*

May I have my bill, please?	**Kan jag få räkningen, tack?**	kahn yaa(g) faw **raik**ningern tahk
Can you get us a taxi?	**Kan ni skaffa oss en taxi?**	kahn nee **skah**fah oss ehn **tahk**si
It's been a very enjoyable stay.	**Det har varit en mycket trevlig vistelse.**	dāy(t) haar **vaa**rit ehn **mewk**er(t) **trāy**vli(g) **vis**terlser

Eating out *Mat och dryck*

Can you recommend a good restaurant?	Kan ni föreslå en bra restaurang?	kahn nee furrerslaw ehn braa rehstorrahng
I'd like to reserve a table for 4.	Jag skulle vilja beställa ett bord för 4.	yaa(g) skewler vilyah berstehlah eht bōō'd fŭrr 4
We'll come at 8.	Vi kommer klockan 8.	vee kommerr klokkahn 8
I'd like breakfast/ lunch/dinner, please.	Jag skulle vilja ha frukost/lunch/ middag, tack.	yaa(g) skewler vilyah haa frewkost/lewnsh/middah(g) tahk
What do you recommend?	Vad rekommende-rar ni?	vaad rehkommernd͞ayrahr nee
Do you have a set menu/local dishes?	Har ni någon meny/lokal specia-litet?	haar nee nawgon mehn͞ew/lookaal spehssiahlit͞ay(t)
Do you have any vegetarian dishes?	Har ni några vege-tariska rätter?	haar nee nawgrah vehgertaariskah rehterr

---

👉	🍽️
Vad önskar ni?	What would you like?
Jag rekommenderar det här.	I recommend this.
Vad önskas att dricka?	What would you like to drink?
Vi har inte ...	We don't have ...
Önskar ni ...?	Would you like ...?

Could we have a/an ..., please?	Kan vi få ..., tack?	kahn vee faw... tahk
ashtray	en askkopp	ehn ahskop
cup	en kopp	ehn kop
fork	en gaffel	ehn gahfehl
glass	ett glas	eht glaass
knife	en kniv	ehn kneev
napkin (serviette)	en servett	ehn sehrveht
plate	en tallrik	ehn tahlrik
spoon	en sked	ehn sh͞ayd

NUMBERS, see page 156/TELLING THE TIME, page 155

Svensk

May I have some ...?	**Kan jag få lite ...?**	kahn yaa(g) faw **lee**ter
bread	**bröd**	brūrd
butter	**smör**	smūrr
lemon	**citron**	sit**rōō**n
oil	**olja**	**ol**yah
pepper	**peppar**	**peh**pahr
salt	**salt**	sahlt
seasoning	**kryddor**	**krew**door
sugar	**socker**	**sok**ker
vinegar	**vinäger**	vin**nai**gerr

Reading the menu *Att läsa matsedeln*

bakverk	**baak**vehrk	pastries
drycker	**drew**kkerr	drinks
efterrätter	**eh**fterrehterr	desserts
fisk	fisk	fish
frukt	frewkt	fruit
fågel	**faw**gerl	poultry
glass	glahss	ice cream
grönsaker	**grūrn**saakerr	vegetables
kött	khurt	meat
ost	oost	cheese
pastarätter	**pahs**tahrehterr	pasta
risrätter	**rees**rehterr	rice
sallader	**sahl**lahderr	salads
skaldjut	skaal**yew**r	seafood
soppor	**sop**poor	soups
smårätter	**smaw**rehterr	snacks
smörgåsar	**smurr**gawssahr	open sandwiches
smörgåsbord	**smurr**gawsbōō'd	smörgåsbord
vilt	vilt	game
vinlista	**veen**listah	wine list
äggrätter	**ehg**rehterr	egg dishes

Breakfast *Frukost*

I'd like...	**Jag skulle vilja ha ...**	yaa(g) **skew**ler **vil**yah haa
bread/butter	**lite bröd/smör**	**lee**ter brūrd/smūrr
cheese	**ost**	oost
eggs	**ägg**	ehg
ham and eggs	**skinka och ägg**	**shin**kah ok ehg
jam/roll	**lite sylt/ett små-franska**	**lee**ter sewlt/eht **smaw**frahnskah

Starters (Appetizers) *Förrätter*

grodlår	**grōōd**lawr	frog's legs
gåslever	**gaws**lāȳverr	goose liver
kaviar	**kahv**yahr	caviar
musslor	**mews**loor	mussels
ostron	**oos**tron	oysters
paté	pah**tōȳ**	paté
sniglar	**sneeg**lahr	snails

Soups *Soppor*

I'd like some soup.	**Jag skulle vilja ha en soppa.**	yaa(g) **skew**ler **vil**yah haa ehn **sop**pah
champinjonsoppa	shamhpin**yōōn**soppah	mushroom soup
fisksoppa	**fisk**soppah	fish soup
hummersoppa	**hew**merrsoppah	lobster soup
kålsoppa	**kawl**soppah	cabbage soup
nässelsoppa	**nehs**serlsoppah	nettle soup
oxvanssoppa	**ooks**svahnssoppah	oxtail soup

blåbärssoppa	sweet bilberry soup; served as a dessert or a
(**blawb**ǣ´ssoppah)	vitamin-packed pick-me-up

Fish and seafood *Fisk och skaldjur*

abborre	**ah**borrer	perch
bläckfisk	**blehk**fisk	octopus
böckling	**burk**ling	smoked herring
flundra	**flewn**drah	flounder
forell	for**rehl**	trout
hälleflundra	**hehler**flewndrah	halibut
hummer	**hew**merr	lobster
kolja	**kol**yah	haddock
krabba	**krah**bah	crab
lax	lahks	salmon
räkor	**rai**koor	prawns (shrimp)
rödspätta	**rūr(d)**spehtah	plaice
sill	sil	herring
sjötunga	**shūr**tewngah	sole
tonfisk	**tōōn**fisk	tuna (tunny)

gravlax
(graavlahks)

salmon marinated with salt, sugar (pepper) and dill; served with a sweet-sour mustard-vinegar-oil sauce with plenty of dill

kräftströmming
(krehftstrurming)

Baltic herring baked with crushed tomatoes and lots of dill; served warm or cold with boiled potatoes

stuvad abborre
(stēēvahd ahborrer)

perch, poached with onion, parsley and lemon; served with boiled potatoes

baked	**ugnstekt**	ewngnstāykt
boiled	**kokt**	kookt
fried	**stekt**	stāykt
grilled	**halstrad, grillad**	hahlstrahd grillahd
whole roasted	**helstekt**	hāylstāykt
underdone (rare)	**blodig**	bloodig
medium	**medium**	māydeeyewn
well-done	**genomstekt**	yāynomstāykt

Meat Kött

beef/lamb	**oxkött/lamm**	ookskhurt/lahm
chicken/duck	**kyckling/anka**	khewkling/ahnkah
pork/veal	**fläskkött/kalv**	flehskkhurt/kahlv
biff	bif	beef steak
björnstek	byūr'nstāyk	roast bear
fläskkorv	flehskkorv	spicy boiled pork sausage
fläskpannkaka	flehskpahnkaakah	thick oven-baked pancake with bacon, served with cranberries
gås	gawss	goose
kalkon	kahlkōōn	turkey
kalvsylta	khalvsewlta	jellied veal loaf
korv	korv	sausage
köttbullar	khurtbewlahr	meat balls
pepparrotskött	pehpahrrōōtskhurt	boiled beef with horseradish sauce
rökt renstek	rūrkt rāynstāyk	roast reindeer
(rökt) skinka	(ruūrkt) shinkah	(smoked) ham
älg	ehly	elk

kåldomar
(kawldolmahr)

cabbage rolls, stuffed with minced meat and rice; served with cream gravy

pytt i panna
(pewt eepahnah)

Swedish hash; chunks of fried meat, sausages, onions and potatoes; served with a fried egg and pickled beetroot

Vegetables and salads *Grönsaker och sallader*

beans	**bönor**	būrnoor
beetroots	**rödbetor**	rūr(d)bāytoor
broccoli	**broccoli**	brokkoli
cabbage	**kål**	kawl
carrots	**morötter**	mōōrurterr
cauliflower	**blomkål**	bloomkawl
cucumber	**gurka**	gewrkah
leeks	**purjolök**	pewryoolūrk
lettuce	**grönsallad**	grūrnsahlahd
mushrooms	**svamp**	svahmp
onions	**lök**	lūrk
peas	**ärtor**	æ'toor
potatoes	**potatis**	pootaatiss
spinach	**spenat**	spehnaat
swede (rutabaga)	**kålrot**	kawlrōōt
tomatoes	**tomater**	toomaaterr

grönsallad
(grūrnsahlahd)

lettuce, cucumber, tomatoes, parsley, dill with oil and vinegar dressing; accompanies the main course

hasselbackspotatis
(hahsserlbahkspoo-
taatiss)

potatoes coated with melted butter, breadcrumbs and sometimes grated cheese, baked

kroppkakor
(kropkaakoor)

potato dumplings with a filling of minced bacon and onions; served with melted butter

raggmunk med fläsk
(rahgmewnk māyd
flaisk)

potato pancake with lightly salted pork served with cranberries

skaldjurssallad
(skaalyēw'ssahlahd)

assorted seafood salad (mostly mussels and shrimps)

västkustsallad
(vehstkewstsahlahd)

assorted seafood salad with mushrooms, tomatoes, lettuce, cucumber, asparagus and dill

Fruit *Frukt*

apple	**äpple**	ehpler
Arctic cloudberries	**hjortron**	yoo'tron
banana	**banan**	bahnaan
blackberries	**björnbär**	byūr'nbær
blackcurrants	**svarta vinbär**	sva'tah veenbær
bilberries (blueberries)	**blåbär**	blawbær
cherries	**körsbär**	khur'sbær
cranberries	**lingon**	lingon
gooseberries	**krusbär**	krēwsbær
grapes	**vindruvor**	veendrēwvoor
grapefruit	**grapefrukt**	"grape"frewkt
lemon	**citron**	sitrōōn
melon	**melon**	mehlōōn
orange	**apelsin**	ahperlseen
peach	**persika**	pæ'sikah
pear	**päron**	pæron
plums	**plommon**	ploomon
raspberries	**hallon**	hahlon
rowanberries	**rönnbär**	rurnbær
strawberries	**jordgubbär**	yōō'dgewbahr
wild strawberries	**smultron**	smewltron

Desserts—Pastries *Efterrätter—Bakverk*

chokladmousse	shoklaa(d)mooss	chocolate mousse
glass	glahss	ice cream
jordgubbar med grädde	yōō'dgewbahr māyd grehder	strawberries with cream
kanelbulle	kahnāylbewler	cinnamon bun
mjuk pepparkaka	myēwk pehpahrkaakah	gingerbread cake
våfflor med sylt	vofloor māyd sewlt	waffles with jam
äppelkaka med vaniljsås	ehperlkaakah māyd vanilysawss	apple cake with vanilla custard

mazarin (mahssahreen)		Sweden's most beloved pastry; almond tart topped with icing
plättar (plehtahr)		small pancakes; eaten with sugar or jam, sometimes whipped cream
toscaäpplen (toskahehplern		stewed apples covered with toffee sauce and almond flakes

Drinks *Alkoholhaltiga drycker*

beer	öl	ūrl
(hot) chocolate	(varm) choklad	(vahrm) shoklaa(d)
coffee	kaffe	kahfer
espresso	en espresso	ehn ehsprehsso
with cream	med grädde	māyd grehder
fruit juice	juice	yōoss
lemonade	en läsk	ehn lehsk
(glass of) milk	(ett glas) mjölk	(eht glaass) myurlk
mineral water	mineralvatten	minerraalvahtern
fizzy (carbonated)	med kolsyra	māyd kawsēwrah
still	utan kolsyra	ēwtahn kawsēwrah
sugar	socker	sokkerr
tea	te	tāy
a cup of	en kopp	ehn kop
with lemon/milk	med citron/mjölk	māyd sitrōōn/myurlk
iced tea	iste	eestāy
wine	vin	veen
red/white	rött/vitt	rurt/vit

| May I have the wine list, please? | Kan jag få vinlistan, tack? | kahn yaa(g) faw veenlistahn tahk |
| I'd like a beer, please. | Jag skulle vilja ha en öl, tack. | yaa(g) skewler vilyah haa ehn ūrl tahk |

Bäska Droppar (behskah droppahr)	bitter-tasting aquavit, flavoured with worm-wood
Herrgårds (Aquavit) (hehrgaw'ds ahkvahveet)	flavoured with caraway seeds and whisky matured in sherry barrels
O.P. (Anderson Aquavit) (oo pāy)	aquavit flavoured with aniseed, caraway seeds and fennel
Punsch (pewnsh)	sweet, strong liqueur made of arrak, sugar and pure alcohol

neat	ren	rāyn
on the rocks	med is	māyd ees
with water	med vatten	māyd vahtern

Complaints *Klagomål*

The meat is ...	**Köttet är ...**	khurtert ær
overdone	**för mycket stekt**	furr **mewker**(t) stāykt
underdone	**inte tillräckligt genomstekt**	inter **til**rehkli(g)t **yāy**nomstāykt
This is too ...	**Det här är för ...**	dāy(t) hær ær furr
bitter/salty/sweet	**beskt/salt/sött**	behskt/sahlt/surt
That's not what I ordered.	**Det där har jag inte beställt.**	dāy(t) dær haar yaa(g) inter ber**stehlt**
The food is cold.	**Maten är kall.**	**maa**tern ær kahl

The bill (check) *Notan*

I'd like to pay.	**Får jag betala?**	fawr yaa(g) ber**taa**lah
What's this amount for?	**Vad står den här summan för?**	vaad stawr den hær **sew**mahn furr
I think there's a mistake in this bill.	**Jag tror att det är ett fel på notan.**	yaa(g) trōōr aht dāy(t)ær eht fāyl paw **nōō**tahn
Is everything included?	**Är allting inräknat?**	ær **ahl**ting **in**raiknaht
Can I pay with this credit card?	**Kan ja betala met det här kreditkortet?**	kahn yaa(g) ber**taa**lah māyd dāy(t) hær kreh**deet**koo'tert
We enjoyed it, thank you.	**Det var mycket gott.**	dāy(t) vaar **mewk**er(t) got

Snacks—Picnic *Mellanmål—Picknick*

I'll have one of those.	**Jag skulle vilja ha en av de där.**	yaa(g) **skewl**er **vil**yah haa ehn ahv dāy dær
to the left/right	**till vänster/höger**	til **vehn**sterr/**hur**gerr
above/below	**ovanför/nedanför**	**aw**vahnfurr/**nāy**dahnfurr
cheese	**ost**	oost
chips (french fries)	**pommes frites**	pom frit
Danish pastry	**wienerbröd**	**vee**nerbrurd
fried sausage	**en grillad korv**	ehn **gril**lahd korv
gherkins (pickles)	**ättiksgurkor**	**eht**iksgewrkah
liver paté	**leverpastej**	**lāy**verrpahstay
spring roll	**vårrulle**	**vawr**rewler

NUMBERS, see page 156

Travelling around *På resa*

Plane *Flyg*

Is there a flight to Luleå?	**Finns det något flyg till Luleå?**	finss day(t) **naw**got flewg til **lew**lay̆aw
What time should I check in?	**Hur dags måste jag checka in?**	hewr dahgss **mos**ter yaa(g) **khehk**ah in
I'd like to ... my reservation.	**Jag skulle vilja ... min reservation.**	yaa(g) **skew**ler **vil**yah ... min rehsehrvah**shoon**
cancel	**annullera**	ahnew**lay̆**rah
change	**ändra**	**ehn**drah
confirm	**bekräfta**	ber**krehf**tah

Train *Tåg*

Where's the railway station?	**Var ligger järn-vägsstationen?**	vaar **lig**gerr **yæ̆'n**vaigsstahshoonern

INGÅNG	ENTRANCE
UTGÅNG	EXIT
TILL TÅGEN	TO THE TRAINS
INFORMATION	INFORMATION

Where is/are (the) ...?	**Var är ...?**	vaar **ær**
booking office	**biljettexpeditionen**	bil**yeht**ehkspehdish**oo**nern
left-luggage office (baggage check)	**effektförvaringen**	eh**fehkt**furrvaaringern
lost property (lost and found) office	**hittegodsexpedi-tionen**	**hit**tergoodsehkspeh-dish**oo**nern
luggage lockers	**förvaringsboxarna**	furr**vaa**ringsboksah'nah
platform 2	**perrong 2**	peh**rong** 2
reservations office	**biljettexpeditionen**	bil**yeht**ehkspehdish**oo**nern
ticket office	**biljettluckan**	bil**yeht**lewkahn
waiting room	**väntsalen**	**vehnt**saalern
I'd like a ticket to Lund.	**Jag skulle vilja ha en biljett till Lund.**	yaa(g) **skew**ler **vil**yah haa ehn bil**yeht** til lewnd
single (one-way)	**enkel**	**ehn**kerl
return (round-trip)	**tur och retur**	tewr ok reh**tewr**
first/second class	**första/andra klass**	**fur'**stah/**ahn**drah klahss

TELLING THE TIME, see page 155

Inquiries *Förfrågningar*

When is the ... train to Uppsala?	**När går ... tåget till Uppsala?**	nær gawr... **taw**gert til **ewp**saalah
first/last/next	**första/sista/nästa**	**fur**ʳstah/**si**stah/**neh**stah
What time does the train to Göteborg leave?	**Hur dags går tåget till Göteborg?**	hewr dahgss gawr **taw**gert til yurter**bory**
Is there a dining car/ sleeping car on the train?	**Finns det någon restaurangvagn/ sovvagn i tåget?**	finss dā̄y(t) **naw**gon rehsstor**rahng**vahngn/ **saw**vahngn ee **taw**gert
Is this the train to Östersund?	**Är det här tåget till Östersund?**	ā̄r dā̄y(t) hā̄r **taw**gert til urster**ʳsewnd**
I'd like a time-table, please.	**Skulle jag kunna få en tidtabell, tack?**	**skew**ler yaa(g) **kew**nah faw ehn **tee(d)**tahbehl tahk
Where can I find a porter?	**Var kan jag få tag på en bärare?**	vaar kahn yaa(g) faw taag paw ehn **bǣ**rahrer
Can you help me with my luggage?	**Kan ni hjälpa mig med bagaget?**	kahn nee **yehl**pah may mā̄yd bah**gaa**shert

Underground (subway) *Tunnelbana*

Where's the nearest underground station?	**Var ligger när- maste tunnelban- estation?**	vaar **li**ggerr **nær**mahster **tew**nerlbaanerstahshōōn
Where do I change for ...?	**Var byter jag för ...?**	vaar **bēw**terr yaa(g) fūrr

Bus—Tram (streetcar) *Buss—Spårvagn*

Which tram (streetcar) goes to the town centre?	**Vilken spårvagn går till centrum?**	**vil**kern **spawr**vahngn gawr til **sehn**trewm
How much is the fare to ...?	**Hur mycket kostar det till ...?**	hewr **mewk**er(t) **kos**tahr dā̄y(t) til
Will you tell me when to get off?	**Kan ni säga till när jag skall stiga av?**	kahn nee **seh**yah til nā̄r yaa(g) skah(l) **stee**gah aav

Boat service *Båt*

When does the boat for ... leave?	**När går båten till ...?**	nawr gawr **baw**tern til
How long does the crossing take?	**Hur lång tid tar överfarten?**	hēwr lawng teed taar **ūr**verrfaa**ʳ**tern
I'd like to take a boat trip.	**Jag skulle vilja göra en båttur.**	yaa(g) **skew**ler **vil**yah **yūr**rah ehn **bawt**tēwr

Taxi *Taxi*

Where can I get a taxi?	**Var kan jag få tag på en taxi?**	vaar kahn yaa(g) faw taag paw ehn **tah**ksi
What's the fare to...?	**Vad kostar det till...?**	vaad **kos**tahr dāy(t) til
Take me to this address.	**Kör mig till den här adressen.**	khurr may til dehn hǣr ahdrehssern
Please stop here.	**Var snäll och stanna här.**	vaar snehl ok **stah**nah hǣr
Could you wait for me?	**Kan ni vänta på mig?**	kahn nee **vehn**tah paw may
I'll be back in 10 minutes.	**Jag är tillbaka om 10 minuter.**	yaa(g) ǣr til**baa**kah om 10 mi**new**terr

Car hire (rental) *Biluthyrning*

I'd like to hire (rent) a car.	**Jag skulle vilja hyra en bil.**	yaa(g) **skew**ler **vil**yah **hew**rah ehn beel
I'd like it for a day/a week.	**Jag vill ha den en dag/en vecka.**	yaa(g) vil haa dehn ehn daa(g)/ehn **veh**kah
What's the charge per day/week?	**Vad kostar det per dag/vecka?**	vaad **kos**tahr dāy(t) pǣr daa(g)/**veh**kah
Is mileage included?	**Är kilometerkostnaden inräknad?**	ǣr khillom**māy**terr-kostnahdern **in**raiknahd
I'd like full insurance.	**Jag vill ha helförsäkring.**	yaa(g) vil haa **hāyl**fur'saikring

Road signs *Vägmärken*

CYKELBANA	Cycle path
EJ MOTORFORDON	No motor vehicles
ENSKILD VÄG	Private road
FARLIG KURVA	Dangerous bend (curve)
HUVUDLED	Main road
KÖR SAKTA	Slow down
LÄMNA FÖRETRÄDE	Give way (yield)
MOTORVÄG	Motorway (expressway)
PARKERING	Parking
TRAFIKOMLÄGGNING	Diversion (detour)
VÄGARBETE	Roadworks (men working)

TELLING THE TIME, see page 155/NUMBERS, page 156

Svensk

Ni har kört fel.	You're on the wrong road.
Kör rakt fram.	Go straight ahead.
Det är där nere till vänster/höger.	It's down there on the left/right.
mitt emot/bakom ...	opposite/behind ...
bredvid/efter ...	next to/after ...
norr/söder/öster/väster	north/south/east/west

Where's the nearest filling station?	Var ligger närmaste bensinstation?	vaar liggerr nærmahster behnseenstahshōōn
Fill it up, please.	Full tank, tack.	fewl tahnk tahk
Give me ... litres of petrol (gasoline).	Kan jag få ... liter bensin?	kahn yaa(g) faw ... leeterr behnseen
super (premium)/regular/unleaded/diesel	högoktanig/lågoktanig/blyfri/diesel	hūrgoktaanig/lawgoktaanig/blewfree/deesserl
How do I get to ...?	Hur kommer jag till ...?	hēwr kommerr yaa(g) til
I've had a breakdown at ...	Jag har fått motorstopp vid ...	yaa(g) haar fot mōōto'stop veed
Can you send a mechanic?	Kan ni skicka en mekaniker?	kahn nee shikkah ehh mehkaanikkerr
Can you mend this puncture (fix this flat)?	Kan ni laga den här punkteringen?	kahn nee laagah dehn pewngtāyringern

Landmarks *Landmärken*

bridge	en bro	ehn brōō
forest	en skog	ehn skōōg
lake	en sjö	ehn shūr
meadow	en äng	ehn ehng
mountain	ett berg	eht bāëry
path	en stig	ehn steeg
river	en flod	ehn flōōd
sea	ett hav	eht haav
valley	en dal	ehn daal
waterfall	ett vattenfall	eht vahternfahl

Sightseeing *Sightseeing*

Where's the tourist office?	**Var ligger turistby-rån?**	vaar **liggerr** tewr**rist**bew'rawn
Is there an English-speaking guide?	**Finns det någon engelsktalande guide?**	finss day(t) **naw**gon **ehng**erlsktaalahnder "guide"
Where is/Where are the ...?	**Var ligger ...?**	vaar **liggerr**
botanical gardens	**botaniska trädgår-den**	boo**taa**niskah **trai(d)**gaw'dern
castle	**slottet**	**slott**ert
cathedral	**domkyrkan**	**doom**khewrkahn
city centre	**(stads)centrum**	**(stahds)sehn**trewm
exhibition	**utställningen**	**ewt**stehlningern
harbour	**hamnen**	**hahm**nern
museum	**museet**	mewss**ay**ert
old town	**gamla stan**	**gahm**lah staan
shopping area	**affärscentrum**	ah**fæ'**ssehntrewm
square	**torget**	**tory**ert
tower	**tornet**	**too'**nert
zoo	**djurparken**	**yewr**pahrkern

Relaxing *Nöjen*

What's playing at the ... Theatre?	**Vad går det på ... teatern?**	vad gawr day(t) paw... tay**aat**er'n
Are there any tickets for tonight?	**Finns det några biljetter till i kväll?**	finss day(t) **naw**grah bil**yeh**terr til ee kvehl
What time does it begin?	**Hur dags börjar det?**	hewr dahgss **burr**yahr day(t)
I'd like to reserve 2 tickets for the show on Friday evening.	**Jag skulle vilja beställa 2 biljetter till föreställningen på fredag kväll.**	yaa(g) **skew**ler **vil**yah ber**steh**lah 2 bil**yeh**terr til **fürr**erstehlningern paw **fray**daa(g) kvehl
Would you like to go out with me tonight?	**Skall vi gå ut i kväll?**	skah(l) vee gaw ewt ee kvehl
Thank you, but I'm busy.	**Tack, men jag är tyvärr upptagen.**	tahk mehn yaa(g) ær tew**vær** ewp**taa**gern
Is there a discotheque in town?	**Finns det något diskotek i stan?**	finss day(t) **naw**got disko**tayk** ee staan
Would you like to dance?	**Skall vi dansa?**	skah(l) vee **dahn**sah
Thank you, it's been a wonderful evening.	**Tack, det har varit en underbar kväll.**	tahk day(t) haar **vaa**rit ehn **ewn**derrbaar kvehl

TELLING THE TIME/DAYS OF THE WEEK, see page 156

Sports *Sport*

What's the admission charge?	**Vad kostar det i inträde?**	vaad kostah dāy(t) ee intraider
Where's the nearest golf course?	**Var ligger närmaste golfbana?**	vaar liggerr nærmahster golfbaanah
Where are the tennis courts?	**Var ligger tennisbanorna?**	vaar liggerr tehnisbaanoo'nah

canoeing	kanot	kahnoot
car racing	biltävling	beeltaivling
cycling	cykel	sewkerl
football (soccer)	fotboll	footbol
(horse-back) riding	ridning	reedning
sailing	segling	sāygling
skiing	skidåkning	sheedawkning
swimming	simning	simning
table tennis	bordtennis	boo'dtehniss
tennis	tennis	tehniss

Can one swim in the lake/river?	**Kan man bada i sjön/floden?**	kahn mahn baadah ee shurn/floodern
Is there a swimming pool here?	**Finns det någon swimmingpool här?**	finss dāy(t) nawgon "swimmingpool" hær
Is there a skating rink near here?	**Finns det en skridskobana i närheten?**	finss dāy(t) ehn skri(d)skoobaanah ee nærhāytern
I'd like to see an ice-hockey match.	**Jag skulle vilja se en ishockeymatch.**	yaa(g) skewler vilyah sāy ehn eeshokkimahtsh
I'd like to ski.	**Jag skulle vilja åka skidor.**	yaa(g) skewler vilyah awkah sheedoor
downhill/cross-country skiing	utförsåkning/längdåkning	ewtfur'sawkning/lehngdawkning
I'd like to hire ...	**Jag skulle vilja hyra ...**	yaa(g) skewler vilyah hewrah
skates	ett par skridskor	eht paar skri(d)skoor
skiing equipment	skidutrustning	sheedewtrewstning
skis	skidor	sheedoor
I'd like to hire a bicycle.	**Jag skulle vilja hyra en cykel.**	yaa(g) skewler vilyah hewrah ehn sewkerl

Shops, stores and services *Affärer och service*

Where's the nearest...?	**Var finns närmaste...?**	vaar finss **nær**mahster
baker's	**ett bageri**	eht baager**ree**
bookshop	**en bokhandel**	ehn **book**hahnderl
butcher's	**en slaktare/ett charkuteri**	ehn **slahk**tarher/eht shahrkewter**ree**
chemist's/drugstore	**en apotek**	eht ahpoo**tayk**
dentist	**en tandläkare**	ehn **tahn(d)**laikahrer
department store	**ett varuhus**	eht **vaar**ewhewss
grocer's	**en livsmedelsaffär**	ehn **livs**mäyderlsahfær
hairdresser's (ladies/ men)	**en frisör (dam-/ herr-)**	ehn fris**ürr** (daam-/hehr-)
market	**en marknad/en torghandel**	ehn **mahrk**nahd/ehn **tory**hahnderl
newsstand	**en tidningskiosk**	ehn **tee(d)**ningskhiosk
post office	**ett postkontor**	eht **post**kontoor
souvenir shop	**en souvenirbutik**	ehn soover**neer**bewteek
supermarket	**ett snabbköp**	eht **snahb**khürp

General expressions *Allmänna uttryck*

Where's the main shopping area?	**Var ligger affärscentrum?**	vaar **liggerr** ahf**æ´s**sehntrewm
Do you have any ...?	**Har ni några ...?**	haar nee **nawg**rah
I'd like a ... one.	**Jag skulle vilja ha en ...**	yaa(g) **skew**ler **vil**yah haa ehn
big	**stor**	st**oo**r
cheap	**billig**	**bil**lig
dark	**mörk**	murrk
good	**bra**	braa
heavy	**tung**	tewng
large	**stor**	st**oo**r
light (weight)	**lätt**	leht
light (colour)	**ljus**	y**ew**ss
rectangular	**rektangulär**	rehktanggewl**ær**
round	**rund**	rewnd
small	**liten**	**lee**tern
square	**kvadratisk**	kvah**draa**tisk
sturdy	**kraftig**	**krah**ftig
Don't you have anything ...?	**Har ni inte någonting ...?**	haar nee **in**ter **naw**gonting
cheaper/better	**billigare/bättre**	**bil**liggahrer/**beh**trer
larger/smaller	**större/mindre**	**stur**rer/**min**drer

Kan jag hjälpa er?	Can I help you?
Vad önskar ni?	What would you like?
Vilken ... önskar ni?	What ... would you like?
färg/form/kvalitet	colour/shape/quality
Det är slut på lagret.	We're out of stock.
Skall vi beställa det åt er?	Shall we order it for you?
Det blir ... kronor, tack.	That's ... crowns, please.
Kassan är där borta.	The cash desk is over there.

How much is this?	**Hur mycket kostar det här?**	hewr **mew**ker(t) **kos**tahr dāȳ(t) hǟr
Please write it down.	**Kan ni skriva det?**	kahn nee **skree**vah dāȳ(t)
I don't want to spend more than ... crowns.	**Jag vill inte lägga ut mer än ... kroner.**	yaa(g) vil **in**ter **leh**gah ēwt māȳr ehn ... **krōō**ner
No, I don't like it.	**Nej, jag tycker inte om det.**	nay yaa(g) **tew**kerr **in**ter om dāȳ(t)
I'll take it.	**Jag tar det.**	yaa(g) taar dāȳ(t)
Do you accept credit cards?	**Tar ni kreditkort?**	taar nee kreh**deet**koo't
Can you order it for me?	**Kan ni beställa det åt mig?**	kahn nee ber**steh**lah dāȳ(t) awt may

Chemist's (drugstore) *Apotek*

aspirin	**aspirin**	ahspi**reen**
condoms	**kondomer**	kon**daw**merr
deodorant	**deodorant**	dāȳodo**rahnt**
insect repellent/spray	**ett insektsmedel/ insektsspray**	eht in**sehkts**māȳderl/ in**sehkts**"spray"
moisturizing cream	**en fuktighetsbe- varande kräm**	ehn **fewk**tighāȳtsbervaar- ahnder kraim
razor blades	**rakblad**	**raak**blaad
shampoo	**ett schampo**	eht **shahm**poo
soap	**en tvål**	ehn tvawl
sun-tan cream	**en solkräm**	ehn **sōōl**kraim
tampons	**tamponger**	tahm**pong**err
toothpaste	**en tandkräm**	ehn **tahn(d)**kraim

NUMBERS, see page 156

black	**svart**	svah't
blue	**blå**	blaw
brown	**brun**	br$\overline{ew}$n
green	**grön**	gr$\overline{u}$rn
grey	**grå**	graw
orange	**orange**	orahnsh
red	**röd**	r$\overline{u}$rd
white	**vit**	veet
yellow	**gul**	g$\overline{ew}$l
light …	**ljus …**	y$\overline{ew}$ss
dark …	**mörk …**	murrk

Clothing *Kläder*

blouse	**en blus**	ehn bl$\overline{ew}$ss
boots	**stövlar**	sturvlahr
dress	**en klänning**	ehn **kleh**ning
gloves	**ett par handskar**	eht paar **hahn(d)**skahr
jersey	**en tröja**	ehn **tru**ryah
scarf	**en scarf**	ehn skaarf
shirt	**en skjorta**	ehn **shoo**'tah
shoes	**skor**	sk$\overline{oo}$r
skirt	**en kjol**	ehn kh$\overline{oo}$l
socks	**ett par sockor**	eht paar **so**kkoor
swimming trunks	**ett par badbyxor**	eht paar **baad**bewksoor
swimsuit	**en baddräkt**	ehn **baa(d)**drehkt
T-shirt	**en T-shirt**	ehn "T-shirt"
trousers	**ett par (lång)byxor**	eht paar **(long)bewk**soor
Can I try it on?	**Kan jag få prova den?**	kahn yaa(g) faw **pr$\overline{oo}$**vah dehn
What's it made of?	**Vad är det gjort av?**	vaad $\overline{ae}$r d$\overline{ay}$(t) y$\overline{oo}$'t aav

cotton	**bomull**	**boo**mewl
denim	**denim**	deh**neem**
lace	**spets**	spehtss
leather	**läder/skinn**	laider/shin
linen	**linne**	**lin**ner
silk	**siden/silke**	**see**dern/**sil**ker
suede	**mocka**	**mo**kkah
velvet	**sammet**	**sah**mert
wool	**ylle**	**ewl**er

Grocer's *Livsmedelsaffär*

What sort of cheese do you have?	**Vad har ni för sorts ostar?**	vaad haar nee fürr so'tss osstahr
half a kilo of tomatoes	**ett halvt kilo tomater**	eht hahlft kheeloo toomaaterr
a litre of milk	**en liter mjölk**	ehn leeterr myurlk
4 slices of ham	**4 skivor skinka**	4 sheevoor shinkah
some bread	**lite bröd**	leeter brürd
a tin (can) of peaches	**en burk persikor**	ehn bewrk pæ'sikkor

Miscellaneous *Diverse*

I'd like a/an/some ...	**Jag skulle vilja ha ...**	yaa(g) skewler vilyah haa
battery	**ett batteri**	eht bahterree
bottle-opener	**en flasköppnare**	ehn flahskurpnahrer
newspaper American/English	**en dagstidning amerikansk/ engelsk**	ehn dahgstee(d)ning ahm(eh)rikaansk/ engerlsk
postcard	**ett vykort**	eht vewkoo't
torch	**en ficklampa**	ehn fiklahmpah
I'd like a film for this camera.	**Jag skulle vilja ha film till den här kameran.**	yaa(g) skewler vilyah haa film til dehn hær kaam(er)-rahn
black and white	**svart-vit**	svah't-veet
colour	**färg**	færy
Can you repair this camera?	**Kan ni laga den här kameran?**	kahn nee laagah dehn hær kaam(er)rahn
I'd like a haircut, please.	**Klippning, tack.**	klipning tahk

Souvenirs *Souvenirer*

candlestick	**en ljusstake**	ehn yewsstaaker
ceramics	**keramik**	khehrahmeek
clogs	**träskor**	træskoor
Dala horse	**en dalahäst**	ehn daalahhehst
glassware	**glas**	glaass
Lapp handicrafts	**sameslöjd**	saamersluryd

At the bank *På banken*

Where's the nearest bank/currency exchange office?	**Var ligger närmaste bank/växelkontor?**	vaar **liggerr nær**mahster bahnk/**vehk**serlkont**ōōr**
I'd like to change some dollars/pounds.	**Jag skulle vilja växla några dollar/pund.**	yaa(g) **skewl**er **vil**yah **vehks**lah **naw**grah **doll**ahr/ pewnd
I'd like to cash a traveller's cheque.	**Jag skulle vilja lösa in en resecheck.**	yaa(g) **skewl**er **vil**yah **lūrs**sah in ehn **rāy**serkhehk
What's the exchange rate?	**Vilken är växelkursen?**	**vil**kern ær **vehk**serlkew'sern

At the post office *Post*

I'd like to send this by ...	**Jag vill skicka det här ...**	yaa(g) vil **shik**kah dāy(t) hær
airmail	**med flyg**	māyd flewg
express	**express**	ehk**sprehss**
A ...-öres stamp, please.	**Ett ...-öres frimärke, tack.**	eht ... **ūr**rerss **free**mærker tahk
What's the postage for a postcard to the U.S.A.?	**Vad är portot för ett vykort till USA?**	vaad ær **po'**tot fūrr eht **vew**kooʼt til **ēw**ehssaa
Is there any post for me?	**Finns det någon post till mig?**	finss dāy(t) **naw**gon post til may

Telephoning *Telefon*

Where's the nearest telephone booth?	**Var finns närmaste telefonkiosk?**	vaar finss **nær**mahster tehleh**fawn**khiosk
May I use your phone?	**Får jag låna telefonen?**	fawr yaa(g) **law**nah tehleh**fawn**ern
Hello. This is ...	**Hallå, det här är ...**	hah**law** dāy(t) hær ær
I'd like to speak to ...	**Kan jag få tala med ...?**	kahn yaa(g) faw **taa**lah māyd
When will he/she be back?	**När kommer han/ hon tillbaka?**	nær **kom**merr hahn/hoon til**vbaa**kah
Would you ask him/ her to call me?	**Skulle ni kunna be honom/henne ringa mig?**	**skewl**er nee **kewn**nah bāy **hon**nom/**heh**ner **ring**ah may
Would you take a message, please?	**Skulle ni kunna lämna ett meddelande?**	**skewl**er nee **kewn**nah **lehm**nah eht **med**dāy**lahn**der

NUMBERS, see page 156

Doctor *Läkare*

Where can I find a doctor who speaks English?	**Var kan jag få tag på en läkare som talar engelska?**	vaar kahn yaa(g) faw taag paw ehn **lai**kahrer som **taa**lahr **eng**erlskah
Where's the surgery (doctor's office)?	**Var ligger läkar- mottagningen?**	vaar **lig**gerr **lai**kahrmōōtaagningern
Can I have an appointment ... ?	**Kan jag få en tid ...?**	kahn yaa(g) faw ehn teed
tomorrow	**i morgon**	ee **mor**gon
as soon as possible	**så snart som möjligt**	saw snaʹt som **mury**li(g)t

Parts of the body *Kroppsdelar*

arm	**armen**	**ahr**mern
back	**ryggen**	**rew**gern
bone	**benen (i kroppen)**	**bāy**nern (ee **krop**pern)
ear	**örat**	**ūr**raht
face	**ansiktet**	**ahn**siktert
finger	**fingret**	**fing**rert
foot	**foten**	**fōō**tern
hand	**handen**	**hahn**dern
head	**huvudet**	**hēw**v(ewd)ert
heart	**hjärtat**	yæʹtaht
knee	**knä(e)t**	knai(er)t
leg	**benet**	**bāy**nert
lung	**lungan**	**lewng**ahn
mouth	**munnen**	**mew**nern
muscle	**muskeln**	**mews**kerln
nerve	**nerven**	**nær**vern
nose	**näsan**	**nais**sahn
shoulder	**skuldran/axeln**	**skewl**drahn/**ahk**serln
skin	**huden**	**hēw**dern
stomach	**magen**	**maa**gern
throat	**halsen**	**hahl**sern
toe	**tån**	tawn
tongue	**tungan**	**tewng**ahn
I've got a/an ...	**Jag har (fått) ...**	yaa(g) haar (fot)
bruise	**ett blåmärke**	eht **blaw**mærker
burn	**ett brännsår**	eht **brehn**sawr
cut	**ett skärsår**	eht **shæ**ʹsawr
insect bite	**ett insektsbett**	eht **in**sehktsbeht
rash	**ett utslag**	eht **ēwt**slaag
sting	**ett stick**	eht stik
swelling	**en svullnad**	ehn **svewl**nahd
wound	**ett sår**	eht sawr

Could you have a look at it?	Skulle ni kunna titta på det?	skewler nee kewnah tittah paw day(t)
It hurts.	Det gör ont.	day(t) yurr oont
I feel ...	Jag känner mig ...	yaa(g) khehnerr may
dizzy	yr	ewr
nauseous	illamående	illahmawehnder
I feel shivery.	Jag har frossbryt-ningar.	yaa(g) haar frosbrewtningahr
I'm diabetic.	Jag är diabetiker.	yaa(g) ær diahbaytikkerr
Can you give me a prescription for this?	Kan ni ge mig ett recept på det här?	kahn nee yay may eht rehsehpt paw day(t) hær
May I have a receipt for my health insurance?	Kan jag få ett kvitto för min sjuk-försäkring?	kahn yaa(g) faw eht kvitto furr min shewkfur'saikring

---

Hur länge har ni känt er så här?	How long have you been feeling like this?
Var gör det ont?	Where does it hurt?
Jag skall ta temperaturen/ blodtrycket.	I'll take your temperature/ blood pressure.
Jag skall ge er en spruta.	I'll give you an injection.
Jag vill ha ett blodprov/ avföringsprov/urinprov.	I want a specimen of your blood/stools/urine.
Ni bör ligga till sängs i ... dagar.	You must stay in bed for ... days.
Jag vill att ni vänder er till en specialist.	I want you to see a specialist.

Can you recommend a good dentist?	Kan ni rekommen-dera en bra tandlä-kare?	kahn nee rehkommerndayrah ehn braa tahn(d)laikahrer
I have toothache.	Jag har tandvärk.	yaa(g) haar tahn(d)værk
I've lost a filling.	Jag har tappat en plomb.	yaa(g) haar tahpaht ehn plomb

Time and date *Klockan och datum*

It's ...	Den är ...	dehn ær
five past one	**fem över ett**	fehm $\overline{u}$rverr eht
ten past two	**tio över två**	teeoo $\overline{u}$rverr tvaw
a quarter past three	**kvart över tre**	kvah't $\overline{u}$rverr tr$\overline{ay}$
twenty past four	**tjugo över fyra**	kh$\overline{ew}$goo $\overline{u}$rverr f$\overline{ew}$rah
twenty-five past five	**fem i halv sex**	fehm ee hahlv sehks
half past six	**halv sju**	hahlv sh$\overline{ew}$
twenty-five to seven	**fem över halv sju**	fehm $\overline{u}$rverh hahlv sh$\overline{ew}$
twenty to eight	**tjugo i åtta**	kh$\overline{ew}$goo ee ottah
a quarter to nine	**kvart i nio**	kvah't ee neeoo
ten to ten	**tio i tio**	teeoo ee teeoo
five to eleven	**fem i elva**	fehm ee ehlvah
noon/midnight	**klockan tolv (på dagen)/midnatt**	klokkahn tolv (paw daagern)/meednaht
in the morning	**på morgonen**	paw morronern
in the afternoon	**på eftermiddagen**	paw ehfterniddahn
in the evening	**på kvällen**	paw kvehlern
during the day	**under dagen**	ewnderr daagern
at night	**på natten**	paw nahtern
yesterday/today	**i går/idag**	ee gawr/eedaa(g)
tomorrow	**i morgon**	ee morron
spring/summer	**vår/sommar**	vawr/sommahr
autumn/winter	**höst/vinter**	hurst/vinterr

Sunday	**söndag**	**surn**daa(g)
Monday	**måndag**	**mon**daa(g)
Tuesday	**tisdag**	**tees**daa(g)
Wednesday	**onsdag**	**oons**daa(g)
Thursday	**torsdag**	**too's**daa(g)
Friday	**fredag**	**fr$\overline{ay}$**daa(g)
Saturday	**lördag**	**l$\overline{ur}$'**daa(g)
January	**januari**	yahnewaari
February	**februari**	fahbrewaari
March	**mars**	mah'ss
April	**april**	ahpril
May	**maj**	mahy
June	**juni**	y$\overline{ew}$ni
July	**juli**	y$\overline{ew}$li
August	**augusti**	ahgewsti
September	**september**	sehp**tehm**berr
October	**oktober**	ok**t$\overline{oo}$**berr
November	**november**	noo**vehm**berr
December	**december**	deh**ssehm**berr

Numbers *Räkneord*

0	**noll**	nol
1	**ett**	eht
2	**två**	tvaw
3	**tre**	trāy
4	**fyra**	fewrah
5	**fem**	fehm
6	**sex**	sehks
7	**sju**	shew
8	**åtta**	ottah
9	**nio**	neeoo
10	**tio**	teeoo
11	**elva**	ehlvah
12	**tolv**	tolv
13	**tretton**	trehton
14	**fjorton**	fyoo'ton
15	**femton**	fehmton
16	**sexton**	sehkston
17	**sjutton**	shewton
18	**arton**	aa'ton
19	**nitton**	nitton
20	**tjugo**	khewgoo
21	**tjugoett**	khewgoeht
30	**trettio**	trehti
40	**fyrtio**	fur'ti
50	**femtio**	fehmti
60	**sextio**	sehksti
70	**sjuttio**	shewti
80	**åttio**	otti
90	**nittio**	nitti
100	**(ett)hundra**	(eht)hewndrah
1000	**(ett)tusen**	(eht)tewssern
first/second	**första/andra**	fur'stah/ahndrah
once/twice	**en gång/två gånger**	ehn gong/tvaw gongerr
a half	**en halva**	ehn hahlvah

Where do you come from? *Varifrån kommer ni?*

Canada	**Kanada**	kahnahdah
Denmark	**Danmark**	dahnmahrk
England	**England**	englahnd
Ireland	**Irland**	irlahnd
Norway	**Norge**	noryer
Scotland	**Skottland**	skotlahnd
Sweden	**Sverige**	sværyer
United States	**USA**	ewehssaa

Signs and notices *Skylter och anslag*

Damer	Ladies
Drag	Pull
Ej ingång	No entrance
Herrar	Gentlemen
Hiss	Lift (elevator)
Ingång	Entrance
Kallt	Cold
Kassa	Cash desk
Ledigt	Free (vacant)
Livsfara	Danger of death
Nödutgång	Emergency exit
Öppet	Open
Reserverat	Reserved
Rökning förbjuden	No smoking
Rökning tillåten	Smoking allowed
Skjut	Push
Stängt	Closed
Stör ej	Do not disturb
Till salu	For sale
Upplysningar	Information
Upptaget	Occupied
Ur funktion	Out of order
Utgång	Exit
Varmt	Hot
Varning	Caution
Varning för hunden	Beware of the dog
Öppet	Open

Emergency *Nödsituation*

Call the police.	Ring polisen.	ring poleessern
Get a doctor.	Hämta en läkare.	hehmtah ehn laikahrer
Go away!	Ge er i väg!	yāy āyr ee vaig
HELP!	HJÄLP!	yehlp
I'm ill.	Jag är sjuk.	yaa(g) ǣr shēwk
I'm lost.	Jag har gått vilse.	yaa(g) haar got vilser
Leave me alone!	Lämna mig ifred!	lehmnah may eefrāy(d)
LOOK OUT!	SE UPP!	sāy ewp
STOP THIEF!	STOPPA TJUVEN!	stoppah khēwvern
My ... has been stolen.	... har stulits.	haar stēwlitss
I've lost my ...	Jag har tappat ...	yaa(g) haar tahpaht
handbag	min handväska	min hahn(d)vehskah
passport	mitt pass	mit pahss
wallet	min plånbok	min plawnbōōk

Guide to Swedish pronunciation *Uttal*

Consonants

Letter	Approximate pronounciation	Symbol	Example	
b,c,d, f,h,l, m,n,p, v,w,x	as in English			
ch	at the beginning of words borrowed from French, like **sh** in **sh**ut	sh	**chef**	sh$\overline{ay}$f
g	1) before stressed **i, e, y, ä, ö**, and sometimes after **l** or **r**, like **y** in yet	y	**ge**	y$\overline{ay}$
	2) before **e** and **i** in words of French origin, like **sh** in **sh**ut	sh	**geni**	sh$\overline{ay}$**nee**
	3) elsewhere, like **g** in **g**o	g	**gaffel**	**gah**ferl
j, dj, g, lj, hj	at the beginning of words always like **y** in yet	y	**ja** **ljus**	yaa y$\overline{ew}$ss
k	1) before stressed **i, e, y, ä, ö**, generally like **ch** in Scottish lo**ch**, but pronounced in the front of the mouth	kh	**köpa**	kh$\overline{ur}$pah
	2) elsewhere, like **k** in **k**it	k	**klippa**	**kl**ippah
kj	like **ch** in lo**ch**, but pronounced in the front of the mouth	kh	**kjol**	kh$\overline{oo}$l
qu	like **k** in **k**it followed by **v** in **v**at	kv	**Lindquist**	lin(d)**kv**ist
r	rolled near the front of the mouth	r	**ryka**	r$\overline{ew}$kah
s	1) in the ending **-sion** like **sh** in **sh**ut	sh	**mission**	mish$\overline{oo}$n
	2) elsewhere, like **s** in **s**o	s/ss	**ses**	s$\overline{ay}$ss
	3) the groups **sch, skj, sj, stj** are pronounced like **sh** in **sh**ut	sh	**schema**	sh$\overline{ay}$mah

sk	1) before stressed **e**, **i**, **y**, **ä**, **ö**, like **sh** in **sh**ut	sh	**shänk**	shehnk
	2) elsewhere, like **sk** in **sk**ip	sk	**skola**	sk$\overline{oo}$la
t	1) in the ending **-tion** like **sh** in **sh**ut or **ch** in **ch**at	sh tsh	**station** **nation**	stahsh$\overline{oo}$n nahtsh$\overline{oo}$n
	2) elsewhere, like **t** in **t**op	t	**tid**	teed
tj	like **ch** in Scottish lo**ch**, but pronounced in the front of the mouth; sometimes with a **t**-sound at the beginning	kh	**tjäna**	khainah
z	like **s** in **s**o	s	**zenit**	s$\overline{ay}$nit

Vowels

a	1) when long, like **a** in car	aa	**dag**	daa(g)
	2) when short, between **a** in cat and **u** in cut	ah	**tack**	tahk
e	1) when long, like **ay** in say	$\overline{ay}$	**sen**	s$\overline{ay}$n
	2) when followed by **r**, like **a** in man; long or short	$\overline{æ}$	**erfara**	$\overline{æ}$rfaarah
	3) when short, like **e** in get	eh	**beck**	behk
	4) unstressed, like **a** in about	er	**betala**	bertaalah
ej	like **a** in mate	ay	**nej**	nay
i	1) when long, like **ee** in b**ee**	ee	**vit**	veet
	2) when short, between **ee** in m**ee**t and **i** in h**i**t	i	**hinna**	hinnah
	3) in a few words, e.g. in the personal pronoun **mig**, like **a** in mate	ay	**mig**	may

o	1) when long, often like oo in soon, but with the lips more tightly rounded	o͞o	**sko**	sko͞o
	2) the same sound can be short	oo	**solid**	soo**leed**
	3) when long, sometimes like **aw** in **raw**, but with the tongue a little higher in the mouth and the lips closely rounded	aw	**son**	sawn
	4) when short, sometimes like **o** in **hot**	o	**korrekt**	korre**hkt**
u	1) when long, like Swedish **y**, but with the tongue a little lower in the mouth, and with a puff of breath at the end	e͞w	**hus**	he͞wss
	2) when short, a little more like the **u** of **put**	ew	**full**	fewl
y	like German **ü** in **über**, or French **u** in **une**; round your lips and try to say **ee** as in **bee**	e͞w; ew	**vy** **syster**	ve͞w **sew**sterr
å	1) when long, like **aw** in **raw**, but with the tongue a little higher in the mouth and the lips closely rounded	aw	**gå**	gaw
	2) when short, like **o** in **hot**	o	**sång**	song
ä	1) when followed by **r**, like **a** in **man**, long or short	ǣ; æ	**ära** **värka**	ǣrah vær**kah**
	2) elsewhere, like **e** in **get**; long or short	ai; eh	**läsa** **bäst**	**lais**sah behst
ö	like **ur** in **fur**, but with the lips rounded and without any **r**-sound; long or short; when followed by **r**, it is pronounced with the mouth a little more open	u͞r; ur	**röd** **köld** **öra**	ru͞rd khurld u͞rrah

English–Danish dictionary

c common gender   *nt* neuter   *pl* plural

A
able, to be kunne 4
above ovenpå 5
accept, to tage 21
address adresse *c* 15
admittance adgang *c* 29
after efter 5, 17
air conditioning klimaanlæg *nt* 6
airmail luftpost *c* 24
American amerikansk 23
amount beløb *nt* 13
and og 5
any nogen 4, 6
anything noget 7, 21
anywhere et eller andet sted 19
April april 27
arm arm *c* 25
art gallery kunstgalleri *nt* 17
ashtray askebæger *nt* 8
aspirin aspirin *c* 22
at ved 5
August august 27
Australia Australien 3
autumn *(fall)* efterår *nt* 27

B
back ryg *c* 25
back, to komme tilbage 24
bad dårlig 5
baker's bager *c* 20
bank bank *c* 24
basic anvendelig 3
bath bad *nt* 6
bathroom badeværelse *nt* 7
be, to være 4
bed seng *c* 6, 26
beer øl *nt* 13
before *(time)* før 5
behind bagved 17
below nedenunder 5
better bedre 5, 7, 21
between mellem 5
bicycle cykel *c* 19
big stor 5, 20
bill *(check)* regning *c* 7, 13
bitter bitter 13
black and white *(film)* sort/hvid 23
black sort 21
blood blod *nt* 26

blood pressure blodtrykket *nt* 26
blouse bluse *c* 22
blue blå 21
boat båd *c* 15
boat service bådfart *c* 15
body legeme *nt* 25
bone knogle *c* 25
booking office pladsreserveringen *c* 14
bookshop boghandel *c* 20
boots støvler *c/pl* 22
botanical gardens botaniske have *c* 17
boyfriend kæreste *c* 3
bra bh *c* 22
breakdown motorstopp *nt* 16
breakfast morgenmad *c* 8
bridge bro *c* 18
brown brun 21
bruise blåt mærke *nt* 25
burn brandsår *nt* 25
bus bus *c* 15
busy optaget 18
but men 5
butcher's slagter *c* 20

C
call, to *(help)* tilkalde 30
call, to *(telephone)* ringe 24
camera kamera *nt* 23
camp, to kampere 6
campsite campingplads *c* 6
can *(tin)* dåse *c* 23
Canada Canada 3
cancel annullere 14
car bil *c* 16
car hire *(rental)* biludlejning *c* 16
cash desk kasse *c* 20, 29
castle borg *c* 17
cathedral domkirke *c* 17
caution forsigtig 29
change ændre 14
change, to *(money)* veksle 24
cheap billig 5, 7, 20
check in, to checke ind 14
check out, to rejse 7
chemist's *(drugstore)* apotek *nt* 20, 22
child barn *nt* 3
city centre byens centrum *c* 17
close, to lukker 17

clothing klæder *c* 22
cold koldt 5, 6, 13, 29
colour farve 20, 23
come, to komme 8
condoms kondomer *nt/pl* 22
confirm bekræfte 14
cotton bomuld *c* 22
credit card kreditkort *nt* 13, 21
crossing overfart *c* 15
cup kop *c* 8
currency exchange office vekselkontor *nt* 24
cut snitsår *nt* 25
cycling cykling *c* 19

D
dance, to danse 18
danger fare *c* 29
dark mørk 6, 20
date dato *c* 7, 27
date of birth fødelsdato *c* 7
day dag *c* 6, 16, 26
December december 27
decision beslutning *c* 6
denim denim *c* 22
Denmark Danmark 29
dentist tandlæge *c* 20, 26
deodorant deodorant *c* 22
department store stormagasin *nt* 20
diabetes sukkersyge *c* 26
diesel diesel *c* 16
dining-room spisesale *c* 7
dinner middag *c* 8
discotheque diskotek *nt* 18
dish ret *c* 8
dizzy svimmel 26
doctor læge *c* 25, 30
doctor's office *(surgery)* konsultation 25
dollar dollar *c* 24
double bed dobbeltseng *c* 6
double room dobbeltværelse *nt* 6
down ned 5
downstairs nedenunder 5
dress kjole *c* 22
drink drikkevare *c* 13
drugstore *(chemist's)* apotek *nt* 20

E
ear øre *nt* 25
early tidligt 5
east øst 17
eight otte 28
emergency exit nødudgang *c* 7, 29

emergency nødstilfælde *nt* 30
England England 29
English *(language)* engelsk 4, 17, 15, 23, 30
enjoy, to nyde 13
enjoyable nyd 7
entrance fee entré *c* 17
entrance indgang *c* 14, 29
evening aften *c* 18, 27
exchange rate vekselkursen *c* 24
exit udgang *c* 14, 29
expensive dyr 5
express expres 24
expression udtryck *nt* 3, 20
eye øje *nt* 25

F
face ansigt *nt* 25
family familie *c* 3
February februar 27
few, a et par 6
filling station benzinstation *c* 16
filling *(tooth)* plombe *c* 26
film film *c* 23
find, to finde 4, 16, 25, 30
fine godt 3, 6
finger finger *c* 25
Finland Finland 29
first class første klasse *c* 14
first første 15, 28
first name fornavn *nt* 7
five fem 28
flight fly *nt* 14
food mad *c* 13
foot fod *c* 25
football *(soccer)* fodbold *c* 19
forbidden ... forbudt 29
forest skov *c* 18
fork gaffel *c* 8
four fire 28
free *(vacant)* ledigt 5
free of charge gratis 29
Friday fredag 27
from fra 5

G
general almindelig 7, 20
gentlemen *(toilets)* herrer *c/pl* 29
get, to få 4, 15
get, to *(fetch)* skaffe 7
girlfriend kæreste *c* 3
glass glas *nt* 8
gloves handsker *c/pl* 22
go away. to gå væk 30
go out, to *(rendez-vous)* gå ud 18

golf course golfbane *c* 19
good afternoon god dag 3
good god 5, 8, 20, 26
good morning god morgen 3
good night god nat 3
good-bye farvel 3
Great Britain Storbritannien 3, 29
green grøn 21
grey grå 21
grocer's købmand 20; madvarer *c* 23
guide guide *c* 17

H
hairdresser frisør *c* 20
half, a halv *c*, halvt *nt* 28
hand hånd *c* 25
handbag håndtaske *c* 30
harbour havn *c* 15, 17
have, to have 6, 7, 23
he han 24
head hoved *nt* 25
health insurance sygeforsikring *c* 26
heart hjerte *nt* 25
heavy tung 21
hello! hallo 24; hello 3
help! hjælp! 30
help, to hjælpe 4, 20
her hende 24
here her 15
hi hej 3
him ham 24
hire, to leje 16, 19
holidays ferie *c* 3
home town by *nt* 7
horse racing hestevæddeløb *nt* 19
hot varm 5, 6, 29
how far hvor langt 4
how hvordan 4
how long hvor længe 4, 14, 15, 26
how much hvor meget 4, 17, 18
hundred hundrede *nt* 28
hurt, to gøre ondt 26
husband mand *c* 3

I
ill syg 30
in i 5
information information *c* 14, 29
injection indsprøjtning *c* 26
inquiries forespørgsler *c/pl* 14
insect bite insektbid *nt* 25
insect spray insekt-spray *nt* 22
inside indenfor 5
introductions præsentationer *c/pl* 3

Ireland Irland 29
island ø *c* 18

J
January januar 27
jersey ulden trøje *c* 22
journey *(trip)* tur *c* 14
July juli 27
June juni 27

K
key nøglen *c* 7
kilo kilo(gram) *nt* 23
knee knæ *nt* 25
knife kniv *c* 8

L
lace knipling *nt* 22
ladies *(toilets)* damer *c/pl* 29
lake sø *c* 18, 19
landmark landmærke *nt* 18
large stor 21
last sidste 15
late sent 5
laundry service tøjvask *c* 6
leather læder *nt* 22
leave, to afgår 15
left venstre 17
left-luggage office (baggage check)
    bagageopbevaring *c* 14
leg ben *nt* 25
letter *(mail)* brev *nt* 24
lift *(elevator)* elevator *c* 7
light *(colour)* lys 21
light *(weight)* let 21
like to, to lyst have 18
linen lærred *nt* 22
litre liter *c* 16, 23
local lokal 8
look at, to *examine* se på 26
lose, to tabe 30
lost faret vild 30
lost property *(lost and found)* office
    hittegodskontor *nt* 14
luggage locker bagageboks *c* 14
lunch frokost *c* 8
lung lunge *c* 25

M
mail post *c* 24
March marts 27
market torvet *nt* 17
match kamp *c* 19

May maj 27
me mig 4
mean, to betyde 4
mechanic mekaniker *c* 16
meet, to træffe 3
mend, to *(fix)* reparere 17
mileage kilometerpenge *c* 16
milk mælk *c* 23
million million *c* 28
mistake fejl *c* 13
moisturizing cream fugtighedscreme *c* 22
Monday mandag 27
morning morgen *c* 27
mountain bjerg *nt* 18
mouth mund *c* 25
muscle muskel *c* 25
museum museum *nt* 17
my min 7

N
napkin *(serviette)* serviet *c* 8
nationality nationalitet *c* 7
nausea *(nauseous)* kvalme *c* 26
near nær 5
nearest nærmeste 16, 19, 20, 24
never aldrig 5
New Zealand New Zealand 29
newsagent bladhandler *c* 20
newspaper avis *c* 23
next næste 15
next to ved siden af 17
night nat *c* 27
nine ni 28
no nej 3
noisy støjende 6
north nord 17
Norway Norge 29
nose næse *c* 25
not ikke 4, 5
nothing ikke noget 5
notice opslag *nt* 29
November november 27
now nu 5
number *(house)* nummer *nt* 7

O
occupation stilling *c* 7
occupied optaget 5, 29
October oktober 27
on på 5
once en gang 28
one en 28
only kun 5
open åben 17, 29

opposite overfor 17
or eller 5
orange orange 21
order, out of i uorden 29
order, to bestille 13, 20, 21
outside udenfor 5

P
pardon, I beg your undskyld 3
parents forældre *pl* 3
park, to parkere 7
parking parkering *c* 16
part del *c* 25
passport pas *nt* 7, 30
path sti *c* 18
pay, to betale 13
per day pr. dag *c* 16
perhaps måske 5
petrol *(gasoline)* benzin *c* 16
place of birth fødested *nt* 7
place sted *nt* 7, 16
plane fly *nt* 14
plate tallerken *c* 8
platform perron *c* 14
play, to spille 18
please vær så venlig 3
police politi *nt* 30
post office posthus *nt* 20, 24
postage porto *c* 24
postcard postkort *nt* 24
pound *(sterling)* pund *nt* 24
prescription recept *c* 26
private privat 29
pull, to trække 29
puncture *(flat)* punktering *c* 17
push, to skubbe 29

Q
quality kvalitet *c* 20
quarter kvart *nt* 27
question spørgsmål *nt* 4
quiet rolig 7

R
radio radio *c* 6
rash udslæt *nt* 25
razor blades barberblade *pl* 22
receipt kvittering *c* 26
recommend, to anbefale 8, 26
rectangular rektangulær 21
red rød 21
regular *(petrol)* normal 16
repeat, to gentage 4
requirements forespørgsler *pl* 7

reservation bestilling *c* 14
reserve, to bestille 8, 18
reserved reserveret 29
restaurant restaurant *c* 8
return *(round trip)* retur 14
riding *(horse-back)* ridning *c* 19
right *(correct)* rigtigt 5
right *(direction)* højre 17
river flod *c* 18, 19
road sign vejskilt *nt* 15
road vej *c* 29
road works vejarbejde *pl* 16
room service service på værelset *c* 6
room værelse *nt* 6
round rund 21

S

sale udsalg *nt* 29
salty saltet 13
Saturday lørdag *c* 27
scarf tørklæde *nt* 22
Scotland Skotland 29
sea hav *nt* 18
seat plads *c* 18
second anden/andet 28
second class anden klasse *c* 14
see, to se 6
send, to sende 16, 24
September september 27
serve, to servere 8
set menu dagens ret *c* 8
seven syv 28
shampoo shampoo *c* 22
shape form *c* 20
she hun 24
shirt skjorte *c* 22
shivers *(shivery)* kuldegysninger *nt* 26
shoe sko *c* 22
shop *(store)* butik *c* 20
shopping area forretningskvarter *nt* 20; indkøbscentret *nt* 17
shoulder skulder *c* 25
shower bruser *c* 6
sign skilt *nt* 29
signature underskrift *c* 7
silk silke *c* 22
single room enkeltværelse *nt* 6
single *(one way)* enkelt 14
six seks 28
skates skøjter *c/pl* 19
skating rink skøjtebane *c* 19
ski ski *c* 19
skiing skiløb *nt* 19
skiing, cross-country langrend *nt* 19
skiing, downhill styrtløb *nt* 19
skiing equipment skiudstyr *nt* 19

skin hud *c* 25
skirt nederdel *c* 22
slice skive *c* 23
slowly, more langsom 4
small lille 5, 21; lyst 6; mindre 21
smoking rygning *c* 29
soap sæbe *c* 22
socks sokker *c/pl* 22
soon snart 5, 25
sort slags *c* 23
South Africa Sydafrika 29
south syd 17
souvenir shop souvenirbutik *c* 20
souvenir souvenir *nt* 23
speak, to tale 4, 24, 25
specialist speciallæge *c* 26
specimen prøve *c* 26
spoon ske *c* 8
sport sport *c* 19
spring forår *nt* 28
square firkantet 21
stamp frimærke *nt* 24
stay ophold *nt* 7
stay, to blive 6
steal, to stjæle 30
sting stik *nt* 25
stock, out of udsolgt 20
stomach mave *c* 25
stop, to standse 15
store *(shop)* butik *c* 20
straight ahead ligeud 17
street gade *c* 7
sturdy solid 21
suede ruskind *nt* 22
summer sommer *c* 28
sun-tan cream solcreme *c* 22
Sunday søndag *c* 27
super *(petrol)* super 16
supermarket supermarked *nt* 20
surgery *(doctor's office)* konsultation *c* 25
surname navn *nt* 7
Sweden Sverige 29
sweet sødt 13
swelling hævelse *c* 25
swimming svømning *c* 19
swimming pool svømmebasin *nt* 19
swimming trunks badebukser *pl* 22
swimsuit badedragt *c* 22

T

T-shirt T-shirt *c* 22
table bord *nt* 8
take, to tage 6, 14, 15, 21

take, to *(duration)* vare 15
tampons tamponer *c/pl* 22
taxi taxa *c* 7, 15
telephone telefon *c* 24
television fjernsyn *nt* 6
tell, to sige 24
temperature temperatur *c* 26
ten ti 28
tennis tennis *c* 19
tennis court tennisbane *c* 19
thank you tak 3
theatre teater *nt* 18
thief tyv *c* 30
third tredje 28
three tre 28
throat hals *c* 25
through gennem 5
Thursday torsdag *c* 27
ticket billet *c* 14
ticket office billetluge *c* 14
tights strømpebukser *pl* 22
tin *(can)* dåse *c* 23
to til 5
today i dag 28
toilet toilet *nt* 6, 7
tomato tomat *c* 23
tomorrow i morgen 25, 28
tongue tunge *c* 25
tonight i aften 18
too for 6, 13
too *(also)* også 5
toothache tandpine *c* 26
toothpaste tandpasta *c* 22
torch lommelygte *c* 23
touch, to røre 29
tour rundfart *c* 15
tourist office turistbureau *nt* 17
town by *c* 18
town centre centrum *nt* 15
translate, to oversætte 4
travel, to rejse 14
trousers bukser *pl* 22
try on, to prøve 21
Tuesday tirsdag *c* 27
twice to gange *pl* 28
twin beds to senge *pl* 6
two to 28

U
under under 5
underpants underbukser *pl* 22
United States USA 3
unleaded blyfri 16
until indtil 5

up op 5
upstairs ovenpå 5
useful nyttig 5

V
vacancies, no alt optaget 29
vacancy ledigt værelse *nt* 6
vacant ledig 29
vegetarian vegetar 8
velvet fløjl *nt* 22
very meget 5

W
wait, to vente 29
waiting room venteværelse *nt* 14
wallet tegnebog *c* 30
want, to ville 18
water vand *nt* 13
waterfall vandfald *nt* 18
Wednesday onsdag *c* 27
week uge *c* 6, 16
west vest 17
what hvad 4, 20
when hvornår 4, 17
where hvor 3, 4, 14, 17
which hvilken 4
white hvid 21
who hvem 4
why hvorfor 4
wife kone *c* 3
wine vin *c* 13
winter vinter *c* 28
with med 3, 5
without uden 5
wonderful virkelig hyggelig 18
wool uld *c* 22
word ord *nt* 5
worse værre 5
wound sår *nt* 25
write down, to skrive ned 21
wrong forkert 5, 17

Y
yellow gul 21
yes ja 3
yesterday i går 28

Z
zero nul 28

English–Finnish dictionary

A

able, to be voida 34
above -n yllä/yli 35, 44
accept, to hyväksyä 53
address osoite 47
admission charge pääsymaksu 51
admittance pääsy 61
after *(time)* -n jälkeen 35
air conditioning ilamastointi 36
airmail lentoposti 56
American amerikkalainen 55
amount summa 44
and ja 35
any yhtään 34
anything else entä muuta/saako olla muuta 52
anything mitään 37
anywhere jossain 51
apple omena 55
April huhtikuu 59
arm käsivarsi 57
arrive, to saapua 46
ashtray tuhkakupi 38
aspirin aspiriini 54
at -n kohdalla 35
August elokuu 59
Australia Australia 33
autumn *(fall)* syksy 59

B

back selkä 57
back, to be *(return)* tulla takaisin 47, 56
bad huono 35
baker's leipomo 52
bank pankki 56
basic perus- 33
bath kylpy 36
bathroom kylpyhuone 37
battery paristo 55
be, to olla 34
bed vuode 36, 56
beer olut 43
before *(time)* ennen -a 35
begin, to alkaa 50
behind -n takana/taakse 35, 49
below -n alla/alle 35, 44
better parempi 35, 37, 53
between -n välissä/välillä 35
beware varoa 61
bicycle (polku)pyörä 51
big suuri 35; iso 53
bigger suurempi 37
bill *(check)* lasku 37, 44

bitter kitkerä 44
black and white *(film)* mustavalkoinen 55
black mustaa 53
blood veri 58
blood pressure verenpaine 58
blouse puseron 54
blue sinistä 53
boat lautta 47
boat service vesiliikenne 47
body ruumis 57
bone luu 57
booking office lipunmyynti 45
bookshop kirjakauppa 52
boots saappaat 54
botanical gardens kasvitieteellinen puutarha 49
boyfriend poikaystävä 33
bra rintaliivit 65
brakes jarruja 48
breakfast aamiainen 38
bridge silta 48, 50
brown ruskeata 53
bruise mustelma 57
burn palohaava 57
bus bussi 46
business trip liikematka 33
but mutta 35
butcher's lihakauppa 52

C

call, to *(help)* kutsua 62
call, to *(telephone)* soittaa 56
camera kamera 55
camp, to leiriytyä 36
campsite leirintäalue 36
can *(tin)* tölkki 55
Canada Kanada 33
cancel peruuttaa 45
car auto 47
car hire *(rental)* auton vuokraus 47
cash desk kassa 52, 61
castle linna 49
cathedral tuomiokirkko 49
caution varo 61
change muuttaa 45
change, to *(money)* vaitoraha 56
charge maksu 47
cheap halpa 35, 53
cheaper halvempi 37
check in, to ilmoittautua 45
check out, to lähteä 37
chemist's *(drugstore)* apteekki 52, 54
city centre keskusta 49
close, to sulkea 49

FINNISH DICTIONARY

Suomi sanakirja

clothing vaatetus 54
coach *(long-distance bus)* bussi 46, 47
cold kylmä 35, 44, 62
colour väri 52, 55
come, to tulla 38
condoms kondomeja 54
confirm vahvistaa 45
cotton puuvillaa 54
credit card luottokortti 44, 53
crossing ylitys 47
cruise risteily 47
cup kuppi 38
currency exchange office valuutanvaihtopaikka 56
cut (viilto)haava 57
cycle racing pyöräkilpailut 51

D
dance tanssi 50
danger vaara 61
dark pimeä 36; tumma 35, 53
date päivä 37; päivämäärä 59
date of birth syntymäaika 37
day päivä 36, 47, 58, 59
December joulukuu 59
decision päätös 36
denim farkkukangasta 54
Denmark Tanska 61
dentist hammaslääkäri 52, 58
deodorant deoderanttia 54
department store tavaratalo 52
diabetic sokeritautinen 58
diesel dieselöljyä 48
dining-room ruokasali 37
dinner päivällinen 38
discotheque disko 50
dizzy huimaus 58
doctor lääkäri 57, 62
doctor's office *(surgery)* vastaanotto 57
dog koira 61
dollar dollari 56
double bed kaksoisvuode 36
double room kahden hengen huone 36
down alas/alhaalla 35
downstairs alakerrassa 35
dress leningin 54
drink juoma 43
drive, to ajaa 48
drugstore *(chemist's)* apteekki 52
during aikana 35

E
ear korva 57
early aikainen 35
east itä 49
eight kahdeksan 60
emergency hätä 62
emergency exit hätäuloskäynti 37, 61
England Englanti 61

English *(language)* englantilainen 34, 49, 55, 57
entrance fee pääsymaksu 49
entrance sisään(käynti) 46, 61
evening ilta 50, 59
exchange rate vaihtokurssi 56
exhibition näyttely 49
exit ulos(käynti) 45, 61
expensive kallis 35
express pika 56
expression ilmaisu 33, 52
eye silmä 57

F
face kasvot 57
family perhe 33
far kaukana 35
fare maksu 46, 47
February helmikuu 59
few, a muutama 35, 36
fill up, to täyttää 48
filling station bensiiniasema 48
filling *(tooth)* paikka 58
film filmi 55
find, to löytää 34, 57
fine *(well)* hyvä 33, 36
finger sormi 57
Finland Suomi 61
Finnish *(language)* suomi 34
first ensimmäinen 46, 61
first class ensimmäinen luokka 45
first name etunimi 37
fitting room sovituskoppi 54
five viisi 60
fjord vuono 50
flight lento 45
food ruoka 44
foot jalka 57
football *(soccer)* jalkapallo 51
for -n suuntaan/-n sijaan 35
forbidden . . . kielletty 61
forest metsä 50
fork haarukka 38
four neljä 60
free *(of charge)* vapaa 61
free *(vacant)* vapaa 35
Friday perjantai 60
from -n suunnasta 35
frost damage kelirikko 48

G
general yleinen 37, 52
gentlemen *(toilets)* miehille 61
get, to *(taxi)* hankkia 37, 47
get off, to *(transport)* nousta pois 46
girlfriend tyttöystävä 33
give, to antaa 58; saada 44, 48
glacier jäätikkö 50
glass lasi 38

gloves hansikkaat 54
go away! mankää tiehenne! 62
go out, to *(rendez-vous)* lähteä ulos 50
golf course golf-rata 51
good hyvä 35, 38, 53, 58
good afternoon (hyvää) päivää 33
good morning (hyvää) huomenta 33
good night hyvää yötä 33
good-bye näkemiin 33
Great Britain Iso Britannia 61
green vihreää 53
grey harmaata 53
grocer's sekatavarakauppa 52, 55
guide opas 49

H
hair-cut tukanleikku 55
hairdresser kampaaja 52
half, a puolikas 61
hand käsi 57
handbag käsilaukku 62
harbour satama 47, 49
have, to -lla on 36, 37, 55; saada 34
he hän 56
head pää 57
health insurance sairausvakuutus 58
heart sydän 57
heavy painava 53
hello hei 33, 56
help, to auttaa 34, 46, 52
help! apua! 62
her hänelle 56
here täällä 47
hi terve 33
him hänelle 56
hire, to vuokrata 47, 51
holiday loma 33
home town kotikaupunki 37
hot kuuma 35, 62
how kuinka 34
how far kuinka kaukana 34
how long kuinka kauan 34, 46, 47, 58
how many kuinka monta 34, 50, 53
how much kuinka paljon 34; paljonko 49, 53
hundred sata 60
hurt, to koskee 58
husband aviomies 33

I
ice hockey jäähockey 15
ill sairas 62
in -n sisässä/-llä 35
include, to sisällyttää 47
included sisältyy 44
information neuvonta 45, 62
injection ruiske 58
inquiries tiedusteluja 46
insect bite hyönteisen purema 57

insect repellent hyttysöljyä 54
inside sisään/sisälle 35
insurance vakuutus 47
introductions esittely 33
Ireland Irlanti 61
island saari 50

J
January tammikuu 59
jersey villatakin 54
journey *(trip)* matka 46
July heinäkuu 29
June kesäkuu 59

K
key avain 37
kilo kilo 55
knee polvi 57
knife veitsi 38

L
lace pitsiä 54
ladies *(toilets)* naisille 62
lake järvi 50, 51
landmark maamerkki 50
large suurta kokoa 53
last viimeinen 46
late myöhäinen 35
leather nahkaa 54
leave, to lähteä 46, 47
left vasen 44, 49
left-luggage office *(baggage check)* matkatavarasäilytys 45
leg sääri 57
lift *(elevator)* hissi 37, 62
light *(colour)* vaalea 35, 53; *(weight)* kevyt 53
like, to pitää 53
like to, to haluta 50
linen pellavaa 54
litre litra 48, 55
little, a vähän 35
local paikallinen 38
look at, to *(examine)* katsoa 58
lose, to kadottaa 62
lost eksynyt 62
lost property *(lost and found)* **office** löytötavaratoimisto 45
lot, a paljon 35
luggage lockers säilytyslokerot 45
lunch lounas 38
lung keuhko 57

M
mail posti 56
main tärkein 52

March maaliskuu 59
market (kauppa)tori 49
match ottelu 51
May toukokuu 59
me minut, minulle 34, 47
mean, to tarkoittaa 34
mechanic korjaaja 48
mend, to *(fix)* korjata 48
menu ruokalista 38
message viesti 56
midnight keskiyö 59
mileage kilometrimäärä 47
milk maito 55
million miljoona 60
minute minuutti 47
mistake virhe 44
moisturizing cream kosteusvoidetta 54
moment, at the hetkellä 52
Monday maanantai 60
morning aamulla 59
mountain vuori 50
mountaineering vuoristokiipeily 51
mouth suu 57
muscle lihas 57
museum museo 49
my minun 37

N

name nimi 56
napkin *(serviette)* lautasliina 38
narrow kapea 48
nationality kansallisuus 37
nauseous pahoinvointi 58
near lähellä/lähelle 35
nearest lähin 48, 51, 52, 56
nerve hermo 57
never ei koskaan 35
New Zealand Uusi-Seelanti 61
newspaper sanomalehti 55
newsstand lehtikioski 52
next seuraava 46, 47
next to vieressä 35, 49
night yö 59
nine yhdeksän 60
no ei 33
noisy meluisa 36
none ei yhtään 35
noon keskipäivä 59
north pohjoinen 49
Norway Norja 61
nose nenä 57
not ei 34, 35
nothing ei mitään 35
notice varoitus 61
November marraskuu 59
now nyt 35
number *(house)* numero 37

O

occupation ammatti 37
occupied varattu 35, 62
October lokakuu 59
on -n päällä/päälle 35
once kerran 61
one yksi 60
only vain 35, 36
open avoinna 62
open, to avata 49
opposite vastapäätä 49
or tai 35
orange oranssia 53
order, to tilata 44, 52, 53
order, out of epäkunnossa 62
outside ulkona/ulos 35
overnight yhden yön 36

P

pardon anteeksi 33
park, to pysäköidä 37
parking pysäköimtipaikka 48
part osa 57
passport passi 37, 62
path polku 50
pay, to maksaa 44
penni *(currency)* penni 56
perhaps ehkä 35
petrol *(gasoline)* bensiini 48
picnic piknik 44
place paikka 37
place of birth syntypaikka 37
plane lento(kone) 45
plate lautanen 38
platform laituri 45
play, to esittää 50
please olkaa hyvä 33
police poliisi 62
porter kantaja 46
post posti 56
postcard postikortti 56
post office posti 52, 56
pound *(sterling)* punta 56
prescription resepti 58
price hinta 36
private oma 36; yksityinen 62
pull, to vetää 62
puncture *(flat)* puhennut rengas 48
push, to työntää 62

Q

quality laatu 52
quarter neljännestä/vartin 59
question kysymys 34
quieter rauhallisempi 37

R

radio radio 36

rash ihottummaa 57
razor blades partakoneen teriä 54
receipt kuitti 58
recommend, to suositella 38, 58
rectangular suorakulmainen 53
red punaista 53
regular *(petrol)* matalaoktaanista 48
repeat, to toistaa 34
requirements tarpeita 37
reservation varaus 36, 45
reservations office paikanvaraus 45
reserve, to varata 38, 50
reserved varattu 62
restaurant ravintola 38
return ticket *(round trip)* menopaluu 45
riding *(horse-back)* ratsastus 15
right *(direction)* oikea 35, 44, 49
river joki 50, 51
road tie 49, 62
road sign liikennemerkki 48
road works tietyö 48
room huone 36
round pyöreä 53

S
sale alennusmyynti/ale 62
salty suolainen 44
Saturday lauantai 60
sauna saunaa 36
scarf huivin 54
Scotland Skotlanti 61
sea meri 50
seat paikkaa 50
second toinen 61
second class toinen luokka 45
see, to nähdä 36
send, to lähettää 48, 56
September syyskuu 59
set menu vakiolista 38
seven seitsemän 60
shampoo shampoota 54
shape muoto 52
she hän 56
shirt paidan 54
shivery puistatuksi 58
shoes kengät 54
shop *(store)* myymälä 52
shopping area ostosalue 49, 2
shoulder olkapää 57
show näytös 50
shower suihku 36
sign kyltti 61
signature allekirjoitus 37
silk silkkiä 54
since alkaen 35
single room yhden hengen huone 36
single ticket *(one-way)* menolippu 45
six kuusi 60
skates luistimet 51

skating rink luistinrata 51
ski, to hiihtää 51
ski jumping mäkihyppy 51
skiing hiihto 51
skiing, cross-country murtomaahiihto 51
skiing, downhill laskettelu 51
skiing equipment hiihtovarusteet 51
skin iho 57
skirt hameen 54
skis sukset 51
slice siivu 55
slowly hitaasti 48
small pieni 35, 36, 53
smoking tupakointi 62
snack välipala 44
soap saippuaa 54
socks (nilkka)sukat 54
soon pian 35
sort laatu 55
south etelä 49
South Africa Etelä-Afrikka 61
souvenir muistoesine 55
souvenir shop matkamuistomyymälä 52
speak, to puhua 34, 56, 57
specialist erikoislääkäri 58
specimen näyte 58
speed limit nopeusrajoitus 48
speed skating pikaluistelu 51
spoon lusikka 38
sport urheilu 51
spring kevät 59
square neliskulmainen 53
stamp postimerkki 56
stay, to pysyä 58; viipyä 36
steal, to varastaa 62
sting pistos 57
stock, out of ei varastossa 52
stomach *(inside/outside)* maha/vatsa 57
stop, to *(catch)* ottaa kiinni 52; pysäkki 47
store *(shop)* myymälä 52
straight ahead suoraan eteenpäin49
street katu 37
sturdy tanakka 53
suede mokkaa 54
summer kesä 59
sun-tan cream aurinkovoidetta 54
Sunday sunnuntai 60
super *(petrol)* korkeaoktaanista 48
supermarket valintamyymälä 52
surgery *(doctor's office)* vastaanotto 57
surname sukunimi 37
Sweden Ruotsi 61
sweet makea 44
swelling turvotusta 57
swim, to uida 51
swimming uinti 51
swimming pool uimaallas 51
swimming trunks uimahousut 54
swimsuit uimapuvun 54

table 172 zoo

T

table pöytä 38
take, to *(buy, accept)* ottaa 36, 53
take, to *(time)* kestää 46, 47
tampons tampooneja 54
taxi taksi 37, 47
telephone puhelin 56
television televisio 36
tell, to kertoa 56
temperature lämpö 58
ten kymmenen 60
tennis tennis 51
tennis court tennis-kenttä 51
test, to kokeilla 48
thank you kiitos 33
theatre teatteri 50
then sitten 35
thief varas 62
third kolmas 61
this tämä 53
three kolme 60
throat *(inside/outside)* kurkku/kaula 57
through läpi 35
Thursday torstai 60
ticket lippu 45
ticket office lipputoimisto 45
tights sukkahousut 54
time kello 59
tin *(can)* tölkki 55
to -n kohdalle 35
today tänään 59
toilet(s) WC(:t) 36, 37
tomorrow huomenna 57, 59
tongue kieli 57
tonight tänä iltana 50
too liian 36, 44
too *(also)* myös 35
toothache hammassärky 58
toothpaste hammastahnaa 54
torch taskulamppu 53
touch, to koskea 61
tourist office matkailutoimisto 48
towards -a kohti 35
tower torni 49
town kaupunki 50
town centre kaupungin keskusta 46
tram *(streetcar)* raitiovaunu 46
translate, to kääntää 34
trousers (pitkät) housut 54
try on, to sovittaa 54
T-shirt T-paidan 54
Tuesday tiistai 60
twice kahdesti 61
twin beds kaksi vuodetta 36
two kaksi 60

U

under alla/alle 35
understand, to ymmärtää 34
United States USA (Yhdysvallat) 33

unleaded lyijytöntä 48
until asti 35
up ylös/ylhäällää 35
upstairs yläkerrassa 35
use, to käyttö 56
useful hyödyllinen 35

V

vacancies, no täynnä 62
vacancy vapaa huone 35
vacant vapaa 62
vegetarian kasvissyöjä 38
velvet samettia 54
very tosi 35

W

wait, to odottaa 47, 62
waiting room odotushuone 45
wallet lompakko 62
want, to haluta 50
water vesi 34
waterfall vesiputous 49
Wednesday keskiviikko 60
week viikko 36, 47
west länsi 49
what mitä 34, 52
when milloin 34, 49
where missä 33, 34, 45, 49
which mikä, kumpi 34
white valkoista 53
who kuka 34
why miksi 34
wife vaimo 33
wine viini 34
winter talvi 59
with mukana 33; -n kanssa 35
without ilman 35
wonderful ihana 50
wool villaa 54
word sana 35
worse huonompi 35
wound haava 57
write down, to kirjoittaa 53
wrong *(incorrect)* väärä 35, 49

Y

yellow keltaista 53
yes kyllä 33
yesterday eilen 59
yet vielä 35

Z

zero nolla 60
zoo eläintarha 49

English–Icelandic dictionary

| *f* feminine | *m* masculine | *nt* neuter |

A

able, to be að geta 66
above fyrir ofan 76
accept, to að taka 85
address heimilisfang *nt* 79, 80
admittance aðgangur *m* 94
after fyrir aftan 80
air conditioning loftræsting *f* 68
airmail flugpóstur *m* 88
a lot mikið 67
American amerísk 87
amount upphæð *f* 76
and og 67
anti-freeze frostlögur *m* 80
any einhver 68
anything eitthvað 69, 84
appointment viðtalstími *m* 89
April apríl *m* 91
arm handleggur *m* 89
arrive, to að koma 78
ashtray öskubakki *m* 70
aspirin aspirín *nt* 86
August ágúst *m* 91
Australia Ástralía 93
autumn *(fall)* haust *nt* 92

B

back bak *nt* 89
bad slæmur 67
baggage farangur *m* 78
baker's bakarí *nt* 84
balcony svalir *f* 68
bank banki *m* 88
bath bað *nt* 68
bathroom baðherbergi *nt* 69
battery *(car)* rafgeymir *m* 80
battery *(small)* rafhlöður *f* 87
be, to að vera 66
beach strönd *f* 81
bed rúm *nt* 68, 90
beer bjór *m* 75
begin, to að byrja 82
behind á eftir 67
below undir 67, 76
better betri 67, 69
between á milli 67
beware varist 94
bicycle hjól *nt* 83
big stór 67, 69, 85

bill *(check)* reikningur *m* 69, 76
bitter beiskur 76
black svartur 85
black and white *(film)* svart-hvít (filma) 87
blood blóð *nt* 90
blood pressure blóðþrýstingur *m* 90
blouse blússa *f* 86
blue blár 85
boat bátur *m* 78
boat service báta þjónusta *f* 78
body líkami *m* 89
bone bein *nt* 89
bookshop bókaverslun *f* 84
boots stígvél *nt* 86
botanical gardens grasagarður *m* 81
boyfriend vinur *m* 65
bra brjóstahaldari *m* 86
brake fluid bremsuvökvi *m* 80
brakes hemlar *m* 79
breakdown bilun *f* 80
breakfast morgunverður *m* 70
bridge brú *f* 79, 81
brown brúnn 85
bruise skráma *f* 89
burn brunasár *nt* 89
bus vagn *m* 78
business viðskipti *nt* 65
busy upptekinn 82
but en 67
butcher's kjötbúð *f* 84
buy, to að kaupa 87

C

call, to *(telephone)* að hringja 88, 94
camera myndavél *f* 87
camp, to að tjalda 68
campsite tjaldstæði *nt* 68
can *(tin)* dós *f* 87
Canada Kanada 93
cancel afpöntun *f*, afturköllun *f* 77
car bíll *m* 79
car hire *(rental)* bílaleiga *f* 79
cash desk kassi *m* 84, 93
cathedral dómkirkja *f* 81
caution varúð *f* 94
change breyting *f* 77
change, to *(money)* að skipta 88
charge greiðsla *f* 79

cheap ódýr 67, 69, 85
check, to að athuga 80
check in, to að skrá sig inn 77
check out, to að skrá sig út 69
chemist's *(drugstore)* apótek *nt* 84, 86
cinema bíó *nt* 82
city centre miðbær *m* 81
close, to að loka 81
clothing fatnaður *m* 86
coach *(long-distance bus)* rúta *f*,
langferðabíll *m* 77
coat kápa *f* 86
cold kaldur 67, 69, 76, 94
colour litur *m* 84
colour (film) lit (filma) 87
come, to að koma 65, 70
condoms smokkur *m* 86
confirm að staðfesta 77
confirmation staðfesting *f* 68
coolant kælivökvi *m* 80
cotton bómull *f* 86
credit card greiðslukort *nt* 76, 85
crossing ferð *f* 78
crown *(currency)* króna *f* 84, 88
cup bolli *m* 70
currency exchange office
gjaldeyrisafgreiðsla *f* 88
cut skurður *m* 89
cycle racing hjólreiðakeppni *f* 83

D
dance dansleikur *m* 82
danger hætta *f* 93
dark dimmur 69, 85
date dagsetning *f* 69, 91
day dagur *m* 68, 79, 90, 91
December desember *m* 91
decision ákvörðun *f* 68
delicatessen sérverslun *f* með tilbúinn
mat *m* 84
denim denímefni *nt* 86
Denmark Danmörk 93
dentist tannlæknir *m* 84, 90
deodorant svitakrem *nt* 86
department store stórverslun *f* 84
diabetic sykursýkis- 90
diesel díselolía *f* 80
dining-room stofa *f* 69
dinner kvöldverður *m* 70
discoteque diskótek *nt* 82
dish réttur *m* 70
dizzy með svima 90
doctor læknir *f* 94
doctor's office *(surgery)* læknisstofa *f*
89
dog hundur *m* 94

dollar dollari *m* 88
double tveggjamanna 68
double bed hjónarúm *nt* 68
down niður 67
downstairs niðri 67
dress kjóll *m* 86
drink drykkur *m* 75
drive, to að aka 79
drugstore *(chemist's)* apótek *nt* 84
during á meðan 67, 91

E
ear eyra *nt* 89
early snemma 67
east austur 80
eight átta 92
emergency neyðarástand 94
emergency exit neyðarútgangur *m* 69
England England 93
English ensk 87
English *(language)* enska *f* 66, 81, 89
enjoy, to að njóta 76
enjoyable ánægjulegur 69
entertainment skemmtanir *f* 82
entrance inngangur *m* 77, 94
evening kvöld *m* 82, 91
exchange rate gengi *nt* 88
exhibition sýning *f* 81
exit útgangur *m* 77; útgöngudyr *f* 94
expensive dýr 67
express hraðpóstur *m* 88
eye auga *nt* 89

F
face andlit *nt* 89
family fjölskylda *f* 65
far langt 67
fax símbréf *nt* 88
February febrúar *m* 91
fee gjald *nt* 81
feel, to að finna 90
few fáir 67, 68
fill up, to að fylla 79
filling *(tooth)* fylling *f* 90
filling station bensínstöð *f* 79
film filma *f* 87
find, to að finna 80,
fine *(well)* vel 65; *(good)* ágætt 68
finger fingur *m* 89
Finland Finnland 93
first fyrstur 78, 93
first class fyrsta farrými *nt* 77
first name skírnarnafn *nt* 69
fishing veiðar *f* 83
fitting room mátunarklefi *m* 85

five fimm 92
fjord fjörður nt 81
flight flug nt 77
food matur m 76
foot fótleggur m 89
football (soccer) fótbolti m 82, 83
forbidden bannaður 94
fork gaffall m 70
four fjórir 92
free laus 94
Friday föstudagur m 91
from frá 67
frost frost nt 79
fur hat loðhattur m 86

G

general almennur 69, 84
gentlemen (toilets) herrasnyrting f 93
get, to að fá 66; (fetch) að ná í 69, 79
get off, to (transport) að fara út úr 78
geyser goshver m 81
girlfriend vinkona f 65
give, to að gefa 76, 80, 90
glacier jökull m 81
glass glas nt 70
gloves hanskar m 86
go away, to fara til 94
go out, to (rendez-vous) að fara út 82
golf course golfvöllur m 82
good afternoon góðan dag m 65
good góður 67, 70, 85, 90
good morning góðan dag m 65
good night góða nótt f 65
good-bye bless 65
Great Britain Stór Bretland 93
green grænn 85
grey grár 85
grocery grænmetisverslun f 84, 87
guide leiðsögumaður m 81

H

hair-cut klipping f 87
hairdresser hárgreiðslustofa f 84
half hálfur 93
hand hönd f 89
handbag handtaska f 94
harbour höfn f 78, 81
have, to að hafa 68, 69, 87
he hann 88
head höfuð nt 89
health insurance sjúkratrygging f 90
heart hjarta nt 89
heavy þungur 85
hello halló 65, 88

help, to að hjálpa 66, 78, 84
help! hjálp! 94
her henni 88
here hér 68, 79
hi hæ 65
him honum 88
hire, to að leigja 79, 83
holiday frí nt 65
home town heimabær m 69
horse-back riding reiðmennska f 83
hot heitur 67, 69, 93
how hvernig 66
how far hversu langt 66
how long hvað lengi 66, 78, 85, 90
how much hvað mikið 66, 81, 82, 85
hundred hundrað 92
hurt, to að finna til 90
husband eiginmaður m 65

I

ice hockey íshokkí nt 83
Iceland Ísland 93
Icelandic Íslensk 65
ill veikur 94
include, to að vera innifalið 79
included innifalið 76
information upplýsingar f 77, 94
injection að fá sprautu f 90
inquiries upplýsingar f 78
insect bite skordýrabit nt 89
insect repellent skordýrafæla f 89
inside inni 67
introduce, to að kynna fyrir 65
introductions kynningar f 65
Ireland Írland 93
island eyja f 81

J

January janúar m 91
jersey prjónapeysa f 86
journey (trip) ferð f 78
July júlí m 91
June júní m 91

K

key lykill m 69
kilo kíló nt 87
km kílómetrar m 79
knee hné nt 89
knife hnífur m 70
krona (currency) krona f 88

L

lace blúnda f 86
ladies *(toilets)* kvennasnyrting f 94
lake stöðuvatn nt 81, 83
landmark kennileiti nt 81
large stór 85
last síðastur 78
late seint 67
leather leður nt 86
leave alone, to að skilja eftir 94
leave, to að fara 78
left vinstri 76, 80
left-luggage office *(baggage check)* óskilafarangur m 77
leg fótur m 89
letter *(mail)* bréf nt 88
lift *(elevator)* lyfta f 69, 94
light *(colour)* ljós 85, *(weight)* léttur 85
like, to að líka við 85
linen lín nt 86
liquor store vínbúð f 84
litre lítri m 80, 87
little, a lítið 67
local þjóðar- 70
look at, to *(examine)* að skoða 90
lost property (lost and found) office tapað fundið 77
lost villtur 94
luggage farangur m 94
luggage lockers geymsluskápar m 77
lunch hádegisverður m 70
lung lungu nt 89

M

mail póstur m 88
main aðal 84
March mars m 91
market markaður m 81
match leikur m 82
May maí m 91
me mér 66, 79
mean, to að þýða 66
mechanic viðgerðarmaður m 80
mend, to *(fix)* að gera við 80
menu matseðill m 70, 71
message skilaboð nt 88
midnight miðnætti nt 91
mileage kílómetragjald nt 79
milk mjólk f 87
million miljón f 93
minute mínúta f 79
mistake mistök 76
moisturizing cream rakakrem nt 86
moment augnablik nt 84
Monday mánudagur m 91
more meira 66

morning morgunn m 91
mountain fjall nt 81
mountaineering fjallganga f 83
mouth munnur m 89
muscle vöðvi m 89
museum safn nt 81
my mitt, minn 65, 69

N

name nafn nt 68, 69, 88
napkin *(serviette)* servétta f, munnþurrka f 70
narrow þröngur 79
nationality þjóðerni nt 69
nauseous óglatt 90
near nálægt 67, 79, 82, 84 ,88
nerve taugar 89
never aldrei 67
New Zealand Nýja Sjáland 93
newsagent blaðasala f 84
newspaper dagblað nt 87
next næstur 78
night nótt f 92
nine níu 92
no nei 65
noisy hávær 69
noon hádegi nt 91
north norður 80
Norway Noregi 93
nose nef nt 89
not ekki 66, 67
nothing ekkert 67
notice tilkynning f 93
November nóvember m 91
now núna 67
number *(house)* númer nt, húsnúmer nt 69

O

occupation starf nt 69
occupied upptekinn 67, 93
October október m 91
oil olía f 80
old gamall 67
once einu sinni 93
one einn 92
only aðeins 67, 68
open opið 94
open, to að opna 81
or eða 67
orange appelsínugulur 85
order, out of bilað 93
order, to að panta 76, 84, 85
outside úti 67

overnight eina nótt f 68

P

park, to að leggja bíl 69
parking bílastæði nt 79
part hluti m 89
passport vegabréf nt 69, 94
path stígur m 81
pay, to að borga 76
per day á dag m 79
perhaps ef til vill 67
petrol (gasoline) bensín nt 79, 80
picnic lautarferð f 76
place staður m 69, 80
place of birth fæðingarstaður m 69
plane flugvél f 77
plate diskur m 70
platform pallur m 77
play, to að leika 82
please afsakið 65
pleased ánægður 65
point of interest athyglisverður staður m 81
police lögregla f 94
porter dyravörður m 78
post office pósthús nt 84, 88
postage póstburðargjald nt 88
postcard póstkort nt 88
pound (sterling) pund nt 88
prescription lyfseðill m 90
price verð nt 68
private einka- 68, 93
public almennings- 88
pull, to að draga 93
puncture (flat) sprungið dekk nt 80
push, to að ýta 94

Q

quality gæði nt 84
quarter fjórðungur m 93; (hour) korter nt 91
question spurning f 66
quieter rólegri 69

R

radio útvarp nt 68
rash útbrot nt 89
razor blades rakvélablöð nt 86
receipt kvittun f 90
recommend, to að mæla með 70, 90
rectangular rétthyrndur 85
red rauður 85
registered mail ábyrgðarpóstur m 88
regular (petrol) venjulegt bensín nt 80

repeat, to að endurtaka 66
requirements kröfur f 69
reservation pöntun 68, 77
reservations office pantanir f 77
reserve, to að panta 70, 82
reserved frátekinn 93
restaurant veitingastaður m 70
return (round trip) báðar leiðir f 77
riding (horse-back) reiðmennska 83
right (correct) réttur 67, 78; (direction) hægri 76, 80
river á f 81, 83
road vegur m 80, 93
road sign vegvísir m 79
room herbergi nt 68
round kringlóttur 85

S

sale útsala f 94
salty saltur 76
Saturday laugardagur m 91
sauna gufubað nt 68
scarf slæða f 86
Scotland Skotland 93
sea sjór m 81
seat sæti nt 82
second annar 93
second class annað farrými. nt 77
see, to að sjá 68
see, to (visit) að heimsækja 90
send, to að senda 80, 88
September september m 91
serve, to að þjóna 70
service þjónusta f 76
set menu fastur matseðill m 70
seven sjö 92
shampoo sjampó nt 86
shape lögun f 84
she hún 88
shirt skyrta f 86
shivery skjálfandi 90
shoe skór m 86
shop verslun f 81, 84
shopping area verslunarsvæði nt 84
shoulder öxl f 89
show sýning f 82
show, to að sýna 85
shower sturta f 68
sign merki nt 93
signature undirskrift f 69
silk silki nt 86
since síðan 67
single einsmanns 68
single (one-way) aðra leiðina f 77
six sex 92
skates skautar m 83

ICELANDIC DICTIONARY

skating rink skautasvell *nt* 83
ski skíði *nt* 83
ski, to að skíða 83
ski jumping skíðastökk *nt* 83
skiing skíðamennska *f* 83
skiing, cross-country skíðaganga *f* 83
skiing, downhill brun *m* 83
skiing equipment skíðabúnaður *m* 83
skin húð *f* 89
skirt pils *nt* 86
slice sneið *f* 87
slowly hægt 66, 79
small lítill 67, 69, 85
smoking reykingar 94
snack smáréttir *m* 76
soap sápa *f* 86
sock sokkar *m* 86
soon bráðum 67
sort tegund *f* 87
South Africa Suður Afríka 93
south suður 80
souvenir minjagripur *m* 87
souvenir shop minjagripaverslun *f* 84
speak, to að tala 66, 88
specialist sérfræðingur *m* 90
specimen sýni *nt* 90
speed limit hraðatakmarkanir *f* 79
speed skating skautahlaup *nt* 83
spoon skeið *f* 70
sport íþróttir *f* 82
spray, insect skordýraeitur *nt* 86
spring vor *nt* 92
square ferhyrndur 85
stamp frímerki *nt* 88
stay dvöl *f* 69
stay, to að dvelja 68, 90
sting sár *nt* eftir stungu *f* 89
stock, out of ekki fáanlegur 84
stolen stolinn 94
stomach magi *m* 89
stop, to að stoppa 79, 94
store *(shop)* verslun *f* 84
straight ahead beint áfram 80
street gata *f* 69
suede rúskinn *nt* 86
summer sumar *nt* 92
sun-tan cream sólkrem *nt* 86
Sunday sunnudagur *m* 91
super *(petrol)* súper bensín *nt* 80
supermarket stórmarkaður *m* 84
surgery *(doctor's office)* læknisstofa *f* 89
Sweden Svíþóð 93
sweet sætur 76
swelling bólga *f* 89
swim, to að synda 83
swimming sund *nt* 83

swimming pool sundlaug *f* 83
swimming trunks sundskýla *f* 86
swimsuit sundbolur *m* 86

T
table borð *nt* 70
take, to að taka 68, 78
tampons tíðatappar *m* 86
taxi leigubíll *m* 69, 79
telegram skeyti *nt* 88
telephone sími *m* 88
television sjónvarp *nt* 68
tell, to að segja frá 88
temperature hiti *m* 90
ten tíu 92
tennis court tennisvöllur *m* 82
tennis tennis *m* 83
test, to að prófa 79
thank you takk fyrir 65
thanks takk 65
theatre leikhús *nt* 82
then þá 67
these þessir hérna 76
thief þjófur *m* 94
third þriðji 93
third, a þriðjungur *m* 93
those þessir þarna 76
three þrír 92
throat háls *m* 89
through í gegnum 67
Thursday fimmtudagur *m* 91
ticket miði *m* 77, 82
ticket office miðasala *f* 77
tights sokkabuxur *f* 86
time tími *m* 91
tin *(can)* dós *f* 87
today í dag *m* 92
toilets snyrtingar *f* 68, 69
tomorrow á morgun *m* 89, 92
tongue tunga *f* 89
tonight í kvöld *nt* 82
too of 69, 76; *(also)* líka 67
toothache tannpína *f* 90
toothpaste tannkrem *nt* 86
torch blys 87
touch, to að snerta 94
tour ferð *f* 78
tourist office ferðaskrifstofa *f* 81
towards í áttina til 67
town borg *f* 82
town centre *(downtown)* miðbær *m* 78
tram *(streetcar)* sporvagn *m* 78
translate, to að þýða 66
travel, to að ferðast 77
trousers síðbuxur *f* 86

íslensk Orðabók

try on, to að máta 85
T-shirt bolur *m* 86
Tuesday þriðjudagur *m* 91
twice tvisvar 93
twin beds tvö rúm *nt* 68
two tveir 92
tyre pressure loftþrýstingur *m* í dekkjum *nt* 80

U

under undir 67
underpants undirbuxur *f* 86
understand, to að skilja 66
unleaded blýlaust 80
up upp 67
upstairs uppi 67
use, to að nota 88
useful gagnlegur 67

V

vacancy laust pláss *nt* 68, 93
vacant laus 67, 94
vacation *(holiday)* frí *nt* 65
vegetarian grænmetisæta *f* 70
velvet flauel *nt* 86
very mjög 67
view útsýni *nt* 68

W

wait, to að bíða 79 ,94
waiting room biðstofa *f* 77
wallet seðlaveski *nt* 94
want, to að vilja 82
water vatn *nt* 75
waterfall foss *m* 81

Wednesday miðvikudagur *m* 91
week vika *f* 68, 79
west vestur 80
what hvað 66, 84
wheel chains keðjur *f* 80
when hvenær 66, 81
where hvar 65, 77, 81
which hver 66
white hvítur 85
who hver 66
why hvers vegna 66
wife eiginkona *f* 65
windscreen water gluggaúði *m* 80
wine vín *nt* 75
winter vetur *m* 92
with með 65, 67
without án 67
wonderful dásamlegur 82
wood skógur *m* 81
wool ull *f* 86
word orð *nt* 67
worse verri 67
wound sár *nt* 89
write down, to að skrifa niður 85
wrong rangur 67, 80

Y

yellow gulur 85
yes já 65
yesterday í gær 92
young ungur 67
your þinn

Z

zero núll 92
zoo dýragarður *m* 81

English–Norwegian dictionary

c common gender	nt neuter	pl plural

A
able, to be kunne 98
above over 99; ovenfor 109
accept, to ta 117
address adresse c 111
admission inngangsbillett c 115
after etter 99, 113
air conditioning air-conditioning 100
airmail med fly 120
a lot mye 99
American amerikansk 119
amount beløp 109
and og 99
any noe 100, 116
anything noe 101, 117
anywhere noe sted 115
appointment time c 121
April april c 123
arm arm c 121
ashtray askebeger nt 102
aspirin aspirin c 118
at ved 99
August august 123
Australia Australia 97
autumn høst c 123

B
back rygg c 121
back, to be komme tilbake 111, 120
bad dårlig 98
baker's bakeri nt 116
bank bank c 120
basic vanlige 97
bath bad nt 100
bathroom bad nt 101
battery batteri nt 119
be, to være 98
bed seng c 100, 122
beer øl nt 108
before (time) før 99
begin, to begynne 114
behind bak 99, 113
below under 99; nedenfor 109
better bedre 98, 101, 117
between mellom 99
bicycle sykkel c 115
bicycling sykling c 115
big stor 98, 117
bigger større 101
bill regning c 101, 109
bitter besk 108
black svart 117
black and white (film) svart-hvitt 119

blister blemme c 121
blood blod nt 122
blood pressure blodtrykk nt 122
blouse bluse c 118
blue blå 117
boat båt c 111
boat trip båttur c 111
body kropp c 121
bone ben nt 121
booking office billettkontor nt 110
bookshop bokhandel c 116
boot støvel c 118
botanical gardens botanisk hage c 113
bottle flaske c 108
boyfriend venn c 97
breakdown motorstopp c 113
breakfast frokost c 102, 103
brown brun 117
bruise blått merke nt 121
burn brannsår nt 121
bus buss c 111
business forretning c 97
busy opptatt 114
but men 99
butcher's slakter c 116

C
call, to (phone) ringe 120, 126
camera apparat nt 119
camp site campingplass c 100
camp, to campe 100
can (tin) boks c 119
Canada Kanada 97
cancel annullere 110
car bil c 101, 112
car hire (rental) bilutleie 112
cash desk kasse c 116, 125
castle slott nt 113
cathedral domkirke c 113
caution forsiktig 125
change, to (money) veksle 120
change, to (transport) bytte 111
cheap billig 98; rimelig 101, 117
check in, to sjekke inn 110
check out, to reise 101
chemist's (drugstore) apotek nt 116, 118
city centre sentrum nt 113
close, to stenge 113
clothing klær pl 118
coat (man's) frakk c 118; (woman's) kåpe c 118
cold kald 98, 108, 125
colour farge c 116, 119

NORWEGIAN DICTIONARY

good bra 98, 102, 117, 122
good afternoon god dag 97
good morning god morgen 97
good night god natt 97
good-bye adjø 97
Great Britain Storbritannia 97, 125
green grønn 117
grey grå 117
grocery matvarehandel *c* 116, 119
guide guide *c* 113

H

hair-cut klipp *c* 119
hairdresser *(ladies)* damefrisør *c* 116
hairdresser *(men)* herrefrisør *c* 116
half en halv 124
hand hånd *c* 121
handbag håndveske *c* 126
harbour havn *c* 113
have, to få 98; har 100, 101, 119, 120
he han 120
head hode *nt* 121
health insurance sykeforsikring *c* 122
heart hjerte *nt* 121
heavy tung 117
hello hallo 97, 120
help, to hjelpe 98, 116
help! hjelp! 126
her hennes 120
here her 111
hi hei 97
him ham 120
hire, to leie 112, 115
holiday *(vacation)* ferie *c* 97
home town hjemsted *nt* 101
hot varm 98, 125
hotel hotell *nt* 100
how far hvor langt 98, 112
how hvor 98
how long hvor lang 98, 111, 122
how much hvor mye 98, 117
hundred hundre 124
hurt, to gjøre vondt 122
husband mann *c* 97

I

ice hockey ishockey *c* 115
Iceland Island 125
ill syk 126
in i 99
include, to inkludere 112
included inkludert 109
information informasjon *c* 110
injection sprøyte *c* 122
inquiries forespørsel *c* 110
insect repellent insektmiddel *nt* 118
inside inne 99
insurance forsikring *c* 112
introduction *(social)* presentasjon *c* 97

Ireland Irland 125
island øy *c* 114

J

January januar *c* 123
July juli *c* 123
June juni *c* 123

K

key nøkkel *c* 101
kilo kilo *nt* 119
knee kne *nt* 121
knife kniv *c* 102
krone *(money)* krone *c* 117

L

lace knipling *c* 118
ladies *(toilets)* damer *c/pl* 125
lake *(inn)*sjø *c* 115
landmark landemerke *nt* 114
large stor 117
last siste 110, 111
late sen 98
leather lær *nt* 118
leave, to gå 111
leave alone, to la være i fred 126
left venstre 109, 113
left-luggage office *(baggage check)*
 bagasjeoppbevaring *c* 110
leg ben *nt* 121
letter *(mail)* brev *nt* 120
lift *(elevator)* heis *c* 101
light *(colour)* lys 117; *(weight)* lett 117
like, to like 117
linen lin *nt* 118
litre liter *c* 112, 119
little, a lite 99
local lokal 102
look at, to *(examine)* undersøke 122
lost mistet 126
lost, to be gå seg bort 126
lost property (lost and found) office
 hittegodskontor *nt* 110
luggage lockers oppbevaringsboks *c* 110
lunch lunsj *c* 102
lung lunge *c* 121

M

mail post *c* 120
main størst 116
many mange 98
March mars *c* 123
market torghandel *c* 113
match *(sport)* kamp *c* 115
May mai *c* 123
me meg 98
meadow eng *c* 114

Norsk ordliste

mean, to bety 98
mechanic mekaniker *c* 113
meet, to treffes 97
mend, to *(fix)* reparere 113
menu spisekart *nt* 103
message beskjed *c* 120
mileage kjørelengde *c* 112
milk melk *c* 119
million million 124
mineral water mineralvann *nt* 108
minute minutt *nt* 111
mistake feil *c* 109
moisturizing cream fuktighetskrem *c* 118
Monday mandag *c* 123
more litt 98
morning morgen *c* 123
mountain fjell *nt* 114
mouth munn *c* 121
muscle muskel *c* 121
museum museum *nt* 113
my min, mitt, mine 97

N
name navn *nt* 97, 120; *(surname)*
etternavn *nt* 101
napkin *(serviette)* serviett *c* 102
nationality nasjonalitet *c* 101
nauseous kvalm 122
near nær 99, 112, 115, 116, 120
neck nakke *c* 121
never aldri 99
New Zealand Ny-Zealand 125
newspaper avis *c* 119
newsstand aviskiosk *c* 116
next neste 110, 111
next to ved siden av 99, 113
night natt *c* 123
nine ni 124
no nei 97
no . . . *(forbidden)* . . . forbudt 112
noisy støyende 100
none ingen 99
north nord 113
Norway Norge 125
Norwegian *(language)* norsk 98
nose nese *c* 121
not ikke 98, 99
nothing ingenting, ikke noe 99
notice *(sign)* oppslag *nt* 125
November november *c* 123
now nå 99

O
occupation *(profession)* yrke *nt* 101
occupied opptatt 99
October oktober *c* 123
on på 99
once en gang 124

one en 124
only bare 99, 100
open, to åpne 113
opposite midt imot 113
or eller 99
orange oransje 117
order, out of i uorden 125
order, to bestille 108, 116, 117
outside ute 99
overnight natten over 100

P
pair par *nt* 118
pardon unnskyld 97
park, to parkere 101
parking parkering *c* 112
part del *c* 121
passport pass *nt* 101, 126
path sti *c* 114
pay, to betale 109
per day pr. dag 112
perhaps kanskje 99
petrol *(gasoline)* bensin *c* 112
picnic picnic *c* 109
place sted *nt* 101
place of birth fødested *nt* 101
plane fly *nt* 110
plate tallerken *c* 102
platform *(station)* perrong *c* 110
play, to *(theatre)* spille 114
please vær (så) snill å . . . , . . . takk 97
pleased hyggelig 97
police politi *nt* 126
post office postkontor *nt* 116, 120
postage porto *c* 120
postcard postkort *nt* 120
pound *(money)* pund *nt* 120
prescription resept *c* 122
private privat 125
pull, to trekke 125
puncture *(flat)* punkteringen 113
push, to *(open)* skyv 125

Q
quarter of an hour kvarter *nt* 123
question spørsmål *nt* 98
quiet rolig 101

R
radio radio *c* 100
rash utslett *nt* 121
rate *(of exchange)* kurs *c* 120
razor blade barberblad *nt* 118
receipt kvittering *c* 122
recommend, to anbefale 102, 122
rectangular rektangulær 117
red rød 117

regular *(petrol)* normal 112
repeat, to gjenta 98
reservation reservasjon c 110
reserve, to bestille 100, 102, 114
reserved reservert 125
restaurant restaurant c 102
return ticket *(round trip)* tur-returbillett c 110
right *(direction)* høyre 109, 113; *(correct)* riktig 99
river elv c 114, 115
road vei c 125
road sign trafikkskilt nt 112
road works veiarbeid, vegarbeid 112
room rom nt 100, 101
round rund 117

S
salty salt 108
Saturday lørdag c 123
sauna badstue c, sauna c 100
scarf skjerf nt 118
Scotland Skottland 125
sea sjø c 114
second annen, andre 124
second class andre klasse c 110
see, to se 100
send, to sende 113, 120
September september c 123
set menu meny c 102
seven sju 124
shampoo sjampo c 118
shape form c 116
she hun 120
shirt skjorte c 118
shoe sko c 118
shop *(store)* butikk c 116
shopping area handlestrøk nt 116
shoulder skulder c 121
show *(theatre)* forestilling c 114
shower dusj c 100
sign *(notice)* skilt nt 125
signature underskrift c 101
silk silke c 118
since siden 99
single enkel 100
single ticket *(one-way)* enkeltbillett c 110
six seks 124
skate skøyte c 115
skating rink skøytebane c 115
ski ski c 115
ski, to gå på ski 115
ski boots skistøvel c 115
ski jumping skihopping c 115
skiing, cross-country langrenn nt 115
skiing, downhill utforkjøring c 115
skin hud c 121
skirt skjørt nt 118
sleeping car sovevogn c 111
slice skive c 119

slowly langsom 98; sakte 112
small liten 98, 100, 117
smoking røyking c 125
snack småretter c/pl 109
soap såpe c 118
socks sokk c 118
soon snart 99, 121
sort slags nt/pl 119
south sør 113
South Africa Sør-Africa 125
souvenir suvenir c 119
souvenir shop suvenirbutikk c 116
speak, to snakke 98, 120, 121
specialist spesialist c 122
specimen *(medical)* prøve c 122
speed skating skøyteløp 115
spoon skje c 102
sport sport c 115
spring vår c 123
square *(town)* plass c, torg nt 113
square *(shape)* firkantet 117
stamp *(postage)* frimerke nt 120
stay, to bli 100
sting stikk nt 121
stock, out of utsolgt 116
stolen stjålet 126
stomach mage c 121
stop, to stanse 111
stop thief! stopp tyven! 126
store *(shop)* butikk c 116
straight ahead rett frem 113
sturdy robust, solid 117
suede semsket skinn 118
summer sommer c 123
sun-tan oil sololje c 118
Sunday søndag c 123
super *(petrol)* super 112
supermarket supermarked nt 116
surgery *(doctor's office)* legekontor nt 121
Sweden Sverige 125
sweet søt 108
swelling hevelse c 121
swim, to svømme 115
swimming svømming c 115
swimming pool svømmebasseng nt 115
swimming trunks badebukse c 118
swimsuit badedrakt c 118

T
table bord nt 102
take, to ta 100, 117
tampons tampong c 118
taxi drosje c 101, 111
telephone booth telefonkiosk c 120
telephone telefon c 120
television TV c 100
tell, to si 100
temperature temperatur c 122
ten ti 124

tennis tennis *c* 115
tennis court tennisbane *c* 115
thank, to takke 97
thanks takk 97
theatre teater *nt* 114
then da 99
there der 98
thief tyv *c* 126
think, to tror 109
third tredje 124
this denne 111
three tre 124
throat hals *c* 121
through gjennom 99
Thursday torsdag *c* 123
ticket billett *c* 110, 114
ticket office billettluke *c* 110
tights strømpebukse *c* 118
time *(clock)* klokken 123
tin *(can)* boks *c* 119
today i dag 123
toilets *(restroom)* toalett *nt* 100, 101
tomorrow i morgen 121, 123
tongue tunge *c* 121
tonight i kveld 114
too for 100, 108; *(also)* også 99
toothache tannpine *c* 122
toothpaste tannpasta *c* 123
torch *(flashlight)* lommelykt *c* 119
tourist office turistkontor *nt* 113
towards mot 99
town by *c* 114
town centre sentrum *nt* 111
train tog *nt* 110
tram *(streetcar)* trikk *c* 111
translate, to oversette 98
trousers langbukser *c/pl* 118
try on, to prøve 118
T-shirt T-skjorte *c* 118
Tuesday tirsdag *c* 123
twice ganger 124
two to 124

U
under under 99
underground *(subway)* t-bane *c* 111
underground station t-banestasjon *c* 111
understand, to forstå 98
United States USA 97
unleaded blyfri 112
until til 99
up opp 99
upstairs oppe 99
us oss 101

useful nyttig 99

V
vacancy ledige rom *nt* 100
vacant ledig 99
vacation ferie *c* 97
valley dal *c* 114
vegetarian vegetar(isk) 102
very meget 99

W
waiting room venterom *nt* 110
wallet lommebok *c* 126
water vann *nt* 108
waterfall foss *c* 114
Wednesday onsdag *c* 123
week uke *c* 100, 112
well bra 97
west vest 113
what hva 98, 113
when når 98, 113
where hvor 97, 98, 110, 113
which hvilken 98
white hvit 117
who hvem 98
why hvorfor 98
wife kone *c* 97
wine vin *c* 108
winter vinter *c* 123
with med 97, 99
without uten 99
wonderful veldig hyggelig 114
wool ull *c* 118
word ord *nt* 99
worse verre 98
wound sår *nt* 121
write, to skrive 117
wrong *(incorrect)* feil 99, 113

Y
yellow gul 117
yes ja 97
yesterday i går 123
yet ennå 99

Z
zero null 124
zoo dyrehage *c* 113

English–Swedish dictionary

c common gender   *nt* neuter   *pl* plural

A

able, to be kunna 130
above ovanför 131, 141
accept, to ta emot 149
address adress *c* 144
after efter 131, 145
air conditioning luftkonditionierung *c* 132
airmail med flyg 152
a lot mycket 131
American amerikansk 151
amount summa *c* 141
and och 131
any några 130, 132
anything något 133; någonting 148
apple äpple *nt* 151
appointment tid *c* 153
April april 155
arm arm *c* 153
ashtray askkopp *c* 134
aspirin aspirin *c* 149
August augusti 155
Australia Australien 129
autumn *(fall)* höst 155

B

back rygg *c* 153
back, to be *(return)* vara tillbaka 144; komma tillbaka 152
bad dålig 131
baggage bagage *nt* 143
baker's bageri *nt* 148
bank bank *c* 152
basic användbar 129
bath bad *nt* 132
bathroom badrum *nt* 133
battery batteri *nt* 151
be, to vara 130
bed säng *c* 132, 154
beer öl *c* 140
begin, to börja 146
behind bakom 131, 145
below nedanför 131, 141
better bättre 131, 133, 148
between mellan 131
beware varning för 157
bicycle cykel *c* 147
big stor 131, 148
bigger större 133
bill *(check)* nota *c* 141; räkning *c* 133
bitter besk 141
black svart 150
black and white *(film)* svart-vit 151

blood blod *nt* 154
blood pressure blodtryck *nt* 154
blouse blus *c* 150
blue blå 150
boat båt *c* 143
boat service båt *c* 143
body kropp *c* 153
bone ben *nt* 153
booking office biljettexpedition *c* 142
bookshop bokhandel *c* 148
boots stövlar *c/pl* 150
botanical gardens botanisk trädgård *c* 146
boyfriend pojkvän *c* 129
breakdown motorstopp *nt* 145
breakfast frukost *c* 134
bridge bro *c* 145
brown brun 150
bruise blåmärke *nt* 153
burn brännsår *nt* 153
bus buss *c* 143
business affär *c* 129
busy upptagen 146
but men 131
butcher's slaktare *c*, charkuteri *nt* 148

C

call, to *(help, telephone)* ringa 152, 157
camera kamera *c* 151
camp, to campa 132
campsite campingplats *c* 132
can *(tin)* burk *c* 151
cancel, to annullera 142
Canada Kanada 129
car bil *c* 144
car hire *(rental)* biluthyrning *c* 144
car racing biltävling *c* 147
cash desk kassa *c* 149, 157
castle slott *nt* 146
cathedral domkyrka *c* 146
caution varning *c* 157
change, to ändra 142
change, to *(money)* växla 152
cheap billig 148
cheaper billigare 133
check in, to checka in 142
check out, to checka ut 133
chemist's *(drugstore)* apotek *nt* 148, 149
children barn *nt/pl* 129
city centre (stads)centrum *nt* 146
clothing kläder *pl* 150
cold kall 131, 132, 141, 157
colour färg *c* 149, 151
come from, to komma från 129

come, to komma 134
condoms kondomer c/pl 149
confirm, to bekräfta 142
cotton bomull c 150
credit card kreditkort c 141,149
crossing överfart c 143
crown (currency) krona c 149, 152
cup kopp c 134
currency exchange office växelkontor nt 152
cut skärsår nt 153
cycling cykel c 147

D
dance, to dansa 146
danger fara c 157
dark mörk 132, 148
date datum nt 133, 155
date of birth födelsedatum nt 133
day dag c 132, 144, 154, 155
December december 155
decision beslut nt 132
denim denim c 150
Denmark Danmark 156
dentist tandläkare c 148, 154
deodorant deodorant c 149
department store varuhus nt 148
diabetic diabetiker c 154
diesel diesel c 145
dining room matsal c 133
dinner middag c 134
discotheque diskotek c 146
dish rätt c 134
dizzy yr 154
doctor läkare c 153, 157
doctor's office (surgery) läkarmottagning c 153
dog hund c 157
dollar dollar c 152
double bed dubbelsäng c 132
double room dubbelrum nt 132
downstairs där nere 131
dress klänning c 150
drink dryck c 140
drugstore (chemist's) apotek nt 148, 149
during under 131, 155

E
ear öra nt 153
early tidig 131
east öster 145
eight åtta 156
emergency nödsituation c 157
emergency exit nödutgång c 133, 157
England England 156
English (language) engelsk 130, 146, 151, 153
enjoy, to njuta 141
enjoyable trevlig 133

entrance ingång c 142, 157
evening kväll c 146, 155
exchange rate växelkurs c 152
exhibition utställning c 146
exit utgång c 142, 157
express express 152
expression uttryck nt 129, 148
eye öga nt 153

F
face ansikte nt 153
family familj c 129
fare pris nt 143, 144
February februari 155
feel, to känna sig 154
few, (a) några 131, 132
fill up, to tanka 145
filling (tooth) plomb c 154
filling station bensinstation c 145
film film c 151
find, to hitta 130, 153
fine (well) bra 129, 132
finger finger nt 153
first class första klass c 142
first först 143, 156
first name namn nt 133
five fem 156
flight flyg nt 142
food mat c 141
foot fot c 153
football (soccer) fotboll c 147
for för 131
for sale til salu 157
forbidden förbjuden 157
forest skog c 145
fork gaffel c 134
four fyra 156
free (vacant) ledig 131, 157
Friday fredag 155
from från 131

G
general allmän 133, 148
gentlemen (toilets) herrar 157
get, to få tag på 130
get, to (fetch) skaffa 133, 144
get lost, to vilsegången 157
get off, to (transport) stiga av 143
girlfriend flickvän c 129
give, to ge 145, 154
glass glas nt 134
gloves handskar c/pl 150
go away, to gå väg 157
go out, to (rendez-vous) gå ut 146
golf course golfbana c 147
good afternoon god middag 129
good bra 131, 134, 148, 154

good morning god morgon 129
good night god natt 129
good-bye adjö 129
green grön 150
Great Britain Storbrittanien 129
grey grå 150
grocer's livsmedelsaffär *c* 148, 151
guide guide *c* 146

H
hair-cut klippning *c* 151
hairdresser frisör *c* 148
half halva *c* 156
hand hand *c* 153
handbag handväska *c* 157
harbour hamn *c* 146
have, to ha 130, 132, 133, 151
he han 152
head huvud *nt* 153
health insurance sjukförsäkring *c* 154
heart hjärta *nt* 153
heavy tung 148
hello hallå 129, 152
help! hjälp! 157
help, to hjälpa 130, 143, 149
her hennes 152
here här 132, 144
hi hej 129
him honom 152
hire, to hyra 144, 147
holiday helgdag *c* 129
home town hemort *c* 133
hot varm 131, 157
how hur 130, 143, 145, 149, 154
how far hur långt 130
how long hur länge 130, 143, 154
how much hur mycket 130, 149
how many hur många 130
hundred hundra 156
hurt, to göra ont 154
husband man *c* 129

I
ice hockey ishockey *c* 147
ill sjuk 157
include, to ingå 144
included inräknad 141
information information *c* 142; upplysning *c* 157
injection spruta *c* 154
inquiries forfrågningar *c/pl* 143
insect bite insektsbett *nt* 153
insect repellent insektsspray *c* 149
insect spray insektsspray *c* 149
inside inne 131
insurance försäkring *c* 144
introduce, to presentera 129

introductions presentation *c* 129
Ireland Irland 156

J
January januari 155
jersey tröja *c* 150
July juli 155
June juni 155

K
key nyckel *c* 133
kilo kilo *nt* 151
knee knä *nt* 153
knife kniv *c* 134

L
lace spets *c* 150
ladies *(toilets)* damer 157
lake sjö *c* 145, 147
landmark landmärke *nt* 145
large stor 148
last sista 143
late sen 131
leather läder *nt*, skinn *nt* 150
leave, to lämna 143
leave alone, to lämna ifred 157
left vänster 141, 145
left-luggage office *(baggage check)* effektförvaring *c* 142
leg ben *nt* 153
letter *(mail)* brev *nt* 152
lift *(elevator)* hiss *c* 133, 157
light *(colour)* ljus 148; *(weight)* lätt 148
like, to tycka om 149
linen linne *nt* 150
litre liter *c* 145, 151
little, a lite 131
local lokal 134
look at, to *(examine)* titta på 154
lose, to tappa 157
lost property (lost and found) office hittegodsexpedition *c* 142
luggage bagage *nt* 157
luggage lockers förvaringsbox *c* 142
lunch lunch *c* 134
lung lunga *c* 153

M
made of gjort av 150
mail post *c* 152
March mars 155
May maj 155
me mig 130, 144
mean, to betyda 130
mechanic mekaniker *c* 145
meet, to träffa 129

mend, to *(fix)* laga 145
menu meny *c* 134; matsedel *c* 135
message meddelande *nt* 152
midnight midnatt *c* 155
mileage kilometerkostnad *c* 144
milk mjölk *c* 151
minute minut *c* 144
mistake fel *nt* 141
moisturizing cream fuktighetsbevarande
    kräm *c* 149
Monday måndag 155
more mer 130
morning morgon *c* 155
mountain berg *nt* 145
mouth mun *c* 153
muscle muskel *c* 153
museum museum *nt* 146
my min, mitt *(pl* mina) 129, 133

N
name namm *nt* 129, 132
napkin *(serviette)* servett *c* 134
nationality nationalitet *c* 133
nauseous illamående 154
near nära 131, 145, 147
nearest närmaste 148, 152
nerve nerv *c* 153
never aldrig 131
newspaper tidning *c* 151
newsstand tidningskiosk *c* 148
next nästa, 143
next to bredvid 131, 143
night natt *c* 155
nine nio 156
no nej 129
none ingen 131
noon klockan tolv (på dagen) 155
north norr 145
Norway Norge 156
nose näsa *c* 153
not inte 130, 131
nothing ingenting, inget 131
notice anslag *nt* 157
November november 155
now nu 131
number *(house)* nummer *nt* 133

O
occupation yrke *nt* 133
occupied upptagen 131, 157
October oktober 155
oil olja *c*
on på 131
once en gång 156
one ett 156
only bara 131, 132
open öppet 157
opposite mitt emot 145

or eller 131
orange orange 150
order, out of ur funktion 157
order, to beställa 141, 149
outside ute 131
overnight över natt 132

P
pardon förlåt 129
parents föräldrar *c/pl* 129
park, to parkera 133
parking parkering *c* 144
part del *c* 153
passport pass *nt* 133, 157
path stig *c* 145
pay, to betala 141
per day per dag 144
perhaps kanske 131
petrol bensin *c* 145
picnic picknick *c* 141
place of birth födelseort *c* 133
place ort *c* 133
plane flyg *nt* 142
plate tallrik *c* 134
platform perrong *c* 142
play, to spela 146
please var snäll och ... 129
pleased trevligt 129
police polis *c* 157
porter bärare *c* 143
post office postkontor *nt* 148; post *c* 152
postage porto *nt* 152
postcard vykort *nt* 152
pound *(sterling)* pund *nt* 152
prescription recept *nt* 154
price pris *nt* 132
private privat 132
pull, to dra 157
puncture *(flat)* punktering *c* 145
push, to trycka 157

Q
quality kvalitet *c* 149
quarter fjärdedel *c* 155, 156
question fråga *c* 130
quieter tystare 133

R
radio radio *c* 132
rash itslag *nt* 153
razor blades rakblad *nt* 149
receipt kvitto *nt* 154
recommend, to föreslå 134;
    rekommendara 154
rectangular rektangulär 148
red röd 150
regular *(petrol)* lågoktanig 145
repeat, to upprepa 130

requirements förfrågningar c/pl 133
reservations office biljettexpedition c 142
reserve, to beställa 134, 146
reserved reserverat 157
restaurant restaurang c 134
return (round trip) tur och retur 142
riding (horse-back) ridning c 147
right (correct) rätt 131
right (direction) höger 141, 145
river flod 145, 147
road sign vägmärke c 144
road väg 145
road works vägarbete pl 144
room rum nt 132
round rund 148

S
salty salt 141
Saturday lördag 155
sauna bastu c 132
scarf scarf c 150
Scotland Skottland 156
sea hav nt 145
second andra 156
second class andra klass c 142
see, to se 132
send, to skicka 145, 152
September september 155
serve, to servera 134
set menu meny c 134
seven sju 156
shampoo shampo nt 149
shape form c 149
she hon 152
shirt skjorta c 150
shivery frossbrytningar 154
shoes skor c/pl 150
shop (store) affär c 148
shopping area affärscentrum nt 148
shoulder axal c 153
show föreställning c 146
shower dusch c 132
sign skylt c 157
signature underskrift c 133
silk siden nt, silke nt 150
single (one-way) enkel 142
single room enkelrum nt 132
six sex 156
skates skridskor c/pl 147
skating rink skridskobana c 147
ski, to åka skidor 147
skiing skidåkning c 147
skiing, cross-country längdåkning c 147
skiing, downhill utförsåkning c 147
skiing equipment skidutrustning c 147
skin hud c 153
skirt kjol c 150
skis skidor c/pl 147
slice skiva c 151

slowly långsamt 130
small liten 131, 132, 148
smoking rökning c 157
snack mellanmål nt 141
soap tvål c 149
socks sockor c/pl 150
soon snart 131
sort sort c 151
south söder 145
souvenir shop souveniraffär c 148
souvenir souvenir c 151
speak, to tala 130, 152, 153
specialist specialist c 154
specimen prov nt 154
spoon sked c 134
sport sport c 147
spring vår 155
square kvadratisk 148
stamp frimärke nt 152
stay vistelse c 133
stay, to stanna 132; bo 154
sting stick nt 153
stock, out of slut på lagret 149
stomach mage c 153
stop, to stanna 144, 157
store (shop) affär c 148
straight ahead rakt fram 145
street gata c 133
sturdy kraftig 148
suede mocka c 150
summer sommar 155
sun-tan cream solkräm c 149
Sunday söndag 155
super (petrol) högoktanig 145
supermarket snabbköp nt 148
surgery (doctor's office) läkarmottagning c 153
surname efternamn nt 133
Sweden Sverige 156
sweet söt 141
swelling svullnad c 153
swim, to simma 147
swimming simning c 147
swimming pool simbassäng c 147
swimming trunks badbyxor c/pl 150
swimsuit baddräkt c 150

T
table bord nt 134
take, to (duration) ta 132, 143, 144, 149
tampons tamponger c/pl 149
taxi taxi c 133, 144
telephone telefon c 152
television TV c 132
temperature temperatur c 154
ten tio 156
tennis tennis c 147
tennis court tennisbana c 147
thank you tack 129

theatre teater *c* 146
then då, sedan 131
there där 130
thief tjuv *c* 157
think, to tro 141
third tredje 156
third tredjedel *c* 156
this den här, det här 149
those de där 141
three tre 156
throat hals *c* 153
through genom 131
Thursday torsdag 155
ticket biljett *c* 142, 146
ticket office biljettluckan *c* 142
time tid *c* 155
tin *(can)* burk *c* 151
today idag 155
toilet toalett *c* 132, 133
tomorrow i morgon 153, 155
tongue tunga *c* 153
tonight i kväll 146
too för 132, 141; *(also)* också 131
toothache tandvärk *c* 154
toothpaste tandkräm *c* 149
torch ficklampa *c* 151
tourist office turistbyrå *c* 146
towards mot 131
town stad *c* 146
town centre centrum *nt* 143
tram *(streetcar)* spårvagn *c* 143
translate, to översätta 130
travel, to resa 142
trousers (lång)byxor *nt/pl* 150
try on, to prova 150
Tuesday tisdag 155
twice två gånger 156
twin beds två sängar *c/pl* 132
two två 156

U
under under 131
understand, to förstå 130
United States USA 129
unleaded blyfri 145
until till 131
upstairs där uppe 131
use, to använda 152
useful användbar 131

V
vacancy ledigt rum *nt* 132, 157
vacant ledig 157
vegetarian vegetarisk 134
velvet sammet *c* 150
very mycket 131

W
wait, to vänta 144
waiting room väntsal *c* 142
wallet plånbok *c* 157
water vatten *nt* 140
waterfall vattenfall *nt* 145
Wednesday onsdag 155
week vecka *c* 132, 144
west väster 145
what vad 130, 149
when när 130
where var 129, 130, 142, 146
which vilken 130
white vit 150
who vem 130
why varför 130
wife fru *c* 129
wine vin *nt* 140
winter vinter 155
with med 129, 131
without utan 131
wonderful underbar 146
wool ylle *nt* 150
word ord *nt* 131
worse sämre 131
wound sår *nt* 153
write down, to skriva 149
wrong *(incorrect)* fel 131, 145

Y
yellow gul 150
yes ja 129
yesterday i går 155

Z
zero noll 156
zoo djurpark *c* 146